UNIVERSITY OF GLAMORGAN
LEARNING RESOURCES CENTRE

Pontypridd, Mid Glamorgan, CF37 1DL
Telephone: Pontypridd (01443) 482626

PARLIAMENTARY ACCOUNTABILITY

Also by Philip Giddings

MARKETING BOARDS AND MINISTERS

Parliamentary Accountability

A Study of Parliament and Executive Agencies

Edited by

Philip Giddings
Lecturer in Politics
University of Reading

for the Study of Parliament Group

First published 1995 by
MACMILLAN PRESS LTD
Houndmills, Basingstoke, Hampshire RG21 2XS
and London
Companies and representatives
throughout the world

ISBN 0–333–63201–X

A catalogue record for this book is available
from the British Library.

10   9   8   7   6   5
04   03   02   01   00

Printed and bound in Great Britain by
Antony Rowe Ltd
Chippenham, Wiltshire

Contents

vi   *Contents*

Preface

This book is based upon the work done by a study group set up by the Study of Parliament Group (SPG) in 1990 to monitor the consequences for Parliament of the Government's Next Steps Initiative. As convenor of the group and editor of the book I have been grateful for the continuing support and encouragement of the SPG and particularly its Executive Committee in seeing the work through to completion. That support has not been merely moral support. The SPG Executive has generously funded the travelling expenses of members of the study group as well as some of the costs of the preparation of the book for publication. For that we are particularly grateful. To avoid misunderstanding I should, nevertheless, make clear at the outset that the SPG does not bear any responsibility for the facts stated or opinions expressed in this book.

That same disclaimer also applies to those who generously gave of their time to talk to the study group and answer our questions about their experience of the Next Steps programme: Don Brereton of the Prime Minister's Efficiency Unit; Mike Goodson, Assistant Auditor General; Giles Radice, MP, of the Treasury and Civil Service Committee; and Peter Ryder, Director of Operations at the Meteorological Office. Peter Kemp, as he then was, gave an illuminating address to the SPG annual meeting in 1991. Priscilla Baines acted as our scribe for these meetings with her customary efficiency and has been a continuing source of encouragement to me as convenor of the group.

To monitor the consequences of development of a programme like the Next Steps means that time must be allowed to reveal what those consequences are. The research, and the book which is based upon it, has therefore inevitably been a long time in the making. I would like, therefore, to pay tribute to the patience and resilience of my colleagues in keeping faith with the project. Most of the initial group who expressed interest in the study have remained with us and contributed to this volume, many of them whilst carrying out heavy commitments elsewhere. The list of contributors is appended to this preface. I am grateful to them all.

I should also like to pay particular tribute to those who have assisted in the task of converting our findings into this book. Sheila Baxter, secretary in the Department of Politics at the University of Reading, did much of the early word processing and Lisa Hasell has brought those early drafts into camera-ready form with remarkable facility. Simon Patrick gave invaluable help with preparation of the tables and other aspects of the design of the book and Paul Evans has generously assisted in proof reading and arranging for preparation of the index, for which we are indebted to Sue Martin.

In the Preface to a book about accountability it is more than ever necessary to make clear who is responsible for what. Broadly speaking, as editor I take responsibility for all matters of editorial policy, within the guidelines helpfully provided by Macmillan, including the structure and balance of the book, as well as (of course) for those chapters which bear my name. For the content of the other chapters, the particular authors, individually or jointly as the case may be, take responsibility. If that leaves the reader with some lingering doubt about precisely who is responsible for particular passages or words in the text, then the reader has been well initiated into the issues raised by a study of accountability.

Reading,   Philip Giddings
October 1994

Contributors

Priscilla Baines is Deputy Librarian of the House of Commons. She joined the Economic Affairs Section of the Research Division of the Library in 1968, became head of section in 1977, head of the Science and Environment Section in 1988 and then Head of the Parliamentary Division. Her publications include contributions to the Study of Parliament Group's *Parliament and Economic Affairs* (1980) and to G. Drewry (ed.), *The New Select Committees: a Study of the 1979 Reforms* (1989).

Gavin Drewry is Professor of Public Administration and Head of the Department of Social Policy and Social Science, Royal Holloway and Bedford New College, University of London. He has been a member of the Study of Parliament Group since 1974 and written or edited several books and many book chapters and academic articles on subjects mainly related to parliamentary practice and procedure, the legislative process, public law and public administration. His books include: as co-author (with Louis Blom-Cooper), *Final Appeal: A Study of the House of Lords in its Judicial Capacity*, (Clarendon Press, 1972), currently being revised; co-author (with Ivor Burton), *Legislation and Public Policy* (Longman, 2nd edition, 1981); editor and principal contributor, *The New Select Committees: a Study of the 1979 Reforms* (Oxford University Press, for the Study of Parliament Group, 2nd edition, 1989); co-author (with Tony Butcher), *The Civil Service Today* (Blackwell, 2nd edition, 1991).

Paul Evans is currently a Clerk in the Public Bill Office of the House of Commons. He has been a Clerk in the House of Commons since 1981 and has worked for the Energy and Health Committees as well as in the Table Office (which deals with Parliamentary Questions) and the Journal Office.

Philip Giddings lectures on Politics at the University of Reading. He is author of *Marketing Boards and Ministers* (Saxon House, 1974) and a number of articles on Parliament and public agencies. He has contributed to several Study of Parliament Group publications, including *The New Select Committees: a Study of the 1979 Reforms* (Oxford University Press, 2nd edition, 1989) and *Parliamentary Questions* (Oxford University Press, 1993), and published articles on the Parliamentary and Health Service Commissioners.

Patricia Greer is now a senior consultant in the public sector group of Price Waterhouse. Previously she was a Research Officer at the Centre for the Analysis of Social Policy, University of Bath, where she carried out a three-year study of Next Steps Agencies funded by the Leverhulme Trust. She was formerly a Senior Analyst in the National Audit Office. Her publications include articles on executive agencies in *Public Administration,* Spring 1992 and Autumn 1993, and *Transforming Central Government* (Open University Press, 1994).

George Jones is Professor of Government at the London School of Economics and Political Science. He has written many articles and chapters on the British prime minister and cabinet, Parliament, public administration and local government. He has given evidence to select committees about their role and about Next Steps agencies. He is the author of *Borough Politics* (Macmillan, 1969), editor of *West European Prime Ministers* (Frank Cass, 1991), and co-author of *Herbert Morrison* (Weidenfeld and Nicolson, 1973), *The Case for Local Government* (Allen and Unwin, 1983) and *The Government of London* (J. Rowntree Foundation, 1991). He is a member of the National Consumer Council and chairman of its Public Services Committee.

Norman Lewis is Professor of Public Law at the University of Sheffield. He has published widely in the public law field, including (with Ian Harden) *The Noble Lie—the British Constitution and the Rule of Law* (1986).

David Natzler has been a member of the Department of the Clerk of the House of Commons since 1975 and is currently a Deputy Principal Clerk. He was Clerk to the Race Relations and Immigration Sub-Committee of the Home Affairs Committee, 1979 to 1981; Clerk to the Social Services Committee, 1981 to 1985; and, after four years in the Table Office, has been Clerk to the Defence Committee since 1989. His publications include chapters in other Study of Parliament Group publications and the latest (14th) edition of *Guide to the Palace of Westminster.*

Robert Pyper is Senior Lecturer in Public Administration at Glasgow Caledonian University. He was formerly Tutor in Politics at the University of Leicester. His Ph. D. thesis (Leicester 1987) was on 'The Doctrine of Individual Ministerial Responsibility in British Government: Theory and Practice in a New Regime of Parliamentary Accountability'. He is author of *The Evolving Civil Service* (Longman, 1991) and numerous journal articles covering a range of topics in the field of UK government and politics. He is Assistant Editor of *Talking Politics*, the journal of the Politics Association.

Paul Silk has been a member of the Department of the Clerk of the House of Commons since 1979. He is now a Deputy Principal Clerk in the Public Bill Office, and from 1989 to 1993 was Clerk of the Home Affairs Select Committee and prior to that of the Energy Committee. He is author of *How Parliament Works* (Longmans, 2nd edition, 1989) and contributor to *Parliament and International Affairs* (Open University Press, 1991) and *Parliament and Information* (Dartmouth, 1991) as well as to a number of journals of Parliamentary interest.

Barry Winetrobe is a member of the Research Division of the House of Commons Library. His research interests are in the field of constitutional (especially Parliamentary) development. From 1991 to 1992 he lectured in Public Law at the University of Aberdeen where he did research into the legal and political aspects of local government finance and produced an article on the history of the poll tax, published in July 1992 issue of *Parliamentary Affairs*.

PART I

The Context of the Initiative

1

The Origins of the Next Steps Programme

Gavin Drewry and Philip Giddings

There is always an element of arbitrariness in purporting to pinpoint the 'origins' of anything. The official birthday of the Next Steps programme was in February 1988. But this event, like all birthdays, has a prehistory—biological and ancestral. Next Steps was conceived some time after 1986, when the Prime Minster's Efficiency Unit was commissioned to undertake a scrutiny of management in the civil service. It has putative parents (Mrs Thatcher and Sir Robin Ibbs—though they are perhaps best regarded as surrogates for the three officials whose names appear as authors of the Next Steps report), at least one identifiable grandparent (Lord Rayner), a great grandfather (Lord Fulton), and even nannies, (Sir Peter Kemp, who was the first Next Steps Project Manager, then Richard Mottram, who succeeded him in July 1992).

We could probably trace the ancestral line back even further, but in the present context Chapter 5 of the Fulton Report on the Civil Service 'The Structure of Departments and the Promotion of Efficiency', (Fulton, 1968) provides a convenient starting point. The report recommended, *inter alia*, the introduction of management by objectives and of accountable management (to be achieved by the introduction of accountable units over a substantial area of executive activity), and an inquiry into the selective 'hiving off' of departmental functions. Some of the relevant paragraphs bear an uncanny similarity to the arguments put forward by the Efficiency Unit, twenty years later, in support of the Next Steps programme. Thus:

> To function efficiently, large organisations, including government departments, need a structure in which units and individual members have authority that is clearly defined and responsibilities for which they can be held accountable. There should be recognised methods of assessing their success in achieving specified objectives. (Fulton, 1968, para. 145)

And:

Accountable management means holding individuals and units responsible for performance measured as objectively as possible. Its achievement depends upon identifying or establishing accountable units within government departments—units where output can be measured against costs or other criteria, and where individuals can be held personally responsible for their performance. (para. 150)

The call (para. 189) for an inquiry into the possibility of hiving off functions (especially the provision of services to the community) to executive boards or corporations drew some of its inspiration from Sweden, to which the Committee had paid a short fact-finding visit. The Committee saw 'no reason to believe that the dividing line between activities for which Ministers are directly responsible and those for which they are not is necessarily drawn in the right place today'. However, it went on to note one potential area of difficulty central to the concern of this study: 'the creation of further autonomous bodies and the drawing of the line between them and Central Government would raise parliamentary and constitutional issues, especially if they affected the answerability for sensitive matters such as the social and educational services'. (para. 190)

Most of the recommendations of the Fulton Committee made little obvious headway. However, two years after the report, the Heath Government's White Paper, *The Reorganisation of Central Government*, promised 'a sustained effort to ensure that ... executive blocks of work will be delegated to accountable units of management, thus lessening the load on the departmental top management.' (Cmnd. 4506, 1970, para. 14) A few hived-off bodies were set up in the 1970s—notably the Civil Aviation Authority (1971), the Procurement Executive (1971), the Property Services Agency (1972), and the Manpower Services Commission (1974). But they remained within the ambit of ministerial control, rather than conforming to the Fulton concept of management by an autonomous board. In 1974, the Royal Ordnance Factories acquired their own trading funds (they were to be privatised in 1984), and the same step was taken a year later with the Royal Mint (which subsequently became a Next Steps agency).

In 1976, the Civil Service Department told the House of Commons Expenditure Committee, in the context of its inquiry into the civil service, that there had been extensive consideration of the possibilities of hiving off elements of departmental work in the aftermath of the Fulton Report and the 1970 White Paper. However, although the theoretical advantages had been recognised, in practice a number of factors had limited its application:

> Activities which were commercial in character and were or could be made wholly or largely self-financing, were found to be uncommon within central Government. In areas of activity which is not self-financing, the requirements of public financial control limit managerial independence. There are difficulties in removing from ministerial responsibility work which has a high policy content, or significant discretionary authority in relation to individual citizens. In areas with a low degree of direct ministerial involvement, there is a risk that the process of hiving off may itself simply add to Ministers' burdens. (Expenditure Committee, 1977, volume II, part I, 23)

This negative opinion was reinforced by a joint memorandum submitted by the Society of Civil Servants and the Civil and Public Services Association, who claimed, *inter alia*, that hiving off was damaging both to industrial relations and to morale in the civil service. The Expenditure Committee concluded that 'hiving off is only viable in limited areas of Government and that it should be approached with caution'; the Committee was 'impressed by the consideration that hiving off necessarily involves a diminution in the area of ministerial control and [it believed] that more attention should be devoted to developing proper control mechanisms for hived off bodies'. (Expenditure Committee, 1977, para. 91)

But the Committee did commend Fulton's hitherto neglected proposal for introducing accountable units, citing evidence from (among others) Sir Derek Rayner (volume II, part II, Q. 1521). And it went on to argue that such units 'should be scaled down to the size most conducive to effective informed control by the officer in charge'. (para. 94)

The Thatcher years: From FMI to Next Steps

The arrival of the Thatcher government signalled a growing preoccupation by government with the 'three Es'—efficiency, effectiveness and economy—and with the creation of a slimmer and fitter civil service. (Drewry and Butcher, 1991, chapter 10; Hennessy, 1989, chapter 14) Management, instead of being seen in Whitehall, as had hitherto been the case, as a secondary level of activity, definitely subordinate to the real work of making policy, was elevated into an important and respectable part of the job description of senior civil servants. Many of the ideas floated by Fulton in the 1960s, and apparently forgotten in the 1970s, resurfaced in new guises in the 1980s. Although it would be a mistake to construct, with benefit of hindsight, the image of a well-crafted efficiency strategy, unfolding throughout the 1980s in accordance with a coherent Thatcher master plan, the launch of the Next Steps programme towards the end of that decade must be set in the wider context of other trends and events.

Immediately after the 1979 election, Mrs Thatcher appointed Sir Derek (now Lord) Rayner, then joint managing director of Marks and Spencer, to advise her, on a part time basis, on ways of improving efficiency and eliminating waste in Whitehall. Rayner had been an adviser to Mr Heath in the run-up to the 1970 election, and had served as the first chief executive of the MOD's Procurement Executive from 1971 to 1973. He was supported by a small team of civil servants, based in the first instance in the Prime Minister's Private Office. In 1983 Rayner was succeeded by Sir Robin Ibbs, an executive director of ICI, and former head of the Central Policy Review Staff. The Efficiency Unit (as it now became) was absorbed into the Management and Personnel Office (set up on the demise of the Civil Service Department)—and later moved again to the Office of the Minister for the Civil Service. In 1988 Ibbs was succeeded as efficiency adviser by Sir Angus Fraser, formerly Chairman of the Board of Customs and Excise; and he in turn was succeeded in 1992 by Sir Peter Levene, who had been Chief of Defence Procurement.

The Efficiency Unit is now part of the Office of Public Service and Science (OPSS), set up in the Cabinet Office after the 1992 general election. In OPSS it sits alongside other units, including the Next Steps Project team (Sir Peter Kemp, the original Project Manager, was made to take early retirement in July 1992 and replaced by Richard Mottram, formerly of the Ministry of Defence), and the Citizen's Charter Unit.

In the first phase of the Efficiency Unit's existence, apart from its work in initiating and coordinating targeted efficiency scrutinies in departments ('Rayner's Raiders'), it was associated with two important linked initiatives that can be regarded as landmarks in the pre-history of the Next Steps programme. The first was DoE's Management Information System for Ministers (MINIS), launched by Michael Heseltine early in 1980, soon after he took office as Secretary of State. Designed to enable ministers to examine who does what, why and what it costs, variations upon the MINIS theme were adopted in various other departments under a variety of picturesque acronyms during the 1980s.

The MINIS principles, allied to devolved budgetary management, were endorsed by the Treasury and Civil Service Committee (TCSC, 1982)—and this endorsement heralded the launching of the Financial Management Initiative (FMI), throughout Whitehall, in May 1982. The declared aims of the FMI were:

> to promote in each department an organisation and system in which managers at all levels have:
>
> (a) a clear view of their objectives and means to assess and, wherever possible, measure outputs or performance in relation to those objectives;
>
> (b) well-defined responsibility for making the best use of their resources, including a critical scrutiny of output and value for money; and
>
> (c) the information (particularly about costs), the training and the access to expert advice that they need to exercise their responsibilities effectively. (Cmnd. 8616, 1982, para. 13)

The FMI was the forerunner of the Next Steps initiative, launched five years later.

Launch of the Next Steps Initiative

At the end of 1986, the Prime Minister asked Sir Robin Ibbs, efficiency adviser and *de facto* director of the Efficiency Unit, to undertake a further review of the possibilities for organisational and managerial reform. The terms of reference of the inquiry were:

> to assess the progress achieved in managing the Civil Service; to identify what measures had been successful in changing attitudes and practices; to identify institutional, administrative, political and managerial obstacles to better management and efficiency that still remain; and to report to the Prime Minister on what further measures should be taken. (Efficiency Unit, 1988, 33)

Thus the review was depicted (and indeed this interpretation is implicit in the short title, Next Steps, by which its outcome has become generally known) as a straightforward incremental progression from the FMI.

However, this interpretation rests on a half-truth. We should not accept at face value the assumption that the Next Steps programme was designed simply as an update of a successful earlier model of organisational reform. Indeed, the FMI is by no means universally regarded as an unqualified 'success'. In 1987, the House of Commons Public Accounts Committee, following up a report by the National Audit Office on the FMI, expressed concern that the Initiative might have lost direction. (Public Accounts Committee, 1987, paras. 20–43) In the first of a series of annual reviews of the Next Steps, the House of Commons Treasury and Civil Service Committee noted some of the criticisms that had been directed at the FMI and declared themselves 'disappointed at evidence of its stunted growth'. (TCSC, 1988, para. 7)

Although the FMI had undoubtedly had a considerable impact both upon the financial processes and the working culture of Whitehall, it had not radically changed the traditional style of central administration. In a television interview, Anne Mueller, Second Permanent Secretary in the Management and Personnel Office, conceded that 'there is still a long way to go in terms of giving greater freedom and discretion to individual departments, and, within departments, to individual line managers'. (quoted in Hennessy, 1989, 615) In the words of Davies and Willman:

> Giving managers the 'right to manage' was the next challenge—how to make sure that budgets really were delegated. This would necessitate 'letting go' by top department officials and the Treasury. While civil servants undoubtedly became more cost-conscious and more managerially minded as a result of FMI, the real devolution of financial management, the development of targets and the switch from targets to outputs never happened. The idea lived to fight another day. (Davies and Willman, 1991, 10)

It would be wrong to ignore the sequential progression from FMI to Next Steps, but one plausible interpretation of the thinking that lay behind the Next Steps initiative is that, rather than building upon a success story, it was 'a gambit to try to revitalise a reform that seemed to have fallen flat'. (Jordan, 1992, 2) FMI had strengthened financial monitoring and control, but had done little to promote managerial initiative.

The Ibbs Report was kept under wraps in the run-up to the 1987 general election, but soon afterwards stories began to appear in the media about some vigorous in-fighting inside Whitehall over proposals for a major shake-up in the structure and configuration of central government departments. This coincided with a Whitehall battle that was being fought at about the same time on another front over Sir Kenneth Stowe's report on the central management of the civil service, the most visible consequence of which was the winding up of the Management and Personnel Office in the late summer of 1987 and the restoration of its civil service manpower, pay and conditions of service responsibilities to the Treasury.

Press reports claimed (more or less accurately, as it transpired) that the Efficiency Unit was advocating the division of the civil service into a small inner core, concerned exclusively with departmental policy advice, with the bulk of departmental functions and civil service jobs concerned with the delivery of public services, being assigned to semi-autonomous (but not fully privatised) agencies—rather on Swedish lines. The Treasury (so it was plausibly rumoured) opposed the scheme because of its perceived implications for weakening central control of departmental expenditure and civil service pay; if so, the outcome of this battle must have diminished the satisfaction of its victory in the context of the Stowe reorganisation. But some senior civil servants (e.g. in the revenue departments) were said to welcome it as offering the prospect of greater autonomy. The civil service unions (who had been generally unhappy about the working of the FMI) apparently had mixed feelings.

In February 1988 a document was published, based on a somewhat watered down version of the Ibbs report—with, unusually, an attribution of authorship to three named officials, Kate Jenkins, Karen Caines and Andrew Jackson. (Efficiency Unit, 1988) It was based on more than 150 interviews with civil servants (including 26 permanent secretaries) and with ministers.

The Efficiency Unit team found that 'the management and staff concerned with the delivery of government services (some 95 per cent of the Civil Service) are generally convinced that the developments towards more clearly defined and budgeted management [they had particularly in mind the FMI] are positive and helpful'. (Efficiency Unit, 1988, para. 3) However, they also detected some concern that senior civil service management 'is dominated by people whose skills are in policy formulation and who have relatively little experience of managing or working where services are actually being delivered'. (para. 4) A senior grade 2 officer was quoted as saying that 'the golden road to the top is through policy and not through management'. The report noted also the size and diversity of the civil service as an impediment to coherent management. (para. 10)

The fact that the service is regulated from the centre means, the report said, that rules and regulations 'are structured to fit everything in general and nothing in particular. The rules are therefore seen primarily as a constraint rather than a support; and in no sense as a pressure on managers to manage effectively'. (para. 11) As for the time-honoured notion of a unified civil service, the report concluded that:

> In our discussions it was clear that the advantages which a unified Civil Service are intended to bring are seen as outweighed by the practical disadvantages, particularly beyond Whitehall itself. We were told that the advantages of an all-embracing pay structure are breaking down, that the uniformity of grading frequently inhibits effective management and that the concept of a career in a unified Civil Service has little relevance for most civil servants, whose horizons are bounded by their local office or, at most, by their department. (para. 12)

The report observed that 'generalised solutions have been the bane of previous attempts at reform' (para. 43) and said that it intended, therefore, to avoid detailed prescriptions. Its core recommendation was that agencies should be established to carry out the executive functions of government within a policy and resources framework set by a department. (para. 19) One key paragraph in particular signalled the radicalism of what was being proposed:

> The aim should be to establish a quite different way of conducting the business of government. The central Civil Service should consist of a relatively small core engaged in the function of servicing Ministers and managing departments, who will be the 'sponsors' of particular government policies and services. Responding to these departments will be a range of agencies employing their own staff, who may or may not have the status of Crown servants, and concentrating on the delivery of their particular service, with clearly defined responsibilities between the Secretary of State and the Permanent Secretary on the one hand and the Chairmen or Chief Executives of the agencies on the other. Both departments and their agencies should have a more open and simplified structure. (para. 44)

The report acknowledged that the size and organisational definition of agencies would necessarily vary from case to case. The main strategic control would lie with the minister and permanent secretary:

... but once the policy objectives within the framework are set, the management of the agency should then have as much independence as possible in deciding how those objectives are met. A crucial element in the relationship would be a formal understanding with ministers about the handling of sensitive issues and the lines of accountability in a crisis. The presumption must be that, provided management is operating within the strategic direction set by ministers, it must be left as free as possible to manage within that framework. (para. 21)

On parliamentary accountability, the authors of *The Next Steps* expressed their belief in the feasibility of Parliament 'through ministers' treating managers as directly responsible for operational matters. Accountability implications were further discussed in a short annex.

On the day of publication, the Prime Minister made a statement in the House of Commons broadly endorsing the report's recommendations. She said that the new agencies would 'generally be within the Civil Service, and their staff will continue to be civil servants', though she later conceded that the word 'generally' did admit the possibility of their being set up outside the civil service in appropriate cases. It has been pointed out that making the new agencies 'part of government' neatly avoided any possible charges of a U-turn that might have been laid against a prime minister who, at the beginning of her term of office, had launched a fierce campaign against quangos. (Pliatzky, 1992)

Mrs Thatcher also said, in reply to a question by Terence Higgins MP (Chairman of the Commons Treasury and Civil Service Committee), that there would be no change in the arrangements for accountability: the work of departmentally-related select committees, the Public Accounts Committee and the Parliamentary Commissioner would not be affected. The Prime Minister announced the appointment of Peter Kemp, former deputy secretary in the Treasury, to act as project manager charged with overseeing the processes of implementation. He was later to be second permanent secretary in the Office of the Minister for the Civil Service (OMCS).

Twelve organisational units—employing in total some 70,000 civil servants—were identified at this stage as particularly promising candidates for agency status. Critics pointed to this cautious beginning as marking a significant victory for Treasury scepticism: it was pointed out that several of the designated agencies, such as HMSO, the Meteorological Office and the Queen Elizabeth II Conference Centre already had many of the semi-autonomous characteristics of agencies; that half the staff employed in the selected agencies worked in the Employment Service (including those working in semi-detached Jobcentres); and that notable omissions (later to be remedied) included the revenue departments and the 500 local social security offices. But other observers accepted the inevitability of gradualism in trying to bring about such significant shifts in the structure and culture of Whitehall: the changes might turn out to be less dramatic than the claims made for them by their proud parents, but they could not in any case be expected to happen overnight.

Mrs Thatcher's announcement in February 1988 was in fact the prelude to a major reorganisation of Whitehall. Within five years 90 Agencies had been established and a further 64 Executive Units set up within Customs and Excise and Inland Revenue, so that by the end of 1993 more than sixty per cent of the civil service was working on Next Steps lines. Moreover, a further 29 candidates for agency status had been announced. The responsible minister, then Mr Waldegrave, thus felt able to speak confidently of the 'far-reaching success of the reform'.

Given the speed and scale of the change, it has to be asked whether it represents a fundamental change to the British system of public administration or is little more than an exercise in organisational cosmetics. Or, perhaps, given the characteristically evolutionary nature of British political institutions, it is something in between.

To address such a question we have to focus our attention on the key characteristic of the concept of agency status as set out by the Prime Minister in February 1988. This is that the executive functions of government ('as distinct from policy advice') should be carried out by executive units clearly designated within departments. Responsibility for day to day operations of such units is delegated to a chief executive, who is responsible for management within a framework of policy objectives and resources set by the responsible minister. As Mrs Thatcher put it replying to questions on her statement in the House of Commons, 'the purpose of the change is to give more responsibility to the manager of the agency'. In contrast to the Fulton proposal for hiving off, Mrs Thatcher made it clear that agencies would generally remain within government departments, their staff would continue to be civil servants and in consequence there would be no change in the arrangements for accountability. Ministers would continue to account to Parliament for all the work of their departments, including the work of agencies.

There is clearly a tension here between greater delegation of responsibility to chief executives and continuing ministerial responsibility to Parliament. Can delegation to the chief executive be genuine if the minister's responsibility for *all* the work of the department, including the agency, remains unchanged? Significant delegation of responsibility from the minister looks like fundamental change. Total ministerial accountability remaining unchanged suggested mere window-dressing. An important issue to be explored, therefore, is the respective roles of chief executive and minister—and their likely intermediary the permanent secretary. If the role of ministers really has changed, what are the implications of that change for Parliament, given that Ministers are the crucial link in the chain of responsibility by which Parliament asserts its control over Government?

Responses from Members of Parliament to Mrs Thatcher's statement made it clear from the outset that the implications for parliamentary accountability would be a major concern. As we shall see, accountability is not always easy to define but parliamentary procedures provide for it in a number of different ways—through questions, written and oral, through the Public Accounts Committee and National Audit Office; through departmental select committees; through the Parliamentary Commissioner for Administration and his related select committee; through adjournment debates, other interventions in debates; as well as MPs' direct contacts with ministers, through correspondence, meetings, lobbies. In these many different way ministers are called to account to Parliament for the work of their departments. To establish whether there has been any significant change in the extent or depth of accountability, therefore, requires a full analysis of wide range of parliamentary activity. It is not sufficient to focus entirely on the more visible aspects such as oral questions or select committee hearings.

It was also clear, both from the Ibbs Report and Mrs Thatcher's statement, that underlying the agency concept is a distinction between 'day to day operations' and 'policy advice', between 'management' (which is for civil servants) and 'policy' (which is for Ministers). This is not a distinction which is recognised in the doctrine of ministerial responsibility, though much (not always successful) play was made with it when Parliament was seeking to incorporate public corporations and nationalised industries into the procedures for ministerial accountability. For in most cases those external bodies had had the respective responsibilities of minister and board set out in a statute or charter. Agencies, by contrast, are largely internal bodies, set up within departments with no statutory underpinning of the duties or responsibilities of ministers and chief executives. Whether the documents setting out the policy and resources framework within which the chief executive is to operate can serve for agencies a purpose similar to that which the statutory provisions give for public corporations and the like is a question which has to be carefully examined.

It is again clear from the Ibbs Report that an important factor in the analysis which led to the agencies proposal was the perception that ministers, and Parliament, were overloaded and that a major contributor to this overload is the conviction that the doctrine of ministerial responsibility makes the minister liable to account for any and every decision or non-decision taken within his department. However detailed or trivial the decision it may be raised with the minister by an MP, either on the floor of the House, by a question or in correspondence. And it is clear that the propensity of MPs to raise matters with ministers has very substantially increased over the last twenty years. (Franklin and Norton, 1993, 17 and 27)

Given that context, most government departments have adopted a pyramid form of organisation to facilitate upward referral of cases and rapid servicing of ministers for their parliamentary duties. Delegation runs counter to the convention and the organisational form as well as to the culture.

The extensive parliamentary duties of many ministers, and the impact of those duties on the senior civil servants who advise them, clearly contribute to overload. It was part of the strategy of the Thatcher Government to reduce that overload by reducing the responsibilities of the state (by direct abolition, privatisation, hiving off) and cutting the size of the civil service. But by the end of Mrs Thatcher's second term it seems to have become clear that further action was needed if a significant reduction of the ministerial burden was to be achieved—so that ministers (and their advisers) could concentrate on their 'proper' function of providing political control and direction to public policy.

It is, therefore, an important part of the underlying logic of the Next Steps Initiative that it should result in a reduction of the load on ministers—a reduction, that is, on the burden arising from parliamentarily originated case-work. This aspect stands in tension with the assertion that ministerial accountability remains unchanged. Mrs Thatcher herself said in answer to questions on her February 1988 statement, that the hope is that MPs will take their cases to the chief executives rather than worry ministers with them, not least because that way they will get a quicker answer (which is not necessarily the same as a satisfactory one).

Parliamentary accountability is not just about constituency cases. Parliamentarians are also concerned to ensure that Government is run efficiently, effectively and, above all, acceptably. MPs will therefore be concerned with, want to enquire into and press for answers about, the way in which Government departments are managed, not least the use to which public resources are put. They will also want to pursue their own and their party's political interests, and to be seen to be doing so. Both concerns, managerial and political, are fundamental to the political culture of a liberal democracy like Britain. Both could be put at risk by a significant reduction in the opportunities to raise matters with ministers. Neither fits easily with a distinction between 'policy' and 'management' or 'day to day operations'. This is no doubt why the Government has insisted that, even though responsibilities have been delegated to chief executives, ministerial accountability for agencies is unimpaired. Parliament itself has, by exercising its scrutinising functions, been testing whether in fact this is so. It is the purpose of this book to examine how successful Parliament has been in that task.

The Plan of the Book

The book is in four parts. In this first part we deal with the *Context of the Initiative*. After this first background-setting chapter, Robert Pyper and Barry Winetrobe analyse the implications of the Initiative for the doctrine of ministerial responsibility and consider what concepts of accountability are appropriate for this form of delegated management.

In Part II we provide a description and critical assessment of the way in which Parliament has monitored the development of the Initiative and the work of agencies since 1988. Philip Giddings in Chapter 4 examines the work of the Commons Treasury and Civil Service Committee, which reported annually on the progress of the Initiative until 1992 and provided an important catalyst for its development. In Chapter 5 David Natzler and Paul Silk look at how the departmentally-related select committees have monitored the work of agencies. In Chapter 6 Priscilla Baines looks at the work of the National Audit Office and Public Accounts Committee, which have special responsibility for financial accountability. Finally, in this part of the book, Paul Evans looks at the ways in which agencies have been dealt with on the floor of the House and particularly at parliamentary questions, which we have already seen are a key indicator of ministerial responsibility, and Philip Giddings looks at agencies and the Ombudsman.

Part III of the book contains case studies of Parliament's handling of the agencies. In Chapter 9 George Jones examines all the agencies operating within one government department—the Department of the

Environment. In Chapter 10 Patricia Greer looks at the impact of the Initiative on parliamentary accountability in relation to the social security agencies, including the Benefits Agency which, with some 70,000 staff, is much the largest of all the agencies currently operating. The size and high political profile of the Benefits Agency makes it a major test of the agency concept. Norman Lewis, in Chapter 11, focuses on the work of the Employment Services Agency, which is responsible for placing unemployed people into jobs or training opportunities and so has extensive direct contact with the public. The significance of changing economic circumstances to the ESA's work makes it an important indicator of the robustness of the framework agreements and performance monitoring which are prominent features of the agency concept.

Finally, in Part IV we bring together the conclusions which have emerged from our case studies and consider to what extent they show the Parliament has effectively addressed the challenge to its accountability mechanisms which the *Next Steps Initiative* has brought. We then look at what the future holds for Parliament's scrutiny of the executive operations as the agency concept is extended to cover the greater part of Whitehall.

References

Davies and Willman, 1991:	Anne Davies and John Willman, *What Next? Agencies, Departments, and the Civil Service*, Institute for Public Policy Research.
Drewry and Butcher, 1981:	Gavin Drewry and Tony Butcher, *The Civil Service Today*, second edition, Basil Blackwell, Oxford.
Efficiency Unit, 1988:	*Improving Management in Government: the Next Steps. Report to the Prime Minister*, HMSO.
Expenditure Committee, 1977:	Eleventh Report of the Expenditure Committee, *The Civil Service*, HC 535, 1976–77.
Franklin and Norton, 1993:	Mark Franklin and Philip Norton, *Parliamentary Questions*, Clarendon Press, Oxford.

Fulton, 1968:   *The Civil Service: Report of the Committee, 1966–68*, Cmnd 3638, HMSO.

Hennessy, 1989:   Peter Hennessy, *Whitehall*, Secker and Warburg.

Jordan, 1992:   Grant Jordan, *Next Steps Agencies: From Managing by Command to Managing by Contract*, University of Aberdeen.

Pliatzky, 1992:   Leo Pliatzky, 'Quangos and Agencies', *Public Administration*, vol. 70(4), 555–63.

PAC, 1987:   Public Accounts Committee, Thirteenth Report, *The Financial Management Initiative*, HC 61, 1986–87.

TCSC, 1982:   Treasury and Civil Service Committee, Third Report, *Efficiency and Effectiveness in the Civil Service*, HC 236, 1981–82.

2

Ministerial Responsibility
and Next Steps Agencies

Robert Pyper

Proposals for the creation of the 'Next Steps' executive agencies seemed to carry with them the possibility of significant change to the theory and practical operation of the doctrine of individual ministerial responsibility. As we have seen in the previous chapter, in its unpublished version, the Ibbs report is said to have proposed fundamental managerial and constitutional change, involving, *inter alia*, the abandonment of individual ministerial responsibility in its traditional form. (Hennessy, 1989, 620) The published report, heavily influenced by the Treasury and Downing Street, was more muted, but still veered between flirting with a form of constitutional radicalism which implied the need to rethink extant notions of ministerial responsibility, and an obvious desire to placate constitutional traditionalists. Compare and contrast the following extracts from the published version:

> Clearly ministers have to be wholly responsible for policy, but it is unrealistic to suppose that they can actually have knowledge in depth about every operational question. The convention that they do is in part the cause of the overload we observed. We believe it is possible for Parliament, through ministers, to regard managers as directly responsible for operational matters. (Efficiency Unit, 1988, para. 23)

> Any change from present practice in accountability would, of course, have to be acceptable to ministers and to Parliament. It is axiomatic that ministers should remain fully and clearly accountable for policy. For agencies which are government departments or parts of departments ultimate accountability for operations must also rest with ministers. (Efficiency Unit, 1988, Annex A, para. 3)

When Margaret Thatcher launched the Next Steps initiative with her Commons statement in February 1988, she made it clear that the government would countenance no alterations to the doctrine of individual ministerial responsibility. (HC Deb, 127, 1149–51) Thatcher, Ibbs, and most academics who have commented on Next Steps, conflate the notion of ministerial accountability *per se* with the wider doctrine of individual ministerial responsibility. This has tended to produce something resembling a dialogue of the deaf, with the originators and custodians of the initiative insisting that Next Steps fits comfortably into existing constitutional arrangements, and the critics asserting that the initiative is doomed to fail precisely because it has not been accompanied by wider constitutional reform.

Thus, the government responded to a constitutional query by the Treasury and Civil Service Select Committee by making it clear that it

> ... does not envisage that setting up Executive Agencies within departments will result in changes to the existing constitutional arrangements. The further delegation of authority to managers inherent in the Next Steps concept concerns internal accountability within departments and does not conflict with the external accountability of Ministers to Parliament. (Cm 524, 9)

On the other hand, hostile commentators have seized on the perceived failure of government to grasp the constitutional nettle as the fatal flaw at the heart of Next Steps. Davies and Willman claim that the Ibbs Report failed to deal with 'the continuing problem of ministerial responsibility', an 'inadequate convention', which 'is incompatible with the managerialist philosophy of Next Steps'. (Davies and Willman, 11, 34 and 27) McDonald writes scathingly of 'the empty notion of ministerial accountability'. (McDonald, 1992, 9) Such critics argue that antipodean or Swedish concepts of ministerial responsibility would be vital prerequisites for successful implementation of Next Steps, while making light of the fundamental differences in political culture between the UK and their model states. McDonald's toleration of the limitations upon the parliamentary accountability of agencies in Sweden ('Swedish MPs are debarred from asking the Minister to intervene in individual cases or indeed to raise any questions about the running of the agencies') seems rather perverse, given her strictures on the British arrangements. (McDonald, 1992, 8–9)

However, it might be argued that the doctrine of individual ministerial responsibility is not necessarily incompatible with the emergence of the Next Steps agencies. In accordance with the spirit of the British constitution, this doctrine had already been subjected to a process of evolutionary change before the advent of Next Steps due in part to the effect of the developing House of Commons select committee system and the introduction of the Parliamentary Commissioner for Administration. Despite the intentions of its creators, Next Steps might have served to emphasise the bogus nature of the policy/administration divide, expose the flawed philosophy of the Armstrong and Osmotherly Memoranda (by which the Government has sought to circumscribe the accountability of civil servants to Parliament), and generally facilitate further evolution of the doctrine. Moreover, those who criticise Next Steps, with blueprints for constitutional upheaval in hand, seem to be guilty of a fundamental misunderstanding of British political culture and in possession of an impoverished notion of individual ministerial responsibility's reality and potential.

Before pursuing this argument, it is important to establish a wide, inclusive perspective of the doctrine.

Individual Ministerial Responsibility: A View of the Doctrine

In simple terms, it can be argued that the doctrine of individual ministerial responsibility might best be understood with reference to four elements (Pyper, 1987):

— Personal (or legal and moral) responsibility
— Role responsibility
— Accountability
— Sanctions

'Responsibility' is a two-sided coin. In the context of government, ministers can be said to be responsible for conducting themselves according to the laws of the land and with respect for the quasi-legal, or even moral, codes of their peers (which, for convenience sake, we can term personal responsibility), as well as for performing a set of reasonably clear roles as policy leaders, departmental managers, departmental ambassadors and legislative pilots (which can be termed role responsibilities). Ministers are responsible to their colleagues in the government (especially the Prime Minister), their party and Parliament. The appropriate sense of 'responsibility to' can be conveyed by the term 'accountability'.

The notion of accountability implies the existence of a controlling agent, a person or body holding sanctions over the office holder. If a minister is said to be accountable to Parliament, to the government as a whole, and to the generality of his or her party, for the effective discharge of role responsibility, and at least for the absence of personal irresponsibility, historical analysis shows that the most significant sanctions holders have been Prime Ministers. (Finer, 1956; Pyper, 1991)

Before attempting to comment on the application of these elements of individual ministerial responsibility in the context of Next Steps, it should be noted that the minister's role responsibility for departmental management provides a link with the civil service. Actions taken by, and negligence on the part of, officials are to some degree within the ambit of this role responsibility of ministers. Civil servants are accountable to ministers, and others, for the performance of certain duties and functions: officials also have role responsibilities for which they are accountable. The extent of *ministerial* accountability for these matters is, of course, a moot point but, to simplify, it can be argued that the concepts of role responsibility, accountability, and sanctions as well as personal responsibility can be applied to civil servants as well as to ministers.

Table 2.1 sets out in summarised form the broad role responsibilities and agents of accountability for ministers and civil servants.

Table 2.1
Role responsibilities and accountability

	Civil servants (agency)	Ministers	Civil servants (parent department)
Roles:	Policy advice Agency management Policy execution	Policy leadership Departmental management Legislative piloting Ambassadorial	Policy advice Departmental management Policy execution
Agents of accountability:	Civil service superiors Ministers Parliament	Government Party Parliament	Civil service superiors Ministers Parliament

Civil service role responsibilities would encompass policy advice, the administration or execution of departmental policy, and departmental management. Accountability is to civil service superiors, ministers and Parliament, albeit in circumstances strictly limited by the Accounting Officer's and Osmotherly Memoranda, which govern the relationship between civil servants and the Public Accounts Committee and the departmental select committees respectively. Disciplinary sanctions are effectively held by hierarchical superiors in the civil service.

In the context of Next Steps, it seems safe to set aside the elements of the doctrine of ministerial responsibility pertaining to personal responsibility and sanctions. The impact of the new agencies would be seen, if at all, in relation to role responsibilities and accountability. The remainder of this chapter will seek to examine the effect of Next Steps on ministerial and civil service role responsibilities, and offer some brief comments on accountability.

Policy Roles of Ministers and Civil Servants

If we accept that government ministers have, as a fundamental aspect of their role responsibility, the need to offer policy leadership, broadly defined, and civil servants are charged with the task of offering policy advice (especially those in the middle to upper reaches of a departmental hierarchy), as well as implementing/executing policy, what conclusions are we able to draw about the effect of Next Steps on these spheres of role responsibility?

Before proceeding, a cautionary note should be sounded. Given the nature of the concepts under discussion in this chapter, it is necessary on occasion for general statements to be made about 'agencies'. However, we must retain an awareness of the diverse forms and characteristics of Next Steps agencies, as well as the dangers of over-simplification.

It would be possible to construct a basic model of the relationship between a Next Steps agency and its parent department which allocates a minimal or non-existent policy advice role to agency officials. Thus, the ministers and senior civil servants in the parent department together formulate policy, which is simply passed on to the agency for efficient, effective and economical implementation in line with the agency's stated objectives. In this light, the extant role responsibilities of ministers and senior civil servants in the parent department for, respectively, policy leadership and policy advice, would remain unaffected by the advent of Next Steps, while the civil servants working in the agencies (even the chief executives and their senior management boards) would have no role responsibility for policy advice *per se.*

However, the Ibbs Report, the Fraser Report and government responses to the Treasury and Civil Service Select Committee have not set out a precise definition of the policy role to be ascribed to agencies. Instead, while there is clearly an underlying assumption that the minister/policy civil servant/administration dichotomy exists, agency framework documents are repeatedly mentioned as the source of information on relationships between particular agencies and their departmental parents.

The framework documents offer us the possibility of two types of policy role for agencies. The minimalist role, as set out above, can be dismissed as a working model. Agency chief executives and management boards have clearly been allocated policy advice roles in relation to the particular sphere covered by the agency in question. As Davies and Willman have noted, this is simple good sense:

> ... it is a reasonable hypothesis that Agencies, particulary in highly specialised areas, will play a substantial, if not always an attributable, role in the formulation of policy. Indeed, it is a nonsense to exclude them, even theoretically, from this exercise. The act of target-setting is, in itself, a matter of policy and if this is to be realistic the experience of the Agency will be a decisive factor. (Davies and Willman, 1991, 33)

Nonetheless, a distinction can be drawn between those agencies and chief executives who have been allocated what might be described as a 'sleeping' role in policy advice (i.e. to provide ministers and senior officials in the parent department with advice as requested, as in the Social Security Benefits Agency Framework Document—see Chapter 10) and those who have been allocated a more pro-active role in this sphere (i.e. to participate fully in the parent department's policy-making machinery, as in the Employment Service Executive Agency Framework Document—see Chapter 11).

As far as the policy role of senior civil servants in the parent department is concerned, the possibility of an enhanced policy role might open up in the long term. As Dunleavy has noted,

> ... some people argue that the policy-administration dichotomy is still there, but it's no longer one between politicians and civil servants, it's between politicians and high civil servants on the one hand, and

management, implementation-oriented, middle range civil servants on the other. (Dunleavy, 1992)

While it may be too early to say that this has happened, or will happen in British government (and the policy role of the Employment Service Agency Chief Executive would seem to challenge Dunleavy's version), it is one possible outcome of Next Steps.

The net effect would seem to be that Next Steps has served to emphasise and, in some cases, develop the extant policy advice role of civil servants (with the potential to do more in this regard over the longer term), while pointing to the continued difficulty in establishing clear demarcation lines between policy advice and the creation of policy.

As far as policy execution/implementation is concerned, the creation of agencies has had the effect of emphasising the importance of this role responsibility for officials working in the outposts of Whitehall departments, while creating a case for those still operating at the heart of the parent department to be more clearly focussed on different sorts of activities. As Greer has commented, 'Next Steps calls for departmental headquarters' senior civil servants to employ a different set of skills. They are to become more strategic'. (Greer, 1992, 227)

The Fraser report indicated that a great deal of ground had still to be covered in this respect, and recommended that,

... the central Departments should review their changing roles in the light of Next Steps and set new staffing levels for these functions. (Efficiency Unit, 1991, 9)

Officials working in the agencies should presumably see the successful implementation of policy as their primary policy role responsibility, for which they will be held accountable to their official superiors within the agency, and, ultimately, to departmental ministers.

Management Roles of Ministers and Civil Servants

Within our basic model of individual ministerial responsibility, it can be seen that ministers and civil servants have traditionally shared role responsibility for departmental 'management' in its varied forms, although one strain of management, financial accounting, falls primarily within the remit of the civil service, personified by the departmental accounting officer.

Despite the shared responsibility, ministers with a penchant for management tend to be a scarce commodity. Michael Heseltine's interest in MINIS and associated matters in the early 1980s was seen by many of his Cabinet colleagues as somewhat perverse. (Hennessy, 1989, 607–608) The transient nature of departmental ministers, allied to the fact that successfully undertaking policy roles is normally seen to be the acid test for a ministerial career, perhaps helps to explain why management functions are generally of greater concern to civil servants than ministers.

Regardless of the precise demarcation line between ministers and officials on managerial issues in any given department, the Ibbs report was reasonably clear, at least in broad terms, about the possible managerial implications of the Next Steps initiative:

Greater freedom to manage should be delegated progressively to individual agencies, depending on the robustness of the framework and their capacity to put the freedom to good use. ((Efficiency Unit, 1988, 11)

As far as the parent departments were concerned:

... senior management will need the same kind of flexibility that we consider necessary for agencies. (Efficiency Unit, 1988, 16)

Furthermore, the rather ambiguous role played by ministers in departmental management could be clarified:

The confusion we observed about the role of Ministers in management should be substantially resolved. Inevitably and rightly it is open to a Minister to get involved in any part of his or her department's business, but in a well-managed department this should normally only be necessary by exception. (Efficiency Unit, 1988, 11)

Thus, a radical reduction in the ministerial role responsibility for management matters was apparently envisaged, not merely in relation to the new agencies, but also, by implication, in the parent department. Additionally, the delegation of key management functions such as recruitment, pay and conditions of service to agency chief executives and their management boards would result in a higher level of managerial autonomy being allocated to officials than heretofore.

In practice, it has become clear from the early experience with agencies that the impact of Next Steps on ministerial and official responsibilities for management has been limited.

As far as the parent departments are concerned, the Fraser Report sounded alarm bells about the paucity of managerial change accomplished since the launching of the initiative. The managerial role, organisational framework and level of staffing in parent departments appeared to have undergone only superficial change, at best, as a result of Next Steps. (Efficiency Unit, 1991)

The managerial autonomy granted to chief executives in relation to matters of recruitment, pay and conditions of service did not differ fundamentally from the 'flexibilities' allowed under a new, service-wide managerial regime, except in a very small number of cases, where arrangements specific to a particular agency would be set out in the framework document. Indeed, there were some indications that the agencies were being tied fairly tightly into the managerial structures and processes of the parent departments.

Successive surveys conducted by Price Waterhouse have indicated a level of concern in agencies about the amount of time given over to discussions with the parent departments over matters relating to targets, budgets and personnel management. (Price Waterhouse, 1991 and 1992). The close department—agency managerial links have also been commented upon by Davies and Willman:

... agencies complained that the amount of control exercised by the centre has increased rather than decreased since they were set up. Departments exert a further brake on Agencies' independence by requirements in the Framework Document that the Agency must procure certain services from the central department ... Where Agencies are based out of London, as with Companies House or the Vehicle Inspectorate, it would be financially advantageous and often more convenient to obtain these services locally. (Davies and Willman, 1991, 31)

The Fraser Report commented unfavourably upon the compulsory provision of services by departments without adequate costing and recommended the introduction of proper charging and invoicing arrangements, and, where possible, value for money comparisons with services on offer from outside the department. (Efficiency Unit, 1991, 16–17)

The introduction of market testing provided yet another illustration of the close managerial links between parent departments and agencies. It has been possible to detect a grumbling resentment on the part of chief executives, who believe that the manner in which market testing was introduced was an infringement upon the concept of devolved management. Agencies and chief executives might have been left to decide upon their own priorities instead of having a quota (25% of all activities) for market testing imposed upon them.

One is led to the conclusion that the early phases of the Next Steps initiative have produced nothing resembling a radical rearrangement of ministerial and civil service role responsibilities in the management sphere.

Legislative Piloting Role of Ministers

The advent of Next Steps agencies brought no change to the ministerial role responsibility for piloting legislation through Parliament. Departmental ministers continued to place Bills before each House, and participate in the process of scrutiny, as before.

Naturally, new legislation will very often have implications for service delivery and policy implementation, and will consequently have an impact on the work of agencies. In this light, chief executives and other senior officials from agencies may accompany ministers to standing committees, in an advisory capacity, as departmental civil servants have been accustomed to doing. However, none of this alters the fact that legislative piloting continues to be a ministerial role responsibility.

Ambassadorial Role of Ministers

The minister *qua* departmental ambassador undertakes three main activities. The first involves acting as an advocate for, a representative of, departmental interests in the Whitehall policy network, up to and including bidding for resources in Cabinet and its committees. The second concerns liaison and consultation with the various client groups of the department and the organised pressure/interest groups associated with these. The third is a public relations function, which sees the minister 'selling' the successes of the department in media appearances, public meetings and ceremonies.

Clearly, in certain types of agency, chief executives would be likely to assume greater responsibility for elements of the minister's ambassadorial role. Those with trading fund status would be likely to rely to a lesser extent on the ministerial 'ambassador' acting as an advocate/bidder for resources than those which came within the departmental vote.

The Fraser Report divides agencies into four groups (Efficiency Unit, 1991, 22): those which 'execute, in a highly delegated way, statutory ... functions derived from the main aims of the department'; those which 'provide services to departments (or other agencies) using particular specialist skills'; those which 'are not linked to any of the main aims of a department'; and those which are fundamental to the mainstream policy and operations of their department. Chief executives of agencies falling within the first three groups are likely to play a significantly greater role than ministers in relation to the second and third types of ambassadorial activity described above. On the other hand, chief executives of agencies in the fourth group are more likely to share key elements of the minister's ambassadorial role, owing to the politically sensitive nature of the agency's activities.

In a general sense, therefore, it can be argued that agencies are likely to have an impact upon this particular aspect of ministerial role responsibility.

Accountability

By offering a broad interpretation of the doctrine of individual ministerial responsibility, we have seen that the concept of ministerial and civil service role responsibilities, encapsulating policy matters, management, legislative piloting and ambassadorial functions, are key elements of the 'responsibility for' aspects of the doctrine, and these can be applied to the activities of parent departments and 'Next Steps' agencies. What of 'responsibility to'?

Earlier, it was argued that the appropriate sense of responsibility to can be conveyed by the term accountability, which has an internal dimension (accountability of ministers to the government as a whole, especially to the Prime Minister, and to the generality of their party; accountability of officials to ministers and to their civil service superiors), and an external dimension (accountability of ministers and officials to Parliament).

Since the major purpose of the rest of this book will be to analyse in detail the accountability of ministers and civil servants to Parliament for their respective role responsibilities in relation to the 'Next Steps' agencies, comments on accountability at this stage will be limited.

Ministers may be held accountable to Parliament in a formal sense via the media of parliamentary questions, departmental select committees, standing committees, the Parliamentary Commissioner for Administration and the Public Accounts Committee. Civil servants have a *de jure* direct accountability to Parliament only through the Public Accounts Committee (as it impinges upon departmental and agency accounting officers). However, it can be argued that developments in parliamentary accountability over the past quarter of a century have produced a new regime of parliamentary accountability in which there has been a move in the direction of a *de facto* direct accountability of officials to Parliament. The questioning of increasing numbers of civil servants in increasing detail by departmental select committees (albeit circumscribed by the Osmotherly Memorandum), and the investigation of official actions by the Parliamentary Commissioner for Administration, together with the new facility for agency chief executives to respond directly to MPs' questions (problematic though that is in some respects), are not insignificant enhancements of the accountability element of our doctrine.

In ten or twenty years' time, it might be possible to conclude that one of the effects of the Next Steps initiative was the creation of an accountability gap which facilitated buck-passing by ministers and chief executives on the model of the nationalised industry chairmen and their sponsoring ministers. On the other hand, the conclusion might be that Next Steps represented another crab-like step in the general direction of improved ministerial and civil service accountability to Parliament for their wide and varied role responsibilities. By examining the early phase of the relationship between the new agencies and Parliament, this book will offer some clues about the most likely outcome.

References

Cm 524, 1988:   *Civil Service Management Reform: the Next Steps: Government Reply to the Eighth Report from the Treasury and Civil Service Committee*, 1987–88, HMSO, November 1988.

Davies and
Willman, 1991:

What Next? Agencies, Departments and the Civil Service, Institute for Public Policy Research, 1991.

Dunleavy, 1992:

Patrick Dunleavy, quoted in Peter Hennessy and Simon Coates, 'Bluehall, SW1?', *Strathclyde Analysis Paper Number 11*, University of Strathclyde, 1992.

Efficiency Unit,
1988:

Cabinet Office Efficiency Unit, *Improving Management in Government: the Next Steps*, HMSO, 1988.

Efficiency Unit,
1991:

Making the Most of Next Steps: the Management of Ministers' Departments and their Executive Agencies, Cabinet Office, May 1991.

Finer, 1956:

'The Individual Responsibility of Ministers', *Public Administration*, Vol 34, No 4, 1956.

Greer, 1992:

Patricia Greer, 'The Next Steps Initiative: the Transformation of Britain's Civil Service', *Political Quarterly*, Vol 63, No 2, April–June 1992.

Hennessy, 1989:

Peter Hennessy, *Whitehall*, Secker and Warburg, 1989.

McDonald, 1992:

Oonagh McDonald: *Swedish Models: the Swedish Model of Central Government*, Institute for Public Policy Research, 1992.

Price Waterhouse,
1991 and 1992:

Price Waterhouse, *Executive Agencies: Facts and Trends*, No 3, March 1991; No 4, March 1992.

Pyper, 1987:

'The doctrine of individual ministerial responsibility in British Government: theory and practice in a new regime of parliamentary accountability', PhD Thesis, University of Leicester, 1987.

Pyper, 1991:   'Ministerial Departures from British Governments, 1964–90: A Survey', *Contemporary Record*, Vol 5, No 2, Autumn 1991.

3

Next Steps and Parliamentary Scrutiny

Barry Winetrobe

Introduction

The Next Steps Initiative has potentially profound implications for the role and function of parliamentary accountability. The scale of the changes made by the Initiative in the structure and operation of central government functions makes it a more fundamental reform of the civil service than any since the War. It can be suggested that Parliament (which for the purposes of this chapter will mean the House of Commons) has developed its methods of scrutiny of the executive, up to and including the select committee reforms of 1979, in an era of reasonably clear ministerial control (direct or otherwise) over central administration and activities, through departments, 'quangos', nationalised industries and so on. The traditional ideas of parliamentary accountability, and even the application of apparent analogies with nationalised industries, may not be appropriate for the brave new world of the executive agency system as conceived in the Initiative.

As is common with reforms of the central government administration, the Initiative has, in general, been implemented without recourse to legislation. Parliament has, therefore, not had the opportunity that the legislative passage of a Bill provides to debate fully the merits of the principle and detail of the Next Steps exercise. Parliament has in practice developed its scrutiny of the Initiative in a pragmatic way. This can mean that the methodology and quality of this scrutiny is dependent on the interest and activity of MPs, either individually or collectively in committees.

It can also mean that, in the absence of an existing framework of appropriate mechanisms, the agenda of scrutiny can, to a large extent, be influenced or even set by the Government. While this chapter, in common with traditional constitutional practice, will talk of 'Parliament' as if it were an autonomous body with one voice, in practice it is the Government which has the role of initiating implementation of procedural changes within Parliament. While this should not be taken to mean that Ministers necessarily force through changes to their own rather than Parliament's benefit (or even that in all cases the interests of 'Parliament' and 'Government' are divergent) it does mean that, even in such important 'House of Commons matters' as scrutiny methods, however much Parliament may propose, it is for the Government to dispose.

It is commonplace to state that the United Kingdom does not have either a written constitution or a formalised system of administrative law in the continental sense. This means that exercises such as the Next Steps Initiative can be considered by the executive, legislature and judiciary as little more than organisational restructuring, with little potential relevance to broad questions of constitutionality or legality. The interests of the public, if they are recognised at all, in the novel changes wrought by the Initiative are to be considered mainly in the consumerist context through the mechanisms of Charters and the like.

The consequence of these initial considerations is that Parliament—with a tradition of acceptance of the 'constitutional' doctrine of the separation of the executive and legislative functions, and in the apparent all-party support for the Initiative in the initial stages—has had to deal with the Initiative, its new executive agencies and slimmed-down core departments, as given. Its perceived role is, therefore, one of analysing how the Initiative affects the existing notions and methods of parliamentary accountability, and then to develop any new or revised methods that may be required to render accountability of the agencies effective.

Accountability

Before we can assess the effectiveness of the parliamentary response to the Next Steps Initiative, we must consider what is meant by the term 'parliamentary accountability'.

Accountability is a rather fluid concept. (Turpin, 1989) For the purposes of this chapter it can be thought of as having two related aspects:

(a)   the existence and direction of the constitutional relationship between two or more parties ('linkages');

(b)   the substance of that relationship ('scrutiny' or 'oversight').

Looking at the first meaning, it can be seen that there are three broad relationships to be considered:

(i)   accountability of agency (or its chief executive) to 'parent' minister,
(ii) accountability of agency (or its chief executive) to Parliament,
(iii) accountability of 'parent' minister to Parliament.

Jordan has remarked that, in the agencies, 'we are told ministerial accountability remains. But in reality it is now accountability to the Minister by the Chief Executive rather than accountability of the Minister to the House of Commons that is now on offer: these are different'. (Jordan, 1992, 13)

Even within these broad relationships there will be 'subsidiary accountabilities', in the sense of responsibility relationships, such as that between a central department and its agencies and minister. For example, the relationship between an agency and its minister may be direct or it may sometimes be through the medium of the department. This is increasingly relevant in the parliamentary select committee context where both ministers and officials may in practice be called to account, not necessarily with one voice. (Turpin, 1989, 64–68)

The development of a quasi-private sector, 'business-like' approach to the civil service since 1979 means that, between agency and department, and between departmental staff and their managers and ministers, the public law concept of accountability consists increasingly of responsibility relationships, such as employee-employer or agent-principal, more familiar to the world of private law. The growing intrusion of 'commercial confidentiality' into hitherto public areas can impede effective accountability through the traditional methods of Parliamentary Questions or select committee investigation. The mixture of more than one of the new methods of service delivery can also complicate the accountability process, where for example an executive agency may itself employ private contractors to undertake operational activities on its behalf. 'Where does the buck stop?' may become an increasingly difficult question for Parliament to answer in its scrutiny of any particular executive operation.

Another important preliminary point to note, in relation to the second form of accountability—scrutiny or oversight—is that Parliament, and especially its committees, at present has two tasks to perform:

(a)   oversight of the Next Steps Initiative itself—the implementation of the programme set in train by the Ibbs report; the effect on the civil service and its staffing, structure and cost as a whole; the role and function of residual 'core departments' and the part they play in the accountability of their agencies to Parliament, and so on;

(b)   oversight of the executive operations of the agencies themselves —Next Steps in action.

It can be assumed that the first task will be finite, or at least a diminishing one, as the Next Steps process will, at some point, be regarded as completed or superseded by a new exercise. However, in the early years of the Initiative it is inevitable that this task will be seen to be predominant, and to some extent part of this task will or should be the creation of the principles and structure of the continuing task of oversight of the agencies' operations.

Agencies, Accountability and Parliament

Consideration of the parliamentary accountability of Next Steps executive agencies is not only important in itself. It also highlights the issue of parliamentary accountability as such. Some would go further and say that it goes to the heart of the role and function of Parliament itself. While the post-war debate on parliamentary reform was to a large degree an attempt to adapt Parliament to the modern scale and form of the 'welfare state' Executive, it culminated in a reform—the 1979 departmental select committee system—which can be regarded as more evolutionary than revolutionary. (Drewry, 1989) Other adaptations of parliamentary practice, such as the expansion of the scale and relative importance of the 'constituency welfare' role of individual Members of Parliament, are a more ad hoc response to the growth and intrusiveness of Government. The Next Steps Initiative has forced Parliament to consider not only the institutional forms of its oversight of the Executive (e.g. *who* and *where* to hold to account for agency activities) but also the fundamental basis of the scrutiny function itself (*how* to hold to account).

Traditionally Parliament has regarded itself as constitutionally most suited to be the body which undertakes this scrutiny of the executive, especially since (as has already been noted) it does not regard itself as part of 'the executive' in terms of policy creation and implementation. So, for example, in addition to the standard methods of parliamentary scrutiny such as questions, debates and committee inquiries, the offices of the

Comptroller and Auditor General (C&AG) and the Parliamentary Commissioner for Administration are by statute linked to Parliament.

The House of Commons Treasury and Civil Service Committee (TCSC) has attempted a continuing examination of the Next Steps Initiative, itself a laudable exercise of its scrutiny powers. The Government has given the appearance of involving Parliament, especially through the medium of the TCSC, in the progress of the Next Steps Initiative. Every opportunity is taken by ministers and senior officials to acknowledge and welcome the active participation of the Committee. In a debate on 20 May 1991 (the first such since the inception of the Initiative three years previously!), the then Minister for the Civil Service, Tim Renton, said that he very much welcomed the Committee's input: 'It is fair to say that the development of Next Steps has been a team effort between the Select Committee and the Government.' (HC Deb 191, 669)

The senior members of the Committee were happy to be associated with this praise. The Labour chairman of the sub-committee dealing with the Initiative, Giles Radice, recognised that MPs 'are usually more comfortable with policy issues than with questions of management, but I ... thought that the Next Steps changes were far too important to be left to the executive alone, and that there should be a parliamentary input ... The Select Committee's close involvement in a major bureaucratic change is, arguably, unique in the relationship between Parliament and the executive.' (HC Deb 191, 683)

The question of accountability of Next Steps executive agencies to Parliament is, according to the ever-growing literature on the Next Steps Initiative, a matter commonly accepted to be of crucial importance. The Ibbs Report itself devotes a whole section to the issue (para. 23 and annex A), albeit in a very provocative way. 'Placing responsibility for performance squarely on the shoulders of the manager of the agency also has implications for the way in which Ministers answer to Parliament for operational issues.' Indeed Ibbs considered that the traditional notion of ministerial responsibility to Parliament 'is part of the cause of the overload we observed. We believe it is possible for Parliament, through Ministers, to regard managers as directly responsible for operational matters and that there are precedents for this and precisely defined ways in which it can be handled. If management in the civil service is truly to be improved this aspect cannot be ignored.' (Efficiency Unit, 1988, para. 23)

In the report's annex this issue was considered in more detail. 'What is needed is the establishment of a convention that heads of executive agencies would have delegated authority from their Ministers for operations of the agencies with the framework of policy directives and resource allocations prescribed by Ministers.' This 'modification of accountability', as the report described it, would also assist in dealing with questions of operational detail and ministerial overload. In addition, MPs should be able to receive a better and quicker service directly from agencies rather than indirectly from ministers.

Accountability, especially the parliamentary variety, is generally regarded as a 'good thing'. Therefore any innovations have to be made to fit into it, and not vice versa. The reason for the hostile reaction to the consideration of parliamentary accountability in the Ibbs Report was that it appeared to suggest that the Efficiency Unit considered parliamentary accountability a disbenefit in the administrative process. 'We do not regard,' responded the TCSC (in suitably bold type), 'parliamentary accountability as a cost which must be weighed in the balance against the benefit of effective management. It is not only important in its own right, it is also an extremely effective pressure for improvement.' (TCSC, 1988, para. 39)

The TCSC discussed accountability extensively in its 1988 report (its first annual scrutiny of Next Steps) under the imposing title of 'Democratic control and accountability'. (paras 39–51) Accountability to Parliament and the public must be 'rigorous', and 'the crucial issue ... is the form which such accountability should take and whether the present arrangements will be appropriate in future'. (para. 39) This indeed is a crucial issue, and the remainder of the report's consideration attempts to deal with some of the relevant accountability linkages, such as the need for agency chief executives to give evidence to select committees on their own behalf (para. 46) and to act as agency accounting officers. (para. 49) Interestingly, changes or developments in non-parliamentary accountability are given a cursory paragraph, despite the assertion that overseas models, such as Sweden, 'would seem to merit the close attention of Government and Parliament'. (para. 50)

The Government decided that discretion was the best policy and simply insisted, in the Prime Minister's words, that 'there will be no change in the arrangements for accountability'. (HC Deb 127, 1151) Indeed, the more recent line is that not only are agencies fully accountable to Parliament through their respective ministers but also that Next Steps has enhanced accountability to Parliament through the publication of relevant information such as framework documents, targets, annual reports and so on. (Next Steps Project Team, 1992) The consideration of parliamentary accountability in agency framework documents appears to reflect the

Government's publicly stated aim that it remains the same, even if in modified form.

However, Greer has questioned the value and relevance of parliamentary accountability in the agency context, fearing that it could interfere with the notion of flexibility which agency status is intended to bring to executive activities. 'If "flexibility" is to be at all meaningful ... it will involve experiment and thereby risk ... If the National Audit Office and the select committees continue their traditional roles of reporting to Parliament on the economy, efficiency and effectiveness of the use of the resources in specific areas, then particularly at the early stages of agency development, they are likely to be accused of stifling innovation, and, consequently, the spirit of the Next Steps Initiative. The potential incompatibility of increased flexibility with parliamentary accountability, therefore, provides agencies and departments with a rationale for attempting to limit the scope of the parliamentary watch-dogs'. (Greer, 1992, 90–91) This reflects the Ibbs Report's comment that 'pressure from Parliament ... encourages a cautious and defensive response which feeds through into management'. (Efficiency Unit, 1988, para. 9)

Prosser, in a similar vein, has suggested (in a pre-Initiative era) that 'the extreme centrality accorded to Parliament as the location for representation and accountability under British constitutional arrangements' is largely responsible for the poverty of consideration in Britain of institutional reform in public law and administration. (Prosser, 1985, 176)

The Next Steps Initiative is but one of a package of developments in the management of the public sector. In a speech to the Institute of Directors on 20 July 1992, the Chancellor of the Duchy of Lancaster, William Waldegrave, set out the Major Government's policy of a 'genuine revolution in Whitehall' as based on four key mechanisms—privatisation, contracting out/market testing, better management, and the application of Citizen's Charter principles. They had not just been reforming government, 'in fact, we have been reinventing it'. By way of example he said that Next Steps agencies were headed by chief executives acting as they would in the private sector, 'only, unlike their private sector counterparts, they are also likely to be hauled up in front of a Parliamentary Select Committee if they haven't delivered'.

The Citizen's Charter, according to Waldegrave, provided the basis for a redefinition of accountability of the public services:

Accountability has been upwards, to Ministers and Parliament; power has been centralised. The Citizen's Charter does not remove that form of accountability—nor should it. But it enhances it by building in addition a pull downwards and outwards—to the local provider, the user and the local community. It gives people information about what they are entitled to and what they can do if their entitlements are not met; it empowers through greater openness and the ending of anonymity and it empowers through public accountability with the publication of both standards and results. (Waldegrave, 1992)

Notwithstanding the Government's protestations of 'business as usual' over parliamentary accountability, there have been a number of areas, perhaps relatively minor in themselves, where change has been successfully pressed on the Government. The most notable of these are the treatment of chief executives' letters to MPs following parliamentary questions (see Chapter 7), and the creation of agency accounting officers.

However, these individual developments in the area of accountability since February 1988 cannot be a substitute for fundamental thinking about the nature of parliamentary accountability in the agency context. Writers such as Drewry (1988, 505) have tackled this issue and the TCSC itself began its involvement in the Next Steps Initiative with the substantial opening salvo noted above (1988, paras. 39–51). But the Committee is hardly a disinterested party in this debate. When it declared that 'the issue of accountability is crucial' (1988, para. 51), it meant that the preservation of accountability is the crucial issue. In other words, the Committee thought that the Initiative would have to be made to fit parliamentary accountability, not, as the Ibbs Report appeared to want, the other way around.

To some degree the search for a proper and effective system for parliamentary accountability reprises the problems which arose over scrutiny of the nationalised industries in the post-war era. There was a clear conflict between Parliament and successive governments (supported by the nationalised industries themselves) over the extent of meaningful parliamentary oversight of what was then a huge segment of the public sector. Problems arose in the areas of traditional scrutiny, such as parliamentary questions, but the crucial issue became the degree to which the C&AG (and, through the PAC, Parliament) could examine the books and records of the nationalised industries. This dispute culminated in the debates over the private member's bill which ultimately became the National Audit Act 1983.

Alternative means of audit and scrutiny of these industries were developed or proposed, including regular references to the Monopolies and

Mergers Commission. However this depended on ministerial, rather than parliamentary initiative, and according to Garner, it benefited government more than it did Parliament. 'Effectively ... efficiency auditing has been introduced in a manner that considerably strengthens ministerial control whilst making only incidental and indirect contributions to accountability to Parliament'. (Garner, 1982, 425) Prosser concluded his study of the nationalised industries by asserting that 'the central point is that the means for accountability and for other forms of democratic legitimacy are not mere optional extras but essential to the success of public ownership'. (Prosser, 1986, 235) While Next Steps agencies are not institutionally identical to the 'old-style' nationalised industries, they may be sufficiently similar for some comparative purposes when examining accountability to Parliament.

Mechanisms such as the regulatory agencies, devised in the 1980s as competition enforcers in the new environment created by widespread privatisation, may develop a more general provenance in the more complex public sector of the future. (Lewis, 1989)

The NAO/PAC Model and Its Application

Parliament at present scrutinises governmental activities, whether performed by agencies, core departments or other relevant institutions, by evaluating them against criteria such as financial probity; 'value-for-money'; efficiency, effectiveness, and economy; and maladministration. The question, then, is whether there is a gap in this web of accountability, involving in some sense a scrutiny of non-financial administrative performance and policy. One possible accountability model, which may provide some assistance in filling this gap, especially in the context of ongoing oversight, is the National Audit Office/Public Accounts Committee relationship, within a context of the departmental select committee system. (The current role of the NAO and the PAC in the scrutiny of executive agencies is considered in Chapter 6) This model benefits from some inherent advantages—the statutory foundation of the NAO; the independence of the C&AG; the staffing levels of the NAO and the strong historical roots of the PAC—which provide it with at least the potential for pursuing a focused and effective form of accountability.

For present purposes, this chapter is not concerned with institutional issues such as the relationship of the two bodies with the departmental select committees. (Procedure Committee 1990, paras. 232–268) What is of interest is the model itself and its potential applicability to the regime of parliamentary scrutiny of agencies. It is an audit model; it is concerned with *ex post facto* scrutiny. Part II of the National Audit Act 1983 empowers the C&AG to carry out 'examinations into the economy, efficiency and effectiveness with which any department ... has used its resources in discharging its functions' although this power does not entitle the C&AG 'to question the merits of the policy objectives of any department ...' [S6(1) and (2)]. This is the 'value for money' audit, now a common feature of public sector financial regulation.

This statutory framework provides a relatively transparent remit for the form of oversight employed by the NAO and the PAC. This means that (policy/administration definitional problems aside) the parliamentary scrutiny bodies have a reasonably clear indication of how they are expected to fulfil their accountability task (in this case, financial accountability) over one area of the policy/administration spectrum.

This suggests that, if there is to be an enhancement of some form of parliamentary accountability applied to agencies, the general instruments of such scrutiny (especially the departmental select committees) may require a similar form of explicit 'mission statement'. At present the committees, in the words of the Commons Standing Order, are empowered simply to examine the expenditure, administration and policy of departments. (Procedure Committee 1990, paras. 13–36) While this broad phrase may have the advantage of flexibility, it may be that in the new world of agencies, contractors and 'core' departments they require a clearer indication of how they are expected to carry out their accountability function, and which methodology (such as audit) they may employ. This could include, for individual departmental committees, the requirement to scrutinise agencies' qualitative and other targets, and to report thereon; to examine issues of agency (or departmental) status, structure, establishment and so on, and to report upon any proposed alterations.

It would be for Parliament itself to determine if more explicit scrutiny duties and powers are required, and if so how they are to be devised and implemented. This could well be undertaken by the Procedure Committee, the springboard for the 1979 reforms.

Traditionally, Parliament has not involved itself routinely in detailed policy formulation, accepting the argument that this is primarily an executive task. In the context of Next Steps agencies, this means that the departmental select committees have apparently accepted, so far, that they can have no direct role in the formulation of agency framework documents (or, presumably, in the appointment of agency chief executives).

However, substantive scrutiny by Parliament could include evaluation of the adequacy and appropriateness of performance targets set out by Government in framework documents (similar issues arise in the context of Citizen's Charter performance indicators). See for example the discussion on agency targets in the TCSC's 1991 report. (TCSC, 1991, paras. 58–69)

In the early days of the Initiative, Giles Radice noted that select committees had been slow to question chief executives about this important issue. 'Part of the problem is that we do not yet have a generally accepted set of performance indicators, so it becomes difficult to ask meaningful questions about the work of agencies. If the performance indicators can be developed perhaps the Select Committees will be in a stronger position. It is important that those Committees can make chief executives responsible for their stewardship'. (HC Deb 191, 686–7)

In particular, there was initial criticism of the relative paucity of quality-of-service compared with financial or efficiency targets. Sir Angus Fraser's report emphasised that it was important for agencies to have 'a handful of robust and meaningful top level output targets' which would include quality of customer service. A main concern of agency and departmental staff was that 'few targets included adequate measures of service quality'. (Efficiency Unit 1991, paras. 2, 4 and 3.3) The government's response to the TCSC's 1991 report was to emphasise the role which the Citizen's Charter would play in enhancing quality of service. (Cm 1761, 9) The NAO and the PAC have also maintained a close interest, as we shall see in Chapter 6.

One aspect of agency activity which the select committees could legitimately scrutinise if they adopted a more 'flexible' view of parliamentary involvement in 'executive' matters is quality of service in terms of the existence and level of the service provided. If executive agencies carry out 'public services', this presumably carries with it the implication that these services need to be undertaken (though not necessarily in the public sector). This is obviously of vital importance to actual or potential 'customers' where the body is in a monopoly or near-monopoly position. Most if not all agencies are in this position and therefore the existence and extent of their service provision is a vital subject of parliamentary scrutiny, not least because such matters are of real interest to users of the services, who are also MPs' constituents.

The former Cabinet Secretary, Lord Hunt of Tanworth, has suggested that there should be established 'an Inspector General of Executive Agencies, who, in consultation with the Head of the Civil Service and the Treasury, could periodically review the performance of each department/agency combination and report to the Prime Minister on how the agencies are managing to combine the drive for greater managerial independence and efficiency with service principally to their customers but also to collective Cabinet government'. (Hunt, 1991, 100) This proposal places the scrutiny function in an executive context. Perhaps what may be needed is the reverse, that is placing supposedly executive functions in a scrutiny context. The NAO/PAC model may provide a method of achieving this.

The major mode of detailed parliamentary accountability is the system of departmental select committees. We have already noted the role of the TCSC in the scrutiny of the Next Steps Initiative. Put very simply there are three types of committee (excluding, for present purposes, standing committees examining proposed legislation from various sources) which have a role in the scrutiny of the executive, including governmental functions carried out by agencies:

(i)   Public Accounts Committee

(ii)   Select Committee on the Parliamentary Commissioner for Administration.

(iii)   Departmental select committees.

The third group can be subdivided into:

(a)   Treasury and Civil Service Select Committee

(b)   Other departmental select committees

As noted above, the PAC works with the C&AG serviced by the National Audit Office. Under existing statutory provisions and parliamentary powers the Initiative, as a process of institutional reform, has been examined by the NAO and PAC. (NAO 1989; PAC 1989) Individual agencies can also be subject to similar audit and scrutiny.

The select committee on the PCA, working with the Parliamentary Ombudsman, who also has statutory functions, operates on a 'maladministration' criterion of scrutiny and assessment, and will deal with complaints against agencies on the same basis as those against other departments within the scope of the PCA's statutory jurisdiction. The literature on the Ombudsman consistently emphasises that, in addition to its complaints redress role, the Ombudsman model is a process for identifying scope for improvement in administrative practice. Rawlings even went so far as to propose that the links between MPs in their 'constituency ombudsman' role, the PCA and the PCA select committee should be formalised so as to unify the two parliamentary functions of redress of grievances and oversight of the executive. (Rawlings, 1986, 137–141) The select committee has already examined the implications of the Citizen's Charter for the work of the PCA. (PCA Select Committee, 1992) The role of the PCA in the Next Steps Initiative is considered in Chapter 8.

There are no statutory rules governing the powers or operation of the departmental select committees. Their existence derives from rather broadly phrased Commons Standing Orders. Although in principle these committees can co-operate with each other and even co-ordinate their activities (so as, for example, to undertake the same sort of enquiry in every subject area at the same time), this has tended (the Liaison Committee notwithstanding) not to be their usual experience since they were set up in their present form in 1979. As regards the Next Steps Initiative, the overall scrutiny of the Initiative has been undertaken by the TCSC (oversight task (a), identified above) and the other subject committees (in addition to the TCSC) are free to examine the agencies within their area (oversight task (b)). Some, such as the Home Affairs Committee in the 1991–92 Parliament, have done so. (Home Affairs Committee, 1991) The work of departmental select committees is examined in more detail in Chapter 5.

At the beginning of this section it was suggested that Parliament may need to evolve some form of scrutiny of policy and administration which mirrors, in a non-financial context, the scrutiny regime of the NAO and the PAC. If so, this implies that such scrutiny should be the responsibility of one or more of the departmental select committees, as their standing orders already authorise them to examine government policy and administration.

If they are to operate according to some external yardstick, equivalent to the financial criteria of the C&AG or the maladministration test of the PCA, rather than by way of ad hoc inquiry, they may well require some form of specialist support beyond that provided at present by specialist advisers and specialist assistants, perhaps mirroring the support provided in their distinctive ways by the PCA and C&AG and their respective offices.

One possible model, which would build upon existing parliamentary structures, would be a full select committee of the House of Commons (in place of the present sub-committee of the TCSC) charged with the parliamentary scrutiny of the machinery of government, the relevant departments such as OPSS and the appropriate divisions of the Treasury. This would cover both agencies and core departments (there appears to be no benefit in Lord Hunt's proposal to treat agencies as a species apart from the rest of the Civil Service). It could be called the Machinery of Government Committee, or, in the interests of familiarity, the Civil Service Committee. Individual departmental committees could report to it on their scrutiny of agencies, and departments, within their remit.

This committee's specialist support, which would perform the role in relation to the Committee that the NAO does for the PAC, could perhaps be called something like the Assessment of Government Office (AGO). Coombes, in his study of the old Nationalised Industries select committee, has described how similar forms of committee support (called, in some cases, 'assessors') were suggested in the 1950s. (Coombes, 1966, 75–81, 206–210) It would have the same statutory status and independence from Government that the NAO has under the National Audit Act 1983, and its head (the Assessor-General?) would have a status, and parliamentary link, similar to that of the C&AG.

To some extent, the departmental select committees are going along a path which may lead to some form of the above system in practice. The 1990 Procedure Committee made a number of recommendations which would allow committees some limited access to the information held by, and the expert staff of, the NAO. While the Procedure Committee was, diplomatically, at pains to reassure the Public Accounts Committee that this was not to be construed as a take-over bid for access to the NAO (hitherto the almost exclusive preserve of the PAC), it is not difficult to envisage a situation in the near future where the 900 staff of the NAO will become an additional, and perhaps essential, regular support for the work of the departmental committees. (Procedure Committee, 1990, paras. 232–268)

Conclusions

This chapter has argued that to consider parliamentary accountability simply in terms of creating and enforcing the linkages between agencies and ministers on the one hand and Parliament on the other should not be the whole story, but simply its first chapter. 'To talk only of links in the system of accountability ... is to risk confining any analysis in a mechanistic, verbal straitjacket, to imply by the choice of words used that the effectiveness of a system of accountability can be evaluated in terms of the appropriate connections being made and the appropriate techniques used'. (Day and Klein, 1987, 29)

The story so far of parliamentary accountability of agencies appears to be one where Parliament has been feeling its way in asserting its scrutiny rights over these new bureaucratic forms, within its existing institutional framework. This is consistent with the evolutionary nature of parliamentary reform as demonstrated by the 1979 select committee reforms. However, in relation to executive agencies, Parliament's actions thus far have concentrated on the first form of accountability, that of defining the accountable relationships between the parties—Parliament, Government and the agencies. See for example the TCSC's initial report: 'We conclude that there must be a modification to the present formal arrangements for accountability. The Chief Executive should give evidence on his own behalf about what he has done as the head of the agency'. (TCSC, 1988, para. 46) This is perhaps an understandable initial impulse on the part of Parliament; a desire to rein in this new beast before it has the chance to escape its accountability clutches. However, Parliament may need to consider seriously further substantive questions of accountability, including analytical tools and institutional mechanisms of scrutiny.

On the surface it would appear that the creation of agency accounting officers is a good example of the success of the existing parliamentary mechanisms to integrate the new governmental bodies into existing processes of accountability. It may be that this success has arisen because it is in an area—financial accountability—where the parliamentary role is recognised and the mechanisms are more clearly established and better understood. The new procedures for publication of chief executive letters to MPs are a step forward in accountability, but one which perhaps demonstrates the present ad hoc development of agency accountability,

Jordan has asserted that 'the Next Steps approach is presented in a constitutional vacuum. Where there should be the delineation of new arrangements, there is a bold empiricism that the detail can be worked out later. There is no sense in the propaganda of change that this is a controversial area. It has been argued that such arrangements could not be better crafted to facilitate blame-avoidance and a confusion of accountability'. (Jordan, 1992, 14)

The TCSC and the PAC have done useful work in monitoring the Next Steps Initiative. They have considered ways in which details of accountability can be improved; the effect of the Initiative on the civil service; the relationship between Next Steps and privatisation; the role and function of core or residual departments and so on. The TCSC has, understandably, taken upon itself the role of chief scrutineer of the Next Steps Initiative, although its pattern of annual reviews was interrupted by the 1992 general election.

However, unless Parliament believes that 'democratic control and accountability' (TCSC, 1988, xvii) is satisfied by an ongoing exercise in monitoring, more detailed self-examination by Parliament may be urgently required. The present successes in improving 'procedural accountability' may properly be regarded as a first step which must be seen as a starting point for constructing a comprehensive web of substantive parliamentary scrutiny of the rapidly changing public sector of the 1990s, including the Next Steps agencies.

Day and Klein have claimed that 'the widespread assumption that direct election can somehow be equated with the effective practice of accountability does not hold water'. (1987, 240) In other words 'democracy' does not of itself ensure the effective control of the service concerned, which is 'the necessary condition for completing the circle of accountability'. (241) Nevertheless this chapter has assumed that, for the foreseeable future, the primary conduit of political accountability (as opposed to legal accountability by way of, say, a reformed administrative law system) in this country, will be the supreme 'democratic' body, Parliament. We may be entering the era of the 'enabling' local authority, but we are still some way away from a fully 'enabling' Whitehall/Westminster system of government. The problem then is to determine whether Parliament can construct the 'tools for assessing the performance of service providers' (Day and Klein, 1987, 241), or whether it leaves this task, as it does at present, to the Executive, and contents itself with exercising a complex form of 'secondary' accountability. In this sense it matters not whether Parliament can deal directly with agencies (by questions, letters or in select committees), as it will be operating within an accountability system designed by the Executive.

Perhaps the search for a new system of parliamentary scrutiny will not result in a radically different method of scrutiny of the Executive. The tentative idea in the previous section of this chapter of a new scrutiny select committee itself suggests that any reform in the near future is unlikely to display a radical departure from the current practices of parliamentary accountability. At least the exercise itself could be a learning experience by providing a relatively rare opportunity for Parliament to re-examine fully its relationship with the rapidly changing Executive. Recent history (Procedure Committee, 1990) implies that Parliament is unwilling to assert for itself any constitutionally novel 'executive' role. However, the whole thrust of change in the civil service since 1979 shows little sign of running out of steam as yet (although it has perhaps become, more recently, a partisan issue) and the combined effect of the Next Steps Initiative, the Citizen's Charter, privatisation, market-testing and so on may ensure that the Executive, which Parliament is 'constitutionally' required to scrutinise, is fundamentally transforming itself before Parliament's very eyes. Parliament must ensure that its scrutiny methods adapt to meet this challenge.

References

Cm 1761:   *The Next Steps Initiative: the Government Reply to the Seventh Report from the Treasury and Civil Service Committee, Session 1990-91*, HMSO, November 1991.

Coombes, 1966:   David Coombes, *The Member of Parliament and the Administration: the Case of the Select Committee on Nationalised Industries*, Allen and Unwin, 1966.

Day and Klein, 1987:   Patricia Day and Rudolf Klein, *Accountabilities*, Tavistock Publications, 1987.

Drewry, 1988:   Gavin Drewry, 'Forward From FMI: the Next Steps', *Public Law*, 1988.

Drewry, 1989:   Gavin Drewry et al, *The New Select Committees*, Clarendon Press, Oxford, 1989.

Efficiency Unit,   Cabinet Office Efficiency Unit, *Improving*
1988:   *Management in Government: the Next Steps*,
                        February 1988.

Efficiency Unit,   *Making the Most of Next Steps: the Management*
1991:   *of Ministers' Departments and their Executive*
                        Agencies, Cabinet Office, May 1991.

Garner, 1982:   M R Garner, 'Auditing the efficiency of the
                        nationalised industries: enter the Monopolies and
                        Mergers Commission', *Public Administration*, Vol
                        60, No 4, Winter 1982.

Greer, 1992:   Patricia Greer, 'The Next Steps Initiative: an
                        Examination of Agency Framework Documents',
                        Public Administration, Vol 70, No 1, Spring
                        1992.

Hunt, 1991:   Lord Hunt of Tanworth, 'The Cabinet and "Next
                        Steps"' in F Vibert (ed), *Britain's Constitutional*
                        Future, Institute of Economic Affairs, 1991.

Jordan, 1992:   Grant Jordan, 'Next Steps Agencies: from
                        management, by command to management by
                        contract?', *Aberdeen Papers in Accountancy,*
                        Finance and Management, W6, 1992.

Lewis, 1989:   Norman Lewis, 'Regulating Non-Government
                        Bodies', in J Jowell and D Oliver (eds), *The*
                        Changing Constitution, OUP, 1989.

NAO, 1989:   National Audit Office, *The Next Steps Initiative*,
                        HC 410, 1988–89, June 1989.

Next Steps Project   *Next Steps Briefing Note*, Cabinet Office Next
Team, 1992:   Steps Project Team, July 1992

PAC, 1989:   Thirty-eighth Report of the Public Accounts
                        Committee, 1988–89, *The Next Steps Initiative*,
                        HC 420, October 1989.

PCA Select
Committee, 1992:
The Implications of the Citizen's Charter for the Work of the Parliamentary Commissioner for Administration, Second Report of 1991–92, HC 158, February 1992.

Procedure
Committee, 1990:
Second Report from the Procedure Committee, *The Working of the Select Committee System*, HC 19, 1989–90, October 1990.

Prosser, 1985:
Tony Prosser, 'Democratisation, Accountability and Institutional Design: Reflections on Public Law', in *Law, Legitimacy and the Constituion*, P McAuslan and J McEldowney (eds).

Prosser, 1986:
Tony Prosser, *Nationalised Industries and Public Control: Legal, Constitutional and Political Issues*, Basil Blackwell, 1986.

Rawlings, 1986:
Rawlings, R, 'Parliamentary Redress of Grievances', in Carol Harlow (ed), *Public Law and Politics*, Sweet and Maxwell 1986.

TCSC, 1991:
Seventh Report from the Treasury and Civil Service Committee, *The Next Steps Initiative*, HC 496, 1990–91, July 1991.

Waldegrave, 1992:
William Waldegrave, *Speech to the Institute of Directors*, Office of Public Service and Science Press Release, 18/92.

PART II
The Process of Scrutiny

4

The Treasury Committee and Next Steps Agencies

Philip Giddings

Introduction

The House of Commons Treasury and Civil Service Committee (TCSC) has played a prominent part in monitoring the Next Steps Initiative (NSI) since its inception in February 1988. In the 1987–92 Parliament the Committee held a series of hearings each summer and published a report at the end of each July to which the Government responded with a Command Paper in the Autumn. In the last two years these appeared at the same time as the publication of the Government's Annual Review of the Next Steps Programme.

The TCSC reviews were conducted through its civil service sub-committee chaired by Giles Radice. In addition to the chairman, prominent roles were taken by John Watts and (after December 1989) John Garrett. It is also noteworthy that the Minister in charge of the NSI from 1988–1990, Sir Richard Luce, became a member of the Committee in March 1991, after his return to the back-benches. Generally speaking the Sub-Committee's proposed reports were accepted by the main Committee, although three paragraphs were excised from the 1991 report when it came before the full committee.

At each year's hearings the sub-committee took oral evidence from the Project Manager, Sir Peter Kemp; from the Minister in charge of OMCS, initially Sir Richard Luce and then Tim Renton; and from the Treasury, in 1988 from the Permanent Secretary, Sir Peter Middleton; after then a group of officials led by the Deputy Secretary, Civil Service Management and Pay, Mr G H Phillips. Apart from 1988, when it was obviously too early, the sub-committee also took oral evidence each year from agency chief executives—five of them in 1991. The Council of Civil Service Unions gave oral evidence twice, in 1989 and 1990, as did the Department of Social Security. The Cabinet Secretary gave evidence in 1988 and the Prime Minister's Adviser on Efficiency gave evidence in 1988 (Ibbs) and

1991 (Fraser). Between three (1990) and six (1988) sessions of oral evidence were held. The sub-committee also received substantial written evidence from Government departments as well as from outside commentators, including academics.

The Committee's reports followed a fairly standard pattern, reviewing progress in the preceding year and exploring general themes (see below). The reports were substantial, but not exceptionally so, comprising between 22 and 32 pages, 18 to 26 recommendations and 111 to 164 pages of published evidence. These reports, with the government's responses, have thus provided a major source of information and opinion about the NSI.

The Themes of the Reports

There are eight general themes in the TCSC's enquiries: the Committee's own role; accountability to Parliament; the shape of the civil service; the role of the Treasury; the pace and durability of the initiative; the relationship between agencies and their 'core departments'; performance indicators; and privatisation. These will be considered briefly in turn.

The Role of the TCSC was explicitly covered in the 1990 report. In general terms, as befits a departmentally-related select committee, it is described as a monitoring role and in this case the regularity of the monitoring was very noticeable. In its 1989 report the Committee described its role as one of 'continuing scrutiny'. More specifically, there were two further aspects to the Committee's role. The first concerned Whitehall politics. In his own evidence the Project Manager welcomed the Committee's continued interest and clearly used it to maintain the NSI's high profile in the face of what one commentator has called 'Whitehall's disbelief system'. The Committee's support has presumably (it would be useful to have direct evidence of this) been helpful to the protagonists of agencies within Whitehall. It is also clear, as has been remarked by Peter Hennessy and Giles Radice himself, that the Committee has been used as a forum for implicit dialogue between top civil service management and the Opposition. It was obviously helpful for the former to know that the NSI had bipartisan support. Such support was formally confirmed by the then Shadow Chancellor's speech to the Royal Institute of Public Administration in May 1991, the substance of which was written into the record in the Committee's 1991 report. (para. 13)

The second aspect of the Committee's particular role was an explicit concern about the *implications for Parliament* of the NSI. This was more than a concern about the mechanics of accountability (discussed below). The Committee also seemed to see itself acting as a guardian of Parliament's interest in decision-making about the organisation of the State, concerned that far-reaching decisions about the shape of Whitehall, having both constitutional and administrative implications, should not be taken without Parliament hearing an account of what is proposed and having an opportunity to express its view. This may be part of the explanation for a tendency in the Committee (and elsewhere) to over-state the radical implications of the NSI. If it was 'the most ambitious attempt at civil service reform in the twentieth century', then Parliament certainly has a legitimate interest—and so has the TCSC as Parliament's 'agent'.

Accountability to Parliament is a recurrent theme of departmentally-related select committees. Essentially this means 'explanatory' accountability and it is not confined to ministers, even if in the strict terms of the Osmotherley rules civil servants see themselves as giving evidence on ministers' behalf. For reasons touched on above, there has been no reluctance on the part of ministers or civil servants to give the TCSC an account of the progress of the NSI—even when, in its initial stages, the progress was slower than forecast and therefore the subject of some criticism. This was as well in view of the TCSC's robust rejection of the negative implications on parliamentary accountability it found in the Ibbs Report—'a view of the work of Parliament and its Committees we do not recognise'. (TCSC, 1988, para. 40)

Perhaps surprisingly in view of governmental responses in other areas, there has been no disposition to treat the NSI as part of the executive's exclusive domain, the re-organisation of which is of no particular concern to Parliament. On the contrary, the Executive, in both its political and bureaucratic guises, has been only too willing to explain to the Committee the whys and the wherefores of this piece of administrative re-organisation. It is noteworthy that without a select committee forum this would have been much more difficult—a debate on the NSI was not held until May 1991, a fact upon which the Committee commented critically more than once.

The Committee also showed particular interest in the mechanics of the accountability—questions, accounting procedures, reports, evidence-giving and the role of (other) departmental committees. The concern about questions, which is dealt with at greater length in Chapter 7, goes to the heart of central rationale of the NSI. If ministers have genuinely delegated functions to named civil servants ('chief executives'), will ministers remain fully responsible to Parliament for the exercise of those functions? The then Prime Minister's statements in 1988 highlighted the ambiguity which some could see here: ministers would remain ultimately responsible but MPs' questions on matters falling within the remit of the chief executive would be passed to the chief executive for reply. If the NSI is to work, delegation to chief executives must be substantial and effective—but not at the cost of parliamentary accountability. The dilemma is that constitutionally—apart from accounting officers—it is only ministers who can be held to account by Parliament. The dilemma is one which the TCSC itself shares, for its reports indicate its desire both to reinforce the authority of chief executives vis-à-vis 'intervention' from the department outside the terms of the framework agreement and to affirm that ministers must remain fully accountable on the Floor of the House.

In practice, many MPs prefer to go direct to the appropriate level of civil service management to deal with constituency cases since they realise that often produces the fastest answer. But neither all constituency cases nor all questions are of this kind, and for those which are not there is a reluctance to be 'palmed off' with a reply from a civil servant rather than the minister. Such reluctance increases and spreads if the line between ministerial and chief executive functions is drawn in different places, as was evident in the McAllion case, which demonstrated the fragility of the division between 'day-to-day operational matters delegated to the Agency' and matters of policy which are for Ministers (an issue not unfamiliar to students of nationalised industries, as Professor Tivey pointed out to the Committee in 1988). One problem here is that the insistence that each framework agreement is tailor-made for each agency/department does precisely mean that the line between agency and 'strictly-ministerial' function will be drawn in different places for different agencies.

Both the TCSC and the Procedure Committee have also been concerned about the availability of answers to PQs which have been re-directed to chief executives. The device of making them available for consultation in the Library was not satisfactory to Members (or to pressure groups and other observers of the parliamentary scene) and the TCSC joined with the Procedure Committee in pressing for some way to be found to include chief executives' responses to PQs in the Official Report, which has now been done. (This issue is dealt with more fully in Chapter 7.)

Both the TCSC and the Procedure Committee have also been concerned that departmentally-related select committees should play a full part in the process of accountability. This was the second recommendation of the TCSC's 1990 report and the issue was picked up again in recommendation xxii of the 1991 Report—and an earlier recommendation in that Report envisaged involving the Chairman of the appropriate select committee when changes were made to an agency's framework document or its annual targets.

On accounting procedures, the TCSC identified at the outset the problem of the accounting officer for executive agencies: if delegation is to be a reality, can the permanent secretary continue as accounting officer, answerable to the PAC? In their 1988 report the TCSC recommended that chief executives should give evidence on their own behalf to select committees on what they had done as heads of agencies and that they should be accounting officers for their agencies. (paras. 46 and 49) In a change which the project manager described as 'quite remarkable ... a breakthrough', the Government accepted this latter recommendation and agreed that chief executives should formally be appointed 'agency accounting officers'. However, the government restated the principle that chief executives give evidence on behalf of their ministers: as Mr Luce put it, 'it will be the minister in charge who carries the ultimate accountability'. (1989, Q 323) This has to be put alongside the project manager's statement that the chief executive 'is accountable for the well-running of his business ... he can be summoned before the Public Accounts Committee, before this Committee and before other Committees, to answer personally for his doings and so on'. (1989, Q 344) A fuller treatment of accounting and audit procedures, including the work of the NAO and the PAC, is given in Chapter 6.

The Shape of the Civil Service: there has from the start of the NSI been a question whether it represents a temporary and superficial or a fundamental and lasting change in the way the civil service is organised. The TCSC had in mind particularly its own disappointment with the Government's previous Financial Management Initiative (FMI) (1988, paras. 6–10) as well as other failures to proceed with the development of 'accountable management' as recommended by the Fulton Report of 1968. The TCSC was clear in its first response to Next Steps that what was needed was a change in the 'culture and attitudes of the civil service ... steps must be taken, and must be seen to be taken, to change the underlying assumptions, and to remould the way government does its business' (1988, paras. 18 and 19). With this in mind the Committee was concerned to encourage Government not to be too cautious about the delegation of responsibilities but to 'display more confidence in the systems they set up, and the managers they appoint. Too much freedom can be reined in, too little may mean the opportunity is lost'.

In their 1989 report—after barely one year's experience of the initiative in operation—the Committee picked up the project manager's assertion that the NSI was more than 'badge engineering'; it was about changing the substance rather than the labels. This emphasis the Committee was happy to endorse and it went on to draw attention to the fact that the NSI represented not only a change in the delivery of Government services but also 'a possibly radically different shape of the Civil Service'. (para. 17)

This was taken further in the Committee's 1991 hearings, when Sir Angus Fraser (Q 343), Mr Phillips from the Treasury (Q 393) and Peter Kemp (Q 415) were questioned specifically about the future shape of the civil service. The particular occasion for such questions was the Fraser report's raising of the issue 'whether there will be at the end of the road a civil service which is still a recognisable entity'—quoted by Giles Radice to Sir Angus Fraser at the start of his evidence. (Q 343) They were not reassured by Sir Angus's view that 'the whole logic of the reforms in the civil service ... was leading us inexorably to the situation where ... a "unified civil service" really is not compatible with the way we are going' (Q 344), a statement which Mr Radice found 'pretty revolutionary'. The Committee were clearly concerned both about what the future shape of the service might be, what might hold it together, and that such a fundamental issue should be widely debated. Hence in their recommendations the Committee commented (para. 31) that it would not be satisfactory if a major change in the structure of the civil service were introduced 'piecemeal, without proper opportunity for full public discussion'.

The Government's response (Cm 1761, 3) was that the NSI was indeed radically altering the organisation of the civil service (it would be interesting to explore whether the difference between 'organisation' and 'structure' is more than semantic) but that the precise shape of the service would necessarily depend upon the demands placed upon it by the government of the day. Nevertheless, the government recognised the importance of public discussion and pointed to the amount of information it had published about Next Steps and to the fact that a debate had been held in the House in May 1991. After the 1992 General Election the Committee decided to undertake a full inquiry into the role of the civil service and identified in its *Interim Report* (para. 4) concern about the implications of the NSI as one of the major issues which would need to be addressed.

The Role of the Treasury was bound to be a matter of considerable interest from the point at which it was first rumoured that the Treasury had fiercely opposed the 'original' version of the Ibbs report and that the statement the Prime Minister eventually made on the NSI was therefore a compromise. This was alluded to by Sir Robin Butler in evidence to the Committee (1988, Q 256) when he spoke of 'Treasury reservations' and 'lively debate' about the implications of the Ibbs proposals for macro-economic policy-making and public expenditure control. But he did assure the Committee that the process of implementation was going 'extremely harmoniously'. Clearly, the Treasury had, and has, a major interest: with its responsibility for civil service pay and conditions as well as public expenditure as a whole, it can hardly remain aloof from proposals for management reform. Sir Peter Middleton pointed out that 'flexibility' on pay might mean 'more pay and more expenditure'. (1988, Q 336) And as the NSI had developed out of the experience of the FMI, no-one could doubt the Treasury's interest.

The Committee's 1988 report indicated three lines of enquiry its subsequent questioning of the Treasury would follow. First, there was concern (1988, para. 28) about the implications of pay flexibility and whether Treasury interest in the expenditure implications of that (e.g. avoiding leap-frogging) would prove to be restrictive. Second, there was concern (1988, para. 30) about central co-ordination, between the Treasury, OMCS and departments, concerns which link back to the Committee's anxieties about the implications for the future shape of the Civil Service. These concerns were underlined in the 1990 report: in terms of agency-department-Treasury relations the Committee were clear that the Treasury's role must be strategic and Departments should be allowed to judge for themselves whether agency outputs were satisfactory in relation to agreed inputs: a proliferation of reporting and monitoring processes would imply too much central control and should be avoided. (para. 76) And on central organisation itself, the Committee recommended the establishment of a unit within OMCS to evaluate these various relationships (para. 80)—picking up a recommendation it had made in 1988 (para. 30) for a 'Management Board' to co-ordinate policy on personnel issues.

The third line of enquiry was concerned with 'controls', particularly those enshrined in agency framework documents. Rightly, the Committee explored the tension between the greater delegation to agency chief executives which is at the heart of the NSI and the continuing need for some central control, particularly—but not only—on expenditure grounds.

This issue was covered under the heading of 'Managerial Independence' in the Committee's 1988 report (paras. 36–38) and featured strongly in the questions to the project manager and the Treasury that year and again in 1989. The Treasury pointed out in evidence (Q 264, 1989) that 'we look out for the kind of financial regime and value for money; that is very important in all cases' and justified its close interest in agency framework documents.

The problem was expressed thus: 'We are not in the business of trying to break up the essence of the Civil Service, but we are in the business of trying to recognise the diversity of its businesses, the different nature of the different problems that are confronted by different departments and trying to attune their internal management and financial control mechanisms to what they need *while at the same time sustaining certain overall common features, both of policy, in the sense of controls on public expenditure, and of the character of the Civil Service*' (1989, Q 273, emphasis added). The Committee was concerned that the Treasury's role should not be too restrictive. Thus it was suggested during the 1991 hearings that there were few 'financially significant' flexibilities available to agencies which did not in fact require Treasury approval. (1991, Q 394) It was also revealed in that session of questioning that the Treasury had insisted on seeing all targets proposed for each agency. (Q 401)

The pace and durability of the NSI was an early concern of the Committee. In part this stemmed from disappointment with the progress made with *FMI* and concern that the 'disbelief system' operating in Whitehall might frustrate the new initiative. Thus in para.10 of its first report (1988) on the NSI the Committee made clear that the pace and extent of change in Whitehall must be improved. The Committee went on to stress the need for a change of culture and attitude in the civil service in order that obstacles to the development of accountable management (advocated in Fulton, 1968) could be overcome. One way in which this might be done, the Committee felt, was the introduction of talent from outside the service.

Having thus expressed their support for the NSI the Committee were disappointed to learn in 1989 (paras. 12 and 13) that progress with the creation of agencies had been slower than hoped for. In support of their disappointment the Committee cited lack of a firm decision from the Home Office about the Passport Agency, the deferral by the DoE of the launch date for Historic Royal Palaces, the delay in establishing the Driver Vehicle Licensing Directorate, though it was one of the first Agency candidates to be announced, and the lack of action with regard to Customs and Excise and the Inland Revenue. (para. 11, 1989) The programme had clearly failed to meet the project manager's first year target.

Nevertheless, the Committee still considered that the NSI represented a real change in the way the civil service was run and that a 'possibly radically different shape of the Civil Service' might emerge from it. The Committee reflected the Council of Civil Service Unions' fears at some of the implications of this, particularly for national pay and grading structures and the right of transferability (1989, paras. 55 and 56), and drew attention to the uncertainty created by the perceived threat that in some cases agency status might be a prelude to privatisation. (1989, paras. 64–65) But these anxieties were firmly placed in the context of the Committee's conviction that central government departments were going to change 'perhaps quite radically' as a result of the NSI. (1989, para. 72)

Concern for the durability of the agency concept was reflected in the Committee's interest in demonstrating the flexibility of framework agreements. Thus in their 1990 Report (para. 20) the Committee underlined the evidence of the Head of the Home Civil Service that 'in the event of a change of government', alteration of the parameters within which the Chief Executive works is 'a simple matter which the system allows for' by concluding that 'we stress that it is always possible to change the objectives of any Framework Agreement'. This displayed the 'non-partisan characteristics' of the NSI.

This theme was taken up at the conclusion of the Committee's 1990 report with explicit commendation of that non-partisan character. Peter Hennessy's reference to 'a piece of transferable technology' operable by governments of any political persuasion was quoted, as was the evidence of Employment Department officials that 'there is nothing in any of the documents to stop a different administration changing the objectives of the Employment Service as soon as it came into office', These comments were explicitly endorsed in the Government's response to the Committee. (Cm 1263, 17)

Having demonstrated the non-partisan character of the agency concept, the Committee proceeded in its 1991 report to place on record the commitment of the Labour Party to continue with the NSI if it were elected to government. In paragraphs 13 and 14 of the 1991 Report the Committee reported in terms the commitment of the then Shadow Chancellor (not in evidence to the Committee, but in a speech to the Royal Institute of Public Administration) not to attempt to reverse the initiative. And the Committee commented (para. 14) that 'in our successive Reports we have been concerned to sustain and develop all party support for the initiative'. In this respect the role of Giles Radice as chairman of the Sub-Committee was crucial.

The relationship between agencies and core departments is a fundamental part of the NSI and arguably one to which too little attention has been paid. A major part of the rationale for agencies is the liberating effect on departmental policy-making that delegation of operational responsibilities to agencies would achieve. The essence of this relationship is expressed in the framework agreement, which the Committee characterised in their 1988 report (para. 38) as a 'contract' between the chief executive and the minister, one which seeks to define the dividing line between policy and execution. The Committee were clear, because of the importance of this dividing line for parliamentary accountability, that framework agreements should be published (para. 42) and the chief executives should be accounting officers for their agencies. (para. 49)

The first point was conceded in the Government's Reply (Cm 524, 9) and the second in a Written Answer on 10 November 1988 (Cols 249–250w)—'a breakthrough' according to the project manager. In these ways the 'independence' of the chief executive was reinforced, with ministerial interventions required to be explicitly justified and on the record—a 'hands-off' approach. The extent of the change this required in core departments was stressed by the Committee in their 1989 Report. (para. 68)

That this 'transparency' in the relationship between chief executives and departments is crucial to the NSI was made clear in the Committee's 1990 Report (para. 14), when the Committee was able to look more closely at framework agreements with more agencies 'up and running'. In this examination it soon became apparent that the procedures for review of framework agreements would be crucial. The quarterly reviews allowed for in the Employment Service's Agreement were described to the Committee by the chief executive as a 'necessary flexibility' rather than an opportunity for interference, but the Committee opined that 'it might seem to give the department a chance to keep a tighter grip on the Agency than is formally allowed for in the agreement'. The protection here, the Committee thought, was in the 'public visibility' of the original targets, an instance of the transparency of framework agreements. (1990, para. 18) But the Committee went on to urge that 'Departments should maintain a self-denying ordinance to ensure that, while review arrangements are available if necessary, they should be used only strategically and not as a vehicle for interference with the running of the agency'. (1990, para. 19)

The Government accepted in their reply that 'control and review arrangements should be operated strategically ... the Minister will set targets and objectives as part of the planning and resource allocation process and thereafter the Agency should be left to deliver them. The Department will wish to ensure the desired results are being achieved, but should not do so in a way which interferes with the clear lines of accountability which have been created. The onus would be on a Department positively to justify any interference with the agreed arrangements, rather than on the Chief Executive to justify his or her independence. Where intervention was judged, exceptionally, to be necessary ... then it should be done explicitly'. (Cm 1263, page 5) That, at least, is the theory, clearly on the record.

The Committee also pursued in their 1990 hearings the question of the effect on core departments of substantial delegation to agencies. Having raised the issue in 1989 (para. 67), the Committee looked in 1990 for evidence that departments were themselves changing the ways they operated and took written evidence from the Departments of Social Security and Transport. Whilst welcoming assurances that departments were committed to 'hands-off' management, the Committee reflected concerns that this might not happen in practice and drew attention to the Civil Service Minister's evidence that there would be reduction in the size of central departments as a result of the NSI. The question in the Committee's mind was whether all this would really have any impact on policy divisions. (1990, para. 62)

These issues were considered at greater length in the 1991 Report, not long after publication of the Fraser Report, but with a rather different emphasis. Now the Committee were concerned that greater clarity in the decision-making process should indicate that responsibility for the choice of targets and the allocation of resources should be clearly attributed to ministers (para. 39) and that managers should have an input into policy-making. The Committee also again reflected unions' concerns about transferability (para. 46): it was important that departments should plan positively for staff to transfer freely rather than become marooned in agencies.

Performance indicators and targets also play an important part in the relationship between departments and their agencies and have been a particular concern for the Committee. In their first hearings in 1988 the Committee established that it would be 'a precondition of setting up an agency that there were sufficient genuine indicators of performance for the monitoring of the agency to be effective' (1988, para. 34, Q 306) and aired the difficulty of moving from quantitative to qualitative targets. Also raised was the important issue of the frequency of monitoring: is it to be annual, quarterly or monthly?

The Minister's reply—I attach importance ... to the annual report of the performance an agency ... Within that ... it might be that secretaries of state may feel that they want more regular reports. [From agencies in my own department] I would certainly want an account quite often from the chief executive. Not to the extent that I interfere with his day-to-day management of the operation—well illustrates the dilemma in this area between effective monitoring and delegation. The Committee took the view that monitoring should probably be quarterly and should be confined to looking at performance against laid down targets. (1988, para. 34) The Government's reply again demonstrated the basic dilemma: 'Stretching performance targets will be set and monitored regularly. The Government's aim is that controls should be few but effective, and it agreed that, provided demanding performance targets are set and monitored, and firm overall controls are maintained, it should be possible to reduce the degree of detailed control of Agencies'. (Cm 524, 7–9)

In their 1990 hearing the Committee returned to some of these issues and was particularly impressed by the amount of work being done in the Treasury and in departments to produce meaningful indicators of agency performance. The Committee was, however, concerned that too much emphasis was being placed on quantitative indicators and too little on quality, although the Chief Secretary assured the Committee that the Government's concern was with effectiveness as much as with efficiency. (1990, para. 23) The Committee also reflected the unions' anxiety that the views of staff should be incorporated in the assessment of agencies' performance.

The Committee took a more extended look at these issues in its 1991 hearings, with the benefit of a rather longer track record for a number of agencies. Drawing on the (main) Committee's work on the new system of Departmental Reports, the Committee was critical of the absence of an agreed terminology in this area. John Garrett was particularly severe in his questioning of the Chief Executive of the Employment Agency on this. (1991, QQ 22–46) The Committee recommended in its report that the Treasury should prescribe a technical vocabulary, such as the one adopted by the NAO. (1991, para. 62)

The Committee was also concerned about the clarity and timing of targets. It is of the essence of targets that it should be clear whether or not they have been achieved and that they should relate to an Agency's declared role. The NHS Estates Agency came in for some criticism here. (1991, para. 63) The Committee also noted critically that while the Treasury's guidance, and the project manager's statements, suggested that targets should relate to financial performance, quality of service and efficiency, many agencies do not have targets in all these areas. (1991, para. 64) In the Committee's view it was unacceptable that an agency (Historic Royal Palaces) should be given a target for financial performance alone, with no reference to efficiency or quality of service. (1991, para. 65) It was also unacceptable that seven agencies should be starting the financial year without firm targets. The Committee recommended that, to ensure targets were set in time, and could be easily and openly referred to, and monitored over time, all agency targets should be published together as a series of parliamentary answers some time before the end of April. (1991, para. 69)

The Government were able to agree to this last recommendation, though they were not so receptive to the Committee's other comments on targets. Thus, while they accepted that ministerially-set targets should always be published, the Government took the view that it was for chief executives to decide whether their own internal management targets should be published. (Cm 1761, 7) And, while the Government agreed that a consistent use of terminology would be 'a desirable element in the openness and accountability which Next Steps seeks to promote', it stopped short of accepting the Committee's view that the Treasury should formally prescribe a technical vocabulary. (Cm 1761, 7–9) Whether, in the event, the Treasury's published guidance on terminology will become *de facto* prescriptive will be a question to which the Committee will presumably return.

Privatisation was bound to be an issue of considerable sensitivity, given the divergence of views between the political parties and the anxieties of the civil service unions. The Committee's role here was to reflect these sensitivities and register the Government's reassurances in a way which would promote rather than hinder the non-partisan character of the NSI. Thus in their first report, the Committee reflected the 'slight confusion' in some quarters about the relationship between Next Steps and privatisation, the Government having said both that the two policies were separate and that agency status might be a step to privatisation. The Committee's view was that 'the essential thing is to avoid uncertainty'. (1988, para. 33)

The Government's response was to reiterate that before an agency is established, alternative options such as privatisation or contracting out will have been considered first. Next Steps 'is primarily about those activities which are to remain *within* Government' (emphasis added). However, as the view on that might change over a period of years, the Government did accept that any firm intention of privatisation should be made clear at the point at which an agency was being set up. (Cm 524, 7)

The Committee repeated the exercise in 1989, the Chairman asking the Project Manager whether, once agency status was granted, privatisation could be ruled out. This gave Peter Kemp the opportunity to re-state, and read into the record again, the text of the Prime Minister's answer to a PQ and the relevant paragraph of the Government's response to the Committee's previous report. He hoped that this would put the matter 'beyond doubt'. (1989, Q 37) The Committee commented that this meant that some uncertainty would 'exist de facto' and that it was therefore vital to avoid, when an agency was established, any uncertainty as to whether its future lay in the public or the private sector. (1989, para. 65)

Uncertainty is also present when established agencies come up for review, generally after three years. It is the Government's declared policy that at this stage what are known as the 'three prior options' are considered: do these functions need to be continued at all? can they be privatised? can they be contractorised? These prior questions, together with the Government's market-testing programme, have significantly increased trade union suspicion that agency status will prove to be a prelude to privatisation. This suspicion, strengthened by the actual privatisation of DVOIT in December 1993, has cast doubt on the degree of the Labour Party's continuing support for the Next Steps programme.

The Committee's Role

Considering all these issues together, it is clear that the Committee has been consistent in its support for the NSI and on occasion sought to force the pace of change. While discharging its function as guardian of the parliamentary interest by registering its concerns about accountability, particularly with regard to parliamentary questions, it avoided making these difficulties an insuperable obstacle to progress, seeking instead to reinforce those forces within Whitehall which were promoting the Initiative. Similarly, while the Committee reflected the anxieties of the Labour Party and the civil service unions about the implications of the NSI for the overall shape of the Service, about staff consultations and pay and conditions and especially about privatisation, it did so in a way which has encouraged rather than discouraged the progress of the programme. Thus, as is pointed out above, the Committee not only performed a regular monitoring—'continuing scrutiny'—role in regard to the NSI, it also acted both as a catalyst for the reforms and as a forum for establishing bipartisan support.

References

Treasury and Civil Service Committee Reports:

TCSC, 1988:   *Civil Service Management Reform: the Next Steps*, Eighth Report of the Treasury and Civil Service Committee, HC 494, 1987-88, HMSO, London, July 1988.

TCSC, 1989:   *Developments in the Next Steps Programme*, Fifth Report of the Treasury and Civil Service Committee, HC 348, 1988-89, HMSO, London, July 1989.

TCSC, 1990:   *Progress in the Next Steps Initiative*, Eighth Report of the Treasury and Civil Service Committee, HC 481, 1989-90, HMSO, London, July 1990.

TCSC, 1991:   *The Next Steps Initiative*, Seventh Report of the Treasury and Civil Service Committee, HC 496, 1990-91, HMSO, London, July 1991.

TCSC, 1993:   *The Role of the Civil Service: Interim Report*, Sixth Report of the Treasury and Civil Service Committee, HC 390, 1992-93, HMSO, London, July 1993.

Government White Papers:

Fulton, 1968:   *Report of the Committee on the Civil Service, 1966-68* (Chairman: Lord Fulton), Cmnd 3638, HMSO, London, 1968.

Cm 524:   *Civil Service Management Reform: the Next Steps—the Government's Reply to the Eighth Report from the Treasury and Civil Service Committee, Session 1987–88*, HMSO, London, November 1988.

Cm 1261:   *Improving Management in Government—the Next Steps Agencies Review, 1990*, HMSO, London, October 1990.

Cm 1263:   *Progress in the Next Steps Initiative—the Government's Reply to the Eighth Report from the Treasury and Civil Service Committee, Session 1989–90*, HMSO, London, October 1990.

Cm 1761:   *The Next Steps Initiative—the Government's Reply to the Seventh Report from the Treasury and Civil Service Committee, Session 1990–91*, HMSO, London, November 1991.

5

Departmental Select Committees and the Next Steps Programme

David Natzler and Paul Silk

Select committees are sometimes elevated into general panaceas for all problems confronting Parliament, and are held up as the only counterweight to the burgeoning power of the executive. It is therefore not surprising that some academic commentators should suggest that select committees offer one way of ensuring that constitutional conventions and the proprieties of ministerial accountability are preserved in the face of the Next Steps programme. Some suggest that the existing departmentally-related select committees should simply add scrutiny of agencies to their existing tasks: others that some new committee should be set up. It is the purpose of this chapter to give an objective summary of the work which departmentally-related select committees have already done with respect to Next Steps agencies, to set out in detail each committee's work (see Annex): and to make an assessment of the factors which may have influenced committees and which will do so in future. (The role of the Treasury and Civil Service Committee is dealt with in Chapter 4 and that of the Public Accounts Committee in Chapter 6.)

The Role of the Select Committees

The departmentally-related select committees have as their principal task under Standing Order No 130 the examination of the 'administration, policy and expenditure' of the department to which each relates. Over a decade and more, each committee has developed its own particular style and pattern of operation, influenced by the nature of the department it scrutinises, the priorities of successive Chairmen and Members, and by the pattern of events in the wider world. Some have tended to concentrate on one or two major subject inquiries each session: others to attempt to submit ministers and their departments to continuous and wide-ranging scrutiny: and others to a mixture of short and long inquiries, not always resulting in Reports to the House. (Procedure Committee, 1990; Drewry, 1989)

In broad terms, it can be said that the select committees have tended to concentrate more on policy than on administration. There has been little consistent effort to monitor departments' expenditure in detail. While many committees now examine and report upon the annual reports produced by departments, and before the production of these in 1991 examined departmental estimates in a rather cursory way, none has engaged in line-by-line or item-by-item scrutiny of the annual Supply Estimates. It is against this background of a general concentration on policy rather than administration or expenditure that the record of select committees in relation to agencies must be judged, and the likely future pattern assessed.

Standing Order No 130 also lays upon select committees the duty of examination of 'associated public bodies', a phrase intended to cover primarily non-departmental public bodies—quangos—and nationalised industries. Although there is no universally accepted definition of an associated public body, it has been interpreted widely enough to include, for example, police and health authorities. A number of committees have reported over the years on non-departmental public bodies. There has been regular examination of nationalised industries by the Energy, Trade and Industry and Transport Committees and a report on the Highland and Islands Development Board by the Scottish Affairs Committee. These inquiries have generally covered a range of administrative and financial aspects of the body concerned rather than concentrating exclusively on policy, reflecting to some extent the practice of the former Select Committee on Nationalised Industries in examining the annual reports and accounts of those industries.

Committees have also devoted some effort to examining the administrative arrangements of the departments themselves. In 1984, for example, the Defence Committee reported on the reorganisation of the Ministry carried out under Mr Heseltine's direction; (Defence Committee, 1984) and the Social Services Committee and its successors, the Health and Social Security Committees, have regularly inquired into the proposals for reforms in NHS and social security administration. The first inquiries undertaken by both the Social Security Committee and the new Science and Technology Committee were into the organisation of the departments whose activities they were to scrutinise. The Welsh Affairs Committee's first inquiry in 1992–93 was into the work of the Welsh Office. The Health Committee took oral evidence in its first year on the organisation and management of the Department of Health and the Department of Health and Social Services (Northern Ireland).

Committees could therefore have been expected to take some interest in the establishment of Next Steps agencies, primarily the policy aspects, but also the implications of agencies for public administration and public expenditure. The Procedure Committee indeed concluded in 1990 that scrutiny of agencies 'ought to play an increasingly important part in the work of the Select Committee'. (Procedure Committee, 1990) The committees certainly do not labour under any formal constraints upon undertaking such work. It has repeatedly been declared that agencies remain accountable to ministers, and that ministers are accountable to Parliament for their activities, through whatever medium that accountability is exercised. Agencies have no independent statutory existence, the Government having carefully eschewed the legislative process in establishing them. The staff of agencies remain civil servants. It would therefore seem that the same conditions of access to papers, and the same conventions on evidence given to select committees as set out in the Osmotherley Rules (Procedure Committee, 1990, 206–238), apply to agency chief executives and their staff as apply to the rest of the civil service. The references in agency framework documents to the conventions which are to be applied when evidence is sought on their work confirm this. In many respects, they are therefore far *more* readily accessible to conventional parliamentary scrutiny than other more evidently autonomous bodies such as Crown corporations, charter bodies, or health authorities, all of whom have other potentially competing lines of accountability. On the same count any frustrations experienced by Committees in their relations with departments may also arise in relations with agencies.

Examining the Agencies

What then have the departmental select committees achieved by way of examination of Next Steps agencies? The general perception is that they have done rather little. There has certainly been no systematic attempt either by select committees as a whole, or by individual select committees, to undertake a conscious programme of inquiries into agencies. Nonetheless, as the details set out in the Annex demonstrate, most committees have had some contact with the work of the agencies. Most committees have either commented on the creation of agencies in the course of inquiries, or have in other ways been in touch with agencies.

The annual Sessional Returns identify witnesses from agencies separately from other civil servants; the Return for 1992–93 shows that 10 of the 16 committees heard oral evidence from 35 agency witnesses, including several Chief Executives. (Sessional Return, 1992–93) Several committees, including Agriculture, Environment and Social Security, have paid visits to agencies. It may also be regarded as indicative of future trends that a number of committees have at one time or another over recent years come into contact with the agencies' predecessors, whether they were then separate organisations or fully integrated into the parent department: and that these contacts generally arose in the course of subject-based inquiries. If committees continue in their past pattern of operation, it would therefore seem likely that they will as a matter of course encounter at least certain aspects of the work of agencies. It can also be observed that the framework which many committees are developing for scrutiny of departments in the context of examination of annual reports could readily be adapted to embrace scrutiny of agencies.

In the early years of Next Steps, the Home Affairs Committee provided an illustration of what a departmentally-related select committee could do. Despite the peripherality of agencies to the mainstream of the work of the Home Office the Committee in the 1987 Parliament was an early convert to the benefits of agency status. In April 1988, the Committee reviewed the government's public expenditure plans. One section of this report dealt with the consequences of the decision to give the Passport Office agency status. Waiting times for passports were at the time growing almost exponentially. Although the Committee expressed no view of its own on the benefits of the new status, it gave prominence to the Permanent Under Secretary's evidence that the management disciplines consequent upon agency status would have an effect on service to the public.

By the following year, the Committee had become more directly favourable to the Next Steps Initiative. In a February 1989 Report on the Forensic Science Service (FSS), the Committee praised its scientific reputation, but were scathing about the administrative problems from which the service suffered: it had 'fallen on hard times'; it could not meet the demand for its work; it was losing some of its best staff; and morale was at rock bottom. In evidence, the Committee had explored the possibility of agency status for the FSS, and was told by the Home Office that this was being considered, although the Minister suggested that the FSS might form part of an agency formed from the whole of the Home Office's Science and Technology Group. The Committee recommended that the status should be given to the FSS by itself, and the Government response agreed that this should happen.

Administrative problems in another area were the subject of more criticism in January 1990. A report on the Criminal Injuries Compensation Board (CICB) suggested means of remedying what the Committee described as the 'scandalous backlog' in compensation claims. Among a number of solutions it proposed, the Committee recommended that 'the possibility of giving the CICB agency status should be studied'. Agency status, in the Committee's view, would give CICB management greater independence and clearer productivity and achievement targets. The Home Office response did not dismiss the possibility of agency status, but favoured other administrative remedies in the short term.

The fact that the Committee had interested itself in the Home Office's first two executive agencies before they achieved this status made it natural for the Committee to return to the subject of agency status in general, and specifically to review the progress the two agency candidates were making towards eradicating the administrative difficulties from which they had been found to suffer. The Committee took written evidence in late 1990 and followed this up with an oral session in January 1991 when the witnesses were the Chief Executives designate of the FSS and the Passport Agency and the Grade 5 Home Office official responsible for the Next Steps programme in the department. This led to a short report in March 1991 entitled simply Next Steps Agencies. (HAC, 1991) This dealt with a number of specific concerns which the Committee had relating to the FSS and Passport Office (as it still remained), but also raised more general issues about the agency programme. According to the Committee, two questions had formed the foundations of their inquiry: whether agency status would produce an improved service to the customer at no extra cost and whether parliamentary accountability would be maintained.

On the latter point, the Committee criticised the 'unnecessary secrecy' which they believed the Home Office had shown in refusing to allow the Committee to see the agencies' draft framework documents. This, they were told, was a central decision, and it was one which the government later justified in its response to the Committee by maintaining that draft framework documents were internal working papers of government and no more to be disclosed to committees than any other draft policy statement. More generally, the Committee believed that the devolution of responsibility and enhanced freedom for agencies (which they welcomed and encouraged) 'should not compromise government accountability to Parliament'. The Committee accepted that there might be changes in practice (for example, letters to MPs might come from chief executives rather than ministers), but 'the overriding principle of ministerial accountability must not be undermined'. The Committee, however, seemed somewhat at a loss to determine itself where the dividing line between ministerial and chief executive accountability should fall, and put the onus on the Home Office to publish a 'leaflet' to explain to MPs and others, by using concrete examples, where the division lay. The Home Office agreed to produce such a leaflet.

For the future, the Committee expressed surprise that there were no further Home Office agency candidates. Though no firm recommendations were made, the possibility of turning into agencies the magistrates' courts service, the directorate of telecommunications, the prison service and (again) the CICB were canvassed. The Committee recommended that the department 'should continue to review the whole breadth of its activities with a view to transferring appropriate sections ... to agency status'. It concluded its report by promising to return to the work of the FSS and Passport Agency when they had received agency status, and to examine other agencies which the Home Office might establish in the future. This declaration of intent was heartily welcomed in the government's response. (Cm 1549)

Why was the Home Affairs Committee so interested in Next Steps? In his evidence to the Procedure Committee in 1989–90, the then Chairman of the Committee, Sir John Wheeler, had pointed out that the Committee had 'generally proceeded by consensus and for that reason had not sought to tackle issues which would arouse direct political confrontation.' Neither Sir John's evidence, nor that of the Home Office, suggested that any difficulties had arisen in the relationship between Department and Committee.

The Procedure Committee subsequently invited Sir John to give oral evidence along with the Chairman of the Defence Committee, Michael Mates, whose evidence had been highly critical of the Ministry of Defence. It is clear that the two Chairmen were intended to be a contrasting pair, and, although the Procedure Committee stopped short of criticising the Home Affairs Committee's record, it is possible to deduce from its report that it believed the Home Affairs Committee was in danger of being 'captured' by the Department it was supposed to monitor. An impressionistic judgement suggests that of all the active departmental select committees in the 1987 Parliament, the Home Affairs Committee was indeed the most generally supportive of government policy.

The Committee did however embrace with more enthusiasm than other Committees the remit of the departmental select committees to tackle administration in Government departments—the very part of their remit which had initially sold the departmental select committee system to Mrs Thatcher in 1979. A regular feature of the Committee's programme was formed by essentially administrative inquiries: subjects like the chaos in the maintenance of criminal records, the administrative delays in the Immigration and Nationality Department, and the extent and control of sick leave in the police service. Other reports on larger topics dealt at length with administrative shortcomings, whether in the Crown Prosecution Service or the lack of co-ordination in the police service. An interest in the mechanics of government and the Next Steps initiative was a natural consequence.

Just before the 1992 election it was announced that the Prison Service was to become an agency, following the lead of its Scottish counterpart. The change took place on 1st April 1993, and thereby brought a very substantial, central and controversial part of the Home Office's responsibilities within the agency framework. The new Home Affairs Committee, under the Chairmanship of Sir Ivan Lawrence, and containing only two members of the former Committee, responded by taking evidence on the Prison Service Agency from the Minister responsible and the Chief Executive on 19th April 1993. While it remains to be seen whether the current Committee will display the interest of its predecessor in administrative matters, it is likely regularly to concern itself with the work of the Prison Service Agency.

It remains, however, broadly true that select committees have as yet undertaken little by way of detailed examination of either the merits of the establishment of agencies or of their operation to date. It is of course early days: the earliest agencies are barely five years old, and many of the more substantial ones have only been established in the last few years. But it may be worth examining both some of the reasons for this absence of activity, and then some possible factors which may lead to greater activity in future.

Setting the Agenda

Select committees set their own agendas and decide their own programmes, based primarily on the sense of priorities which each Member brings to the deliberations of a committee. The salient question before committee members may therefore be not whether committee scrutiny of agencies would prove interesting or instructive—that is not in doubt—but whether such activity should take priority over the many other possible inquiries competing for a committee's attention. While any general advice emanating from the Liaison Committee, composed of select committee chairmen, or from the Procedure Committee, as in its 1990 report, may have some influence, committees jealously guard their independence of action. Only the House of Commons itself can oblige a committee to undertake an inquiry or class of inquiries, a power it has not used in respect of departmental Committees. There would therefore have to be some powerful reasons to persuade departmental committees to inquire into particular agencies rather than into broader subjects. In the 1992–93 Session, for example, the Agriculture Committee inquired into banana imports and fisheries; the Defence Committee into cuts in the Army and the Royal Navy; the Environment Committee into energy efficiency; and the Social Security Committee into the operation of pension funds. These Committees would have had to decide whether to devote less of their limited time and resources to these subjects, and more to inquiries into the administrative arrangements of, for example, the Hydrographic Office, Ordnance Survey, or the Intervention Board for Agricultural Produce.

Agencies still represent, for most committees, a small part of their department's area of responsibility, whether measured by expenditure or staff numbers. Although the figures for 1992–93 show that 62 per cent of civil servants work in agencies, many of these come from two Departments—Employment and Social Security—and the figures include Inland Revenue and Customs and Excise, which are organised internally on agency lines. For most committees, agencies do not represent the most politically interesting part of departmental life, as chapter 9 illustrates with regard to the Department of the Environment. As Winetrobe notes in Chapter 3 above, scrutiny of administration rather than policy is not normally an attractive option. Where there is no evidence to suggest that there are particular matters of controversy within an agency's responsibility, committees may have considered that to prioritise scrutiny of them over other matters would be imprudent, and would indeed be a way of permitting the Government, through the administrative arrangements it makes for relatively minor parts of its empire, to set the agendas of committees.

There are three further negative factors which are worth examining. First, it has been argued that steady parliamentary scrutiny of agencies might in some way undermine the very purposes for which they were established. While ministers remain in theory wholly accountable for agencies, and the agencies remain an integral part of the civil service, they were established at least in part to encourage greater management freedom and initiative, and to release management from day-to-day political control. Unlike nationalised industries, they were not established by statute, even by subordinate legislation, and are entirely creatures of the prerogative, able to be wound up and reabsorbed within departments at the stroke of a pen. Nonetheless, there are some parallels to be drawn with the nationalised industries of earlier years, and with the controversy over the establishment in 1956 of the Select Committee on the Nationalised Industries. (Coombes, 1966, 44–45) It could therefore be seen as counter-productive if excessive civil service or ministerial supervision of agencies were to be replaced by select committees taking a close interest. Put simply, if part of the rationale for agencies was to distance identifiable executive and administrative functions from day to day ministerial oversight, in order to encourage initiative, risk-taking and responsible management, it might be seen as counter-productive for select committees to inquire into the pricing of commercially available weather forecasts or the profits from sales of the produce of prison farms.

Secondly, select committees may with justice be wary of permitting their agendas to be set as the result of Government initiatives, with the risk that they are tied up in scrutiny of what may prove to be transient administrative arrangements when they would be better occupied on other matters of greater political moment and impact on the world at large. This is not to suggest that departments would set out deliberately to skew a committee's agenda in this way. Some committees may nonetheless have sensed that the creation and work of agencies may signify rather less than meets the eye, and prove eventually to be a side-show on which they do not wish to waste their time.

Thirdly, the close involvement of the Treasury and Civil Service Committee in the process of establishment of agencies and the implications for the theory and practice of parliamentary accountability may have had the paradoxical side-effect of discouraging departmental select committees from scrutinising them. Agencies may have come to be seen as a Treasury and Civil Service Committee 'topic', although as Chapter 4 has shown that Committee's interests have been in the agency programme as a whole rather than the operation of individual agencies. The close involvement of the National Audit Office (NAO) and, prospectively, of the Committee of Public Accounts (PAC), as described in Chapter 6 by Priscilla Baines, may also lead departmental select committees to regard agencies as peripheral to their own remit, particularly if NAO Reports on individual agencies are taken up by PAC rather than being offered as possible bases for a departmental select committee inquiry. As Baines notes, the NAO has already produced one report assessing the effects of agency status on its performance, on the Vehicle Inspectorate. One way forward would be for an explicit convention that the NAO's reports on individual agencies be taken up by the relevant departmental select committee. In 1990 the Procedure Committee recommended that ways should be found for enabling the NAO's resources to be drawn upon by departmentally-related Select Committees. (Procedure Committee, 1990, para. 267) In any event, the NAO is likely to provide the House, and thus departmental select committees, with useful analytical and critical material on agencies which may act as a stimulus to further scrutiny.

The Case for More Scrutiny

Whatever the difficulties or disincentives, there are several good reasons for select committees to do more by way of examination of agencies. In the first case, while opinions may differ as to the real significance of the Next Steps programme, it is the Government's principal administrative reform of the past decade, covering all departments. That fact alone may be thought to put some onus on committees to provide a well-informed parliamentary input into assessment of the merits of the programme, drawing on detailed knowledge of agencies' work against an understanding of the political and financial background peculiar to each department. Only the departmental select committees can do this; and it may be thought particularly appropriate that they should do so in view on the one hand of their watchdog role, and on the other of the claims made for agencies in terms of increasing Government's efficiency and effectiveness.

Secondly, it may be considered that the very fact of the distancing of the day to day running of agencies from ministerial control should act as an incentive for Parliament to ensure that the public interest, both in the mass and in particular cases, is not neglected. All agencies have a direct impact on the public, as employers, consumers and producers of goods or services, and there is some prospect that their release from civil service constraints may free them to make managerially attractive but unpopular decisions. There may well be a role for Parliament here, and specifically the select committees, as protector of the public interest. Parliament must ensure that Government is not left with the impression that the creation of agencies is a means of solving awkward political dilemmas at the stroke of a pen.

Thirdly, there is no doubt that the division and separation of various departmental functions into separate agencies has facilitated the task of scrutiny. Framework documents, the publication of comprehensible and measurable targets and lengthy annual reports make agencies much easier, and so arguably more cost effective, to scrutinise than the rest of a department. The relatively high individual profiles which agency chief executives are supposed to possess, in some cases equivalent more to that of a junior minister rather than a senior civil servant, may also serve to present a more visible target for committees.

Conclusions

Departmental select committees are likely to take an increasing interest in agencies over the next decade, both in the course of their general programmes of work, and as discrete inquiries. There are a number of possibilities: examination of chief executives and their annual reports; scrutiny of the choice of targets as well as their attainment; analysis of the effects of agency status on a particular activity; relation with the sponsoring department; and so on. Winetrobe's suggestion in Chapter 3 of a single overarching mission statement may prove unrealistic: but there may be some value in at least broad agreement on a common line of approach. It has, however, to be accepted that any prioritisation of such work is bound to mean less of something else: and it remains to be seen how each committee resolves that dilemma.

References

Cm 1549: Government Reply to the Third Report from the Home Affairs Committee, Session 1990–91, *Next Steps Agencies*, May 1991.

Coombes, 1966: David Coombes, *The Member of Parliament and the Administration: the Case of the Select Committee on the Nationalised Industries*, Allen and Unwin, 1966.

Defence Committee, 1984:	Third Report from the Defence Committee, HC 584, 1983–84, *Ministry of Defence Re-organisation.*
Drewry, 1989:	Gavin Drewry, (ed), *The New Select Committees: A Study of the 1979 Reforms*, Clarendon Press, 1989.
HAC, 1991:	Third Report from the Home Affairs Committee, HC 177, 1990–91, *Next Steps Agencies*, March 1991.
Sessional Return, 1991:	HC 271, 1990–91.
Sessional Return, 1992:	HC 18, 1991–92.
Sessional Return, 1993:	HC 280, 1993–94.

ANNEX

Department Select Committees' Scrutiny of Executive Agencies
1988–1993

Agriculture

The Agriculture Committee has to date had little to do with the MAFF Agencies, which are relatively few in number and not of great policy significance. Evidence was heard from the Chief Executive of the Intervention Board in 1991 and 1993 as part of the Committee's annual inquiry into the Departmental Report, and a visit was paid in March 1991 to the Central Veterinary Laboratory Service laboratories at Weybridge in connection with the salmonella inquiry. It has also taken evidence from a range of quangos. It has, for example, on several occasions had contact with the Public Health Laboratory Service, including formal oral evidence as part of its inquiry into salmonella, and a visit to Colindale in February 1991. It heard from a number of other quangos in the course of its fish farming inquiry.

4th Report, 1988–89, *Fish Farming in the UK*, HC 141.

1st Report, 1989–90, *Salmonella in Eggs—A Progress Report,* HC 33.

5th Report, 1989–90, *Bovine Spongiform Encephalopathy (BSE),* HC 449.

2nd Report, 1992–93, *MAFF/Intervention Board Departmental Report 1993*, HC 636.

Defence

The Ministry of Defence is responsible for a number of agencies, including the Meteorological Office and the Defence Research Agency, run on classic Next Steps lines, and a number of Defence Support Agencies, run internally on Next Steps lines but remaining within the defence chain of command, and generally employing both civilian and military personnel. (This distinction was ended in 1993.) The Defence Committee has not examined any of these agencies in detail, but has commented on them in the context of its Annual Report on the Government's Statement on the Defence Estimates. In its 1990 report, the Committee set out briefly the proposals then being made, noting that the Met Office and Hydrographic Office had become the department's first agency and Defence Support Agency respectively in April 1990. The Committee, quoting from the Hydrographic Office's Framework Document and oral evidence thereon, concluded a touch sceptically that the real significance of the introduction of defence support agencies remained to be seen. It also expressed the hope that innovative research would be maintained once the Defence Research Agency achieved agency status.

In 1991, the Committee recounted progress in setting up further agencies: calling for prompt and full publication of framework documents, performance targets and annual reports, it also warned that, once the process was complete, the department would have to be able to demonstrate that the anticipated improvements had indeed been achieved.

In 1992, the Committee restricted itself to commenting on the extent to which chief executives of agencies and defence support agencies were obliged to reduce manpower in line with the prevailing 20 per cent reductions in the department, concluding that any direction given to chief executives to cut civilian manpower by 20 per cent would call into question the supposed degree of management autonomy given to these bodies.

8th Report, 1989–90, *Statement on the Defence Estimates 1990*, HC 388.

11th Report, 1990–91, *Statement on the Defence Estimates 1991*, HC 394.

1st Report, 1992–93, *Statement on the Defence Estimates 1992*, HC 218.

Education

It is hardly surprising that the Education Committee (formerly the Education Science and Arts Committee) paid no attention to the one small agency within its area of responsibility—the Teachers' Pensions Agency. The Committee has, however, published regular reports on the Department of Education and Office of Arts and Libraries' expenditure plans, and held scrutiny sessions with a variety of public bodies, such as the School Examinations and Assessment Council and the Arts Council, National Curriculum Council and the Office for Standards in Education.

Employment

The Employment Service Agency was one of the largest of the first tranche of agencies to be created. Its Chief Executive gave evidence at scrutiny sessions held by the Employment Committee in Sessions 1989–90, 1990–91, and 1991–92: in 1992–93 the Deputy Chief Executive and others gave evidence at a session on the work of the Service, which had been proceeded by a visit to Bermondsey and Lambeth. Policy questions dominated these occasions, though some administrative matters were raised. No reports were produced, in line with the general pattern adopted by the Committee, which regularly held similar one-off sessions on the Employment Department Group, the Health and Safety Commission and Executive, ACAS and the Equal Opportunities Commission.

Another evidence session showed the Committee's interest in administrative matters with high political profile: the evidence taken on the privatisation of the Skills Training Agency just before the General Election in 1992. In the case of the Skills Training Agency, it was never entirely clear on what basis the employees passed straight from the civil service to the private sector. The move was politically controversial, and the Committee concentrated on the issue of the terms under which civil servants who were transferred from the Skills Training Agency were hired. The Committee also heard evidence from HM Customs and Excise in the course of its inquiry into employment in the horseracing industry.

Minutes of Evidence, *The Employment Service*, HC 147, 1989–90.

Minutes of Evidence, *The Work of the Employment Service*, HC 267, 1990–91.

Minutes of Evidence, *The Work of the Employment Service*, HC 235, 1991–92.

Minutes of Evidence, *Sale of the Skills Training Agency*, HC 281, 1991–92.

Minutes of Evidence, 31 March 1993, *The Work of the Employment Service*, HC 598-i, 1992–93.

Energy

No agencies came within the responsibility of the Department of Energy. The Committee did hold regular evidence sessions with the gradually diminishing number of nationalised industries within its remit, and displayed some interest in administrative matters, as in its Reports of Session 1988–89 on the Department of Energy's spending plans and on the Report and Accounts of British Nuclear Fuels.

Environment

Although the Environment Committee has not yet formally inquired into any of the Department of the Environment's (DOE) five Agencies (see Chapter 9), it has twice taken evidence from one in the course of a subject-based inquiry, and from another before it became an agency. In the course of its 1990–91 inquiry into indoor pollution, the Committee visited the Building Research Establishment at Garston, Watford in January 1991 and heard formal oral evidence there from the Chief Executive and others, primarily on the Establishment's environmental assessment methods rather than its operation specifically as an agency: and again in June 1993 as part of its inquiry into Energy Efficiency in Buildings. In 1985–86 the Committee had similarly heard a session of oral evidence from two DOE Planning Inspectors as part of its inquiry into aspects of the planning system. The Committee has in past years inquired regularly into the range of DOE's non-departmental associated bodies, including the Sports Council, the Property Services Agency and the British Board of Agrément, as well as into the annual DOE Estimates: and published a major Report in 1993 on the Housing Corporation.

On 24 April 1991 while examining the DOE's Property Holdings vote, the Committee devoted a substantial part of its questioning of witnesses to various detailed issues connected with the QEII Conference Centre. It returned to the Agency in 1993 and called for review of its targets in view of its continuing deficit. The Committee has also shown itself closely interested in the possibilities of agency status; in its Report of 1991–92 on the Government's proposals for an Environment Agency, it examined in some detail the future structure of the Agency, although it seems likely that it will in fact be an NDPB rather than an executive agency. It also commented in 1993 on the progress of Property Holdings towards agency status.

5th Report, 1985-86, *Planning: Appeal, Call-In and Major Public Inquiries*, HC 181.

4th Report, 1990-91, *DOE, Property Holdings and PSA Service Estimates 1991-92 and DOE Annual Report 1991*, HC 389.

6th Report, 1990-91, *Indoor Pollution*, HC 61.

1st Report, 1991-92, *The Government's Proposals for an Environment Agency*, HC 55.

3rd Report, 1992-93, *DOE, Property Holding and PSA Service Estimates 1993-94 and DOE Annual Report 1993*, HC 629.

4th Report, 1992-93, *Energy Efficiency in Buildings*, HC 648.

Foreign Affairs

Of the two small agencies within its ambit, the Foreign Affairs Committee has in the past reported on one specifically, and on the other more generally. It drew attention to funding cuts for Wilton Park in its First Report of 1982-83. In its Fourth Report of the same session on the ODA's Scientific and Special Units, the Committee, endorsing the conclusions of its Overseas Development Sub-Committee, called for a number of options to be explored for the future structured management of these units, including 'a strategy of decentralisation which would encourage the units to operate in a more 'entrepreneurial' manner'. The Natural Resources Institute became an agency in 1990. The Committee has also taken a consistent interest in the principal quangos associated with the FCO, notably the British Council and the BBC World Service, generally in the context of regular inquiries into departmental estimates and expenditure.

1st Report, 1982-83, *The Wilton House International Conference Centre (Wilton Park)*, HC 117.

4th Report, 1982-83, *The Overseas Development Administration's scientific and special units*, HC 25.

Health

The Committee has not had occasion in its relatively short existence to take evidence from the three relatively minor agencies within its sphere of responsibility, but has regularly taken evidence from a range of NHS organisations.

Home Affairs

The Home Affairs Committee's dealings with agencies within its remit are discussed at length in the main chapter above, pp 74 to 77.

1st Report, 1987–88, *The Government's Public Expenditure Plans 1988–89 to 1990–91*, HC 340.

1st Report, 1988–89, *The Forensic Science Service*, HC 26.

Cm 699, *The Government's Reply to the 1st Report from the Home Affairs Committee, HC 26, 1988–89*, 1989.

2nd Report, 1989–90, *Compensating Victims Quickly: the Administration of the Criminal Injuries Compensation Board*, HC 92.

Cm 1153, *The Government's Reply to the 2nd Report from the Home Affairs Committee, HC 92, 1989–90*, 1990.

3rd Report, 1990–91, *Next Steps Agencies*, HC 177.

Cm 1549, *The Government's Reply to the 3rd Report from the Home Affairs Committee, HC 177, 1990–91*, May 1991.

Minutes of Evidence, 19 April 1993, *The Prison Service*, HC 612–i.

National Heritage

The Committee was first established in 1992. Although it did not hear evidence in Session 1992–93 from either of the Department of National Heritage's two agencies—Royal Parks and Historic Royal Palaces—it did hear oral evidence in November 1992 from HM Customs and Excise in its inquiry into the draft Seventh VAT Directive and the export of works of art.

1st and 2nd Reports, 1992–93, *Exports of Works of Art: Draft Seventh VAT Directive*, HC 249.

Science and Technology

There are no agencies within the Committee's remit.

Scottish Affairs

The Committee was not established in the 1987–92 Parliament. In Session 1992–93, the Committee did not undertake any inquiries into policy areas for which Scottish Office agencies were directly responsible. It did, however, take oral evidence from the Scottish Prison Service.

1st Report, 1993–94, *Drug Abuse in Scotland*, HC 62–I, II and III.

Social Security

The Benefits Agency and the Contributions Agency between them employ the vast majority of DSS staff, and are among the largest agencies of all. (see Chapter 10) It is therefore not surprising that the Social Security Committee, established in January 1991, should have begun to inquire into them. One of its first inquiries was into the organisation and administration of the DSS. Oral evidence was heard on 25 June 1991 from the Chief Executives of the Benefits Agency and the IT Services Agency; the former witness was again examined together with Ministers on 12 November 1991. The Committee visited the local offices at Archway Tower, Islington on 3 December 1991. No report was in the event published. The Committee had also heard oral evidence on 19 March 1991 from, among others, the Benefit Agency's Director of Strategic Policy and Planning, which was used in its November 1991 Report on the Department's Annual Departmental Report.

The Social Security Committee was closely associated with the birth of the DSS's fifth Agency, the Child Support Agency, the proposals for which it examined in detail in its Third Report of Session 1990–91. The Committee had called for the possibility of its establishment as part of the Inland Revenue to be kept under review. It was in fact established as a DSS Agency, and the Government reply to the Committee referred to the challenging targets which would be set. In Session 1992–93, as part of its inquiry into Disability Benefit, the Committee heard evidence from the Chief Executive of the Benefit Agency and an Area Director, and subsequently visited the Disability Living Allowance Unit at North Fylde in Lancashire. As the session drew to an end, it heard oral evidence from the Chief Executive and a Regional Operations Director of the Child Support Agency, as the opening shot of an inquiry into the operation of the Child Support Act, which had become the subject of considerable public controversy. Thereafter, and separately, it heard evidence from the Minister and his officials, in which the relationship between Department and Agency were explored as well as more contentious issues.

3rd Report, 1990–91, *Changes in Maintenance Arrangements: the White Paper "Children Come First" and the Child Support Bill*, HC 277.

Cm 1691, *The Government's Reply to the 3rd Report of the Social Security Committee, HC 277, 1990–91*, November 1991.

1st Report, 1991–92, *Public Expenditure on Social Security*, HC 18.

Minutes of Evidence, 25 June 1991, *The Organisation and Administration of the Department of Social Security*, HC 550-i, 1990–91.

Minutes of Evidence, 12 November 1991, *The Organisation and Administration of the Department of Social Security*, HC 19–iii, 1991–92.

3rd Report, 1992–93, *Disability Benefits: the Delivery of Disability Living Allowance and Disability Working Allowance*, HC 284.

Minutes of Evidence, 6 and 13 July 1994, *The Operation of the Child Support Act*, HC 470–iv and v.

Trade and Industry

The Trade and Industry Committee showed little enthusiasm for administrative inquiries between 1987 and 1992. Though it took evidence during the Parliament from nationalised industries such as the Post Office and British Shipbuilders, as well as the Securities and Investment Board, it concentrated on large policy-orientated inquiries. In Session 1992–93, however, in the course of its inquiry into the British Aerospace Industry, it heard oral evidence from the Chief Executive of the Defence Research Agency, who appeared together with a Minister and officials of the Ministry of Defence: and evidence was heard in November 1993 on Warren Spring Laboratory prior to its merger with AEA Technology.

3rd Report, 1992–93, *British Aerospace Industry*, HC 563.

Minutes of Evidence, 23 November 1993, *National Engineering Laboratory and Warren Spring Laboratory*, HC 34, 1993–94.

Transport

During the 1987–1992 Parliament, the Transport Committee frequently took evidence from the nationalised industries and public bodies within its remit, and held regular inquiries into the Government's Expenditure Plans for transport. These inquiries paid some attention to the agencies under the department's aegis. The Committee took written evidence from the Transport Road Research Laboratory as part of a policy inquiry into road provision, before it had become an agency.

1st Report, 1989–90, *Roads for the Future*, HC 198.

Minutes of Evidence, 9 March 1994, *Privatisation and De-regulation of Department of Transport Agency Work*, HC 137-i.

Treasury and Civil Service

The Treasury and Civil Service Committee, and in particular its Sub-Committee, has played a critical role in the establishment of Next Steps agencies, and in consideration of the principles and practices which are to govern parliamentary accountability and scrutiny, as set out in Chapter 4. The Committee has called for departmentally-related select committees to play a full part in the process of accountability. The TCSC, as the Committee responsible for monitoring the Treasury and the Office of Management and the Civil Service, and now for the civil service aspect of the Office of Public Services and Science, has a number of agencies within its own ambit, including two of the largest, the Inland Revenue and the Customs and Excise; five Agencies which are Government Departments; and smaller ones including the Civil Service College and the Valuation Office. It is therefore instructive to examine how much scrutiny the Committee has been able to give to these agencies.

Prior to the establishment of agencies, the Committee took evidence at a single sitting in 1987–88 from the Inland Revenue, the Royal Mint and the Central Office of Information as the main component of its inquiry into public expenditure and Estimates, and in 1988–89 from HMSO in the course of its annual Next Steps inquiry. It also heard evidence from the Department of National Savings in preparation for its report on that Department, and from the Valuation Office on which it made a separate Report, recommending its establishment as an executive agency. In its 1989 Report, it criticised the lack of action on Customs and Excise and the Inland Revenue. (see Chapter 4, p. 62–63) Since the first agencies were established, it has taken evidence in 1990–91 from HMSO and the Civil Service College as part of its inquiry into Next Steps Agencies and also heard evidence from the Royal Mint in the course of its inquiry into Notes and Coins. In 1992–93 the Sub-Committee heard evidence in the course of its inquiry into the Civil Service from the Civil Service College on 8 June, and on 16 June the Chief Executive of the Recruitment and Assessment Services Agency gave evidence, primarily as a Civil Service Commissioner.

Evidence from a range of Treasury and Civil Service Agencies has therefore been taken, often in the context of subject inquiries. More extensive evidence has, however, been heard from chief executives of, and more recommendations have been made on, agencies within other Departments, such as Social Security and Transport. The Committee has not undertaken a full-scale inquiry into a Treasury and Civil Service Agency, and to that extent has not established a template for regular scrutiny of agencies by other departmentally-related select committees.

7th Report, 1987–88, *Public Expenditure and Estimates*, HC 506.

8th Report, 1987–88, *Civil Service Management Reform: the Next Steps*, HC 294.

5th Report, 1988–89, *Developments in the Next Steps Programme*, HC 348.

2nd Report, 1989–90, *The Work of the Valuation Office*, HC 223.

6th Report, 1989–90, *Public Expenditure: the Department of National Savings and the Chancellor's Departments Annual Report*, HC 466.

3rd Report, 1990–91, *The System of Notes and Coins*, HC 481.

7th Report, 1990–91, *The Next Steps Initiative*, HC 496.

8th Report, 1989–90, *Progress in the Next Steps Initiative*, HC 481.

Welsh Affairs

The Welsh Office is wholly responsible for only one agency (Cadw: Welsh Historic Monuments), though it shares ownership of two other Agencies—the Agriculture Development and Advisory Service (ADAS) and the Planning Inspectorate. During the 1987–92 Parliament, the Welsh Affairs Committee showed no particular interest in the administration of the department, nor in the matters within the agencies' responsibilities—though the agencies were not established until the end of the Parliament. Evidence was, however, regularly taken from a range of associated public bodies both of the Welsh Office and other departments. Only the Chairman of the Committee in the previous Parliament serves on the Committee nominated in July 1992. This may be a factor in an apparent change of approach since the 1992 election.

The Committee's first inquiry and first Report focused on the administration of the Welsh Office. Memoranda were sought from all three agencies, and oral evidence taken from Cadw and ADAS. The Chairman's draft report, which suggested that there might be fewer candidates for agencies in Wales partly because of the number of non-departmental public bodies in Wales and possibly because of the relatively small size of the Department, was amended during formal consideration following a division along party lines (6 Conservatives voting against 2 Labour and 1

Plaid Cymru Member) to include a recommendation that further consideration be given to the establishment of new agencies or the conversion of some existing NDPB's into agencies where this was appropriate.

The Committee's second inquiry was directly into the area for which Cadw is responsible, and the report into the *Preservation of Historic Buildings and Ancient Monuments* included a substantial chapter on Cadw, encouraging it to adopt a more independent position, and discussing the extent to which it was constrained by its status as an agency. A further inquiry into Rural Housing included oral evidence from the Planning Inspectorate. It is perhaps fortuitous that two policy areas which interest the Committee—historic monuments and rural housing—cut directly into the areas of responsibility of Welsh Office agencies; but it is noteworthy that the Committee began the Parliament with two inquiries both of which had administrative significance.

1st Report, 1992-93, *The Work of the Welsh Office*, HC 259.

2nd Report, 1992-93, *The Preservation of Historic Buildings and Ancient Monuments*, HC 403.

3rd Report, 1992-93, *Rural Housing*, HC 621.

6

Financial Accountability: Agencies and Audit

Priscilla Baines

Introduction

At one level, the Next Steps initiative and the creation of the executive agencies might have been expected to make little difference to the work of the National Audit Office (NAO) or the Committee of Public Accounts (PAC), because the agencies have remained very largely funded by voted money. The NAO was set up under the National Audit Act 1983 and reports to the House of Commons. It is answerable to the House of Commons through the Public Accounts Commission and its reports are considered by the Public Accounts Committee. The Office's primary functions are to audit the accounts of over five hundred publicly-funded bodies and to ensure the propriety and regularity of those bodies' expenditure. Under S.6 of the 1983 Act, it is also entitled to investigate the efficiency, effectiveness and economy of public bodies. The agencies' continued dependence on voted money has meant that their new status has not directly affected their relationship with the NAO, which remains responsible for auditing their accounts and may also carry out value for money studies of their operations. In her February 1988 statement, the then Prime Minister, Mrs Thatcher, assured the House of Commons that the normal rules of accountability and audit should apply to the agencies and that the NAO should have the same role in relation to them as it had in relation to government departments.

The agencies and their accounting officers

In practice, as we have seen in Chapter 4, questions about how the agencies' financial accountability to Parliament should operate have persistently exercised the Treasury and Civil Service Committee (TCSC) during its regular reviews of the implementation of the Next Steps initiative; the matter remains the subject of some as yet inconclusive debate. The creation of the agencies has added a new dimension to the perennial arguments about the nature and extent of *ministerial* accountability to Parliament while the Committee, and others, have sought to establish how far the agencies themselves, in the form of their chief executives, can be held to be directly accountable *financially* to Parliament. At an early stage, the TCSC scored what was seen at the time by the first Next Steps Project Manager, Peter Kemp, as 'a quite remarkable change ... a breakthrough' when it persuaded the government that chief executives should also be accounting officers. That innovation has, however, so far largely failed to clarify the position. Following that decision, in January 1990 the Treasury issued a revised Accounting Officer Memorandum which contained specific provision for the Next Steps agencies but which in effect left the division of responsibilities to be laid down by departmental accounting officers in the context of agency framework documents:

Accounting Officer for Next Steps Agencies

23. Where an agency established under the Next Steps initiative is a separate department, or where it remains part of a department but has its own vote or is a Trading Fund, the Treasury appoints the Chief Executive as Accounting Officer in the normal way. The relationship of such a Treasury-appointed Accounting Officer, where the agency is part of a department, with his Minister and with the departmental Accounting Officer will be analogous to that of an additional Accounting Officer as described above, but in particular will stem from the allocation of responsibilities between the agency and the department in the agency framework document.

24. Where an agency remains part of a department and is financed from one or more subheads of departmental votes, it is for the departmental Accounting Officer to designate the Chief Executive as Agency Accounting Officer. When he does so, he should send the Chief Executive a letter, in a form approved by the Treasury, defining the relationship between the Chief Executive's responsibilities as Agency Accounting Officer and his own as departmental Accounting Officer. This relationship will again be determined by the allocation of responsibilities between the agency and the department in the agency framework document.

25. The Chief Executive of an agency is liable to be summoned to give evidence to the Public Accounts Committee on the discharge of those responsibilities which have been allocated to him. Where his appointment is that of an Agency Accounting Officer the Committee will probably wish to take evidence both from him and the departmental Accounting Officer. Where an agency remains part of a department but the Chief Executive is appointed Accounting Officer by the Treasury the PAC will similarly have the opportunity, if they wish, to take evidence from the departmental Accounting Officer as well as the Chief Executive. (reproduced in PAC, 1990a)

The Fraser Report (Efficiency Unit, 1991) pointed out that to make chief executives act as accounting officers created uncertainty about the respective responsibilities of agency chief executives and permanent secretaries. The report recommended that the Treasury's Accounting Officer Memorandum (presumably the revised version of January 1990), then under review, should be amended 'to clarify the respective accounting officer responsibilities of chief executive and Permanent Secretaries'. The TCSC similarly hoped that the review of the memorandum would resolve the uncertainty identified in the Fraser Report and added: 'If problems arise from a blurring of responsibilities, we assume that they will come to the attention of our colleagues on the Public Accounts Committee and that the Committee will take appropriate action to ensure the necessary clarity is restored'. (TCSC, 1991, para. 88)

Up to July 1993 there had been only one occasion when a permanent secretary and chief executive appeared before the PAC and were questioned by the Committee specifically about the relationship between the parent department and the agency. That was when the Permanent Secretary of the Department of Transport and the Chief Executive of the Vehicle Inspectorate gave evidence on 6th July 1992 about the NAO's report on *The Vehicle Inspectorate*. (NAO, 1992; PAC, 1993a) (The reports are discussed in more detail below.) The two witnesses generally appeared to understand their respective roles and shared the responses to the questioning, with the Chief Executive answering the majority of the questions, particularly on operational matters. He stated categorically that agency status meant that the relationship with the parent department was much clearer, with much more clearly defined roles for the agency than previously. (PAC, 1993a, QQ 13 and 283) He also emphasised that the Vehicle Inspectorate had a very precise financial framework in terms of its sources of revenue and lack of freedom to set charges for its services. (QQ 86 and 234)

There was no suggestion by either witness that the financial relationship between the department and the agency had been found to cause particular problems. It had, however, been made clear in the NAO's report on the Inspectorate that there were several aspects of the Inspectorate's framework document, such as the requirement to follow civil service rules on pay and grading, which had been found to be unduly restrictive and where the Chief Executive confirmed to the PAC that he was exploring the possibility of change with the department, as part of a general review of the document. (QQ 89–100) The members of the Committee made only one obvious attempt to divide the two officials (in relation to their responsibility for monitoring performance, QQ 130–155), while the question of their respective financial responsibilities was not raised, possibly because that factor did not emerge as causing particular difficulties.

There were two earlier occasions when the Permanent Secretary of the Department of Social Security, Sir Michael Partridge, accompanied by the then Chief Executive designate of the Social Security Benefits Agency, Mr Michael Bichard, gave evidence to the PAC. Mr Bichard was treated very much as though the Agency was already in operation and answered questions accordingly (both occasions were in February 1991 and the Agency was formally set up in April 1991). Again, there appeared to be a good understanding between the two witnesses about where their respective responsibilities lay but Sir Michael replied to the large majority of the questions. The Committee members did not make any obvious attempts to drive wedges between the two officials and the question of the status of the Agency did not arise, although the performance of its local offices did. (PAC, 1991a and 1991b)

The same two witnesses appeared again before the PAC on 7th December 1992 (by which time Mr Bichard was substantive Chief Executive of the Benefits Agency) with other Department of Social Security officials and were questioned about an NAO report on *Quality of Service* (NAO, 1993a), together with a follow-up memorandum by the Comptroller and Auditor General. The good understanding between them appeared to be maintained but on that occasion Mr Bichard answered a much larger share of the questions, probably because much of the questioning was concerned with operational matters. The questions were almost entirely concerned with problems of service delivery which had been identified in the NAO's report (an aspect of the NAO's involvement with the agencies which is discussed further below) rather than with the relationship between the two Accounting Officers or the effects of agency status. (PAC, 1993b) On a subsequent occasion when the PAC examined the same pair about the Department of Social Security's Appropriation Accounts, a more traditional type of PAC inquiry, there were no questions about their respective roles or about the Agency's status. (PAC, 1993c)

As there has not been an occasion where a permanent secretary and a chief executive have been publicly required to justify the division of their responsibilities as accounting officers, it remains to be seen whether there are genuine difficulties over that particular aspect of their respective roles and whether the PAC will have to take any of the 'appropriate action' identified by the TCSC—whatever form such action might take. To a considerable extent, such difficulties are part of the wider question of the general relationship between the agencies and their core departments (a point which was raised in some detail by the PAC in relation to the Department of Transport and the Vehicle Inspectorate), although they are also potentially significant in their own right in terms of the agencies' financial accountability to Parliament. As the TCSC's concern with the need for clarity over their responsibilities illustrates, accounting officers play an important part in the system of financial accountability to Parliament. It is therefore at least arguable that if such a visible part of the system fails, then other more fundamental parts may be seriously wrong.

The NAO and the agencies: certification audits and value for money reports

The NAO has actively sought from the start to be closely involved in such matters as the form of the agencies' accounts and has had to devote increasing resources to auditing those accounts. As the Comptroller and Auditor General himself acknowledged in evidence to the PAC, the creation of the agencies has caused an increase in the actual number of audits to be undertaken and hence in the volume of routine work for the NAO. Each agency which has been carved out of a government department is required to submit separate accounts which have to be individually audited each year, whereas previously the audit would have been carried out as part of that of the parent department and their transactions would not necessarily have been looked at every year. (PAC, 1992)

Initially, the NAO faced the practical problem that the precise number of candidates for agency status and when they would be set up were uncertain, so that the number of accounts to be audited and resources required could only be guesses. In the Office's 1989–90 to 1993–94 Corporate Plan, provision was made for a modest increase (from 476 to 485) in the number of accounts audited because the government had accepted the Efficiency Unit's recommendations for the establishment of agencies—an expurgated version of that Corporate Plan was published in the PAC's 4th Report for Session 1988–89. (PAC, 1989a) The 1990–91 to 1994–95 Corporate Plan said that clearer pictures had begun to emerge of the likely number of agencies (about 80 were then known to be planned) although uncertainties still remained about the timing of their creation. (PAC, 1990b)

By the time the NAO's 1991–92 to 1995–96 Corporate Plan was presented to the PAC in July 1990, the need to respond positively to changes in government structure, particularly the Next Steps Initiative, was listed as one of the main aspects of the NAO's overall strategy. A net increase was forecast in certification audits by 1995–96 from around 465 to 530 accounts, mainly due to the creation of over 80 Next Steps agencies. Para. 1.12 of the 1991–92 Plan said:

> The Next Steps reforms have continued to gain momentum since the 1989 Plan and a somewhat clearer picture has now emerged of their likely impact, particularly on certification audit and on the need for the NAO to respond with assistance in establishing new forms of account and the associated systems. This is reflected in the Plan.

In evidence to the PAC, the Comptroller and Auditor General said that the agencies' accounts did not pose any particular problems for the NAO. While it was not for the NAO to tell the agencies what accounting system they should have or how they should arrange their financial affairs, the NAO was concerned that the agencies should have proper systems of accounts from the start. There had been or would be meetings between the NAO and the chief executive and financial staff of every agency so that all the agencies knew from the beginning what the NAO's requirements as auditors would be. (PAC, 1991c, QQ 4915 and 4934) The C&AG told the PAC on 25th November 1991 that he was catering for the number of agency accounts to rise to 90 by 1996-97 and that he would have oversight of 46 in 1992-93. (PAC, 1992) The NAO's 1992 Annual Report noted that by April 1992 over 70 agencies had been established and commented:

'When a new agency is set up it often needs help in reviewing its accounting and financial management systems to ensure that its accounts can be prepared quickly and accurately and are auditable. We have provided help and advice to many agencies in this way'.

The C&AG's assurances to the PAC that auditing the Next Steps agencies poses no real problems for the NAO may be literally true but does not tell the whole story. Apart from the actual increase in workload for the NAO, even certification audit may not be entirely straightforward where a framework document does not lay down clear divisions between the finances of an agency and those of its parent department. Confusion in that area may have wider repercussions. There may also be difficulties where agencies are unwilling to cooperate with the NAO over such matters as the form of accounts. The NAO has a specific function in examining and assessing financial targets and in ensuring that financial performance measures are reflected in published accounts, even though it cannot insist on the adoption of a particular form of accounts. It can also look at performance indicators, but only where there are specific financial performance indicators which appear in published accounts, and in theory it cannot question the validity of other performance indicators, although in practice this limitation does not appear to be rigorously applied. The NAO nevertheless has to operate largely behind the scenes when dealing with the agencies over such matters and some of its ability to persuade agencies to choose, for example, realistic financial targets and performance indicators must depend on the traditional 'birch in the cupboard' threat of an adverse report by the C&AG followed by a rebuke from the PAC and a Minute from the Treasury.

The C&AG hinted at such an approach when he said to the PAC 'What I have been concerned to do is to provide the advice from the viewpoint of the Office as to the kind of requirement we shall put upon them in order to do our work'. (PAC, 1991c, Q 4934) With the emphasis in the Next Steps Initiative on such aspects of performance as improved quality of service and greater efficiency, performance measurement and targets are obviously sensitive areas for both the agencies and the NAO. The agencies may find themselves subject to conflicting pressures from Ministers anxious to present agencies' results in the best possible light and from the NAO's concern to ensure that proper financial performance measures are adopted and reflected in published accounts.

By July 1993, the NAO had published eight value for money reports on the agencies, which adopted a variety of approaches. The first, *The Next Steps Initiative* (NAO, 1989), was a useful but largely descriptive account of the early arrangements made by five departments to identify candidates and set up agencies and of the work of the Next Steps Project Team. It was subsequently endorsed, but again in very bland terms, by the PAC. (1989b) A report on *HM Land Registry* (NAO, 1991) was a follow-up of an earlier study in 1987 and a subsequent PAC report, both of which had contained strong criticisms of the Land Registry, particularly its standards of service and the level of fees. The Registry had acquired agency status in July 1990 but its financial regime had not been changed. The 1991 NAO report found substantial improvements in the Registry's performance and concluded that its agency status 'provides the opportunity to press ahead with further initiatives ... The aim is to enhance the efficiency of its operations and to benefit the public through improved quality of service'. (NAO, 1991, Summary and Conclusions, para. 4) The PAC subsequently commented that the 'productivity targets set [for the Land Registry] seemed to be little more demanding than in the past' but nevertheless went on:

> We are encouraged by the Registry's positive attitude to improving productivity and performance and the measures it is taking to make the most of the opportunities flowing from 'Next Steps' status and the prospective move to a Trading Fund regime. We note the intention to consult the Lord Chancellor's Department, the Treasury and the National Audit Office in working out these arrangements. (PAC, 1991d, paras. 36 and 39)

A very similar approach was adopted in a report published in April 1993 on *Manpower Planning in the Home Office*. (NAO, 1993c) That was also a follow-up of earlier reports by the NAO and PAC on manpower planning in five government departments, of which the Home Office was one. As far as the Passport Agency was concerned, the NAO commented favourably on the improvement in various aspects of the Agency's performance but nevertheless concluded that there was room for further progress in such areas as the use of differential pricing to save manpower and the need to pay more attention to reducing unit costs. Although the PAC had suggested in its earlier report that agency status was a possible way of improving performance, the NAO did not specifically attribute any of the progress which it identified as resulting from the change of status.

The Vehicle Inspectorate

The NAO report on *The Vehicle Inspectorate* (NAO, 1992) was specifically concerned with the Inspectorate's progress since becoming an agency. It showed clearly how the NAO viewed both its own role in relation to the agencies and the agencies' own priorities and possible development. It was seen as a model for future reports on the agencies. It was the first report to date (July 1993) on an executive agency where the traditional NAO/PAC/Treasury Minute cycle had been completed. In the course of that cycle, it became clear that there were considerable differences between the bodies involved about where specific responsibilities should lie and some wider arguments arose which have yet to be resolved.

The introductory chapter of the NAO's report explained that as both the first agency and one of the first trading funds, the Inspectorate was:

> at the forefront of the implementation of the Next Steps Initiative. Whilst every agency is different, the National Audit Office consider that other agencies will find much that the Inspectorate have done relevant to their own development. This Report, therefore, examines the steps that the Inspectorate have taken to improve the quality of their service and efficiency, the two main goals of the Next Steps Initiative. It seeks to draw together conclusions arising out of this examination to look at the future challenges facing the Inspectorate, as an indication of similar challenges likely to be faced by other maturing agencies. (para. 1.12)

The emphasis in the report on quality of service and its measurement, as well as on the NAO's more traditional concern with cost efficiency, was clearly deliberate: the NAO were 'keen to identify whether the Inspectorate's service had improved and whether it has become more efficient'. (Summary and Conclusions para. 6)

The report referred to many aspects of the Inspectorate's work, starting with the basic framework within which all the agencies, as exemplified by the Inspectorate, had to work. It looked at both the 'freedoms and flexibilities accorded to the Inspectorate' and the constraints imposed by its framework document. It also considered the Inspectorate's relationship with its 'customers', the Department of Transport as the primary customer on the one hand and, on the other, those at the receiving end of its work, mainly the operators of heavy goods vehicle and public service vehicle fleets and the owners of MOT testing garages. It analysed the ways in which the Inspectorate's performance in terms of service to both categories of customer could be assessed and whether there had been any measurable improvement in performance. The report contained some criticisms of how the Inspectorate had introduced some new customer service initiatives without doing sufficient market research or costing before they were introduced, but generally endorsed the Inspectorate's efforts to devise suitable performance measures which would provide genuine indicators of the levels of service provided. It also considered the Inspectorate's efficiency targets and reviewed performance against those targets, as well as how the Inspectorate's management structure had been changed following agency status.

The report's overall conclusions about how the Inspectorate had performed as an agency were generally favourable:

> The Inspectorate, with the support of the Department of Transport, have done well since they became an agency in 1988. They have developed the way they deliver their service to their customers and have improved their efficiency significantly. In doing so the Inspectorate have introduced a large number of initiatives and changes in a relatively short period. (Summary and Conclusions, para. 17)

And:

> ... the National Audit Office consider that Agency status has had a telling beneficial impact on performance achieved. Agency status has also helped to clarify the Department's requirements as a customer for the Inspectorate's services and as their 'owner' in setting targets. (para. 18)

Despite this recognition of the benefits of agency status, there was a significant, if paradoxical, qualifying observation that:

> The extent to which these improvements (in quality of service and efficiency) were the direct result of agency status is, however, difficult to determine. The National Audit Office consider that the flexibilities (such as financial and contractual delegation) offered by agency status, although useful, do not in themselves account for the changes that have taken place in the Inspectorate. These changes could have taken place without the additional delegated powers that agency status brings.

Agency status had, however, provided a catalyst without which the changes in the Inspectorate might well not have taken place at all and would not have proceeded at the same pace. 'The National Audit Office consider that it was this change in attitude rather than the extra delegated powers that made the difference'. (Summary and Conclusions, paras. 8 and 9)

In the context of the practical improvements which, the Inspectorate recognised, might still be introduced, there was a further, equally fundamental, qualification in the conclusion that 'Even with those practical improvements, however, the National Audit Office consider that without policy changes the scope for radical improvements will become exhausted and management may find further gains more difficult'. (para 20) The report also explicitly acknowledged (in para. 12) that there were significant differences between agencies and market-led businesses and that agencies were constrained by their status, particularly their need to conform with the terms of their framework documents. There were therefore finite limits to what agency status as such could achieve in terms of improved quality of service and efficiency, unless the framework documents could be revised in order to give the agencies greater freedom.

The PAC generally welcomed the report when it heard evidence on 6th July 1992 from the Permanent Secretary to the Department of Transport and the Chief Executive of the Vehicle Inspectorate. In his opening remarks, the Chairman, Robert Sheldon, said:

> We are rather pleased with the way in which the National Audit Office have carried out this first inquiry [into the agencies]. We will be looking at a number of points as a benchmark for some of the future Next Steps agencies that will be presenting evidence before this Committee. They range widely and some of them will have some of the characteristics of this Agency and some will have quite different ones. It may come to be looked upon as one of the ways in which the Committee of Public Accounts concerns itself with the Next Steps agencies and the matters that are likely to interest us. (PAC, 1993a, Q 1)

The PAC's subsequent questioning pursued several themes, some of them concerned with detailed aspects of the Inspectorate's performance and some with more general topics such as the effect of agency status and the relationship with the Department of Transport. The improved clarity of that relationship emerged in several contexts, with both witnesses emphasising their perception of the existence of a 'contract' between the two bodies (QQ 14 and 35–36) and the Inspectorate's much greater freedom of action as a result of being an agency. The Chief Executive said that the new status had resulted in a marked change in the Inspectorate's 'culture' and a much more focused approach to its work (QQ 64, 187, 217–220, 283 and 285), while both he and the Permanent Secretary claimed, when challenged on whether agency status had been essential for the changes to be made, that many of the arrangements for the agency could not have been applied without the change of status (QQ 261 and 283–4). Some members of the Committee expressed concern over the long list in the NAO report of constraints on the Inspectorate which appeared to contradict the claims of greater freedom and flexibility (QQ 15–16, 89–91 and 235) and drew attention to the Inspectorate's desire for more operational freedom in certain areas (see, for example, QQ 20 and 192–7). The Chief Executive emphasised that he did not see running an agency as the equivalent of running a market-led business (Q 89) but saw his job as being 'to provide a service' within the terms laid down by the operation's owner and principal customer (the Department of Transport) (QQ 93–97).

Several members of the Committee questioned the witnesses in some detail about performance indicators, including quality of service indicators, and targets, with some concern being expressed about how the targets were derived and imposed on the Inspectorate. Questioning on that point revealed clearly that the PAC, like the NAO, saw such matters as quality of service as being inseparable from specifically financial aspects of the Inspectorate's performance. In adopting this approach, both bodies followed the Treasury's view that the two cannot be considered in isolation:

> Improving quantity and quality of service is the key aim of Next Steps and of the Citizen's Charter. True value for money judgements, i.e. those which genuinely balance inputs and outputs, can only be made by assessing both together. This is particularly so in those areas where the agency is a monopoly supplier where quality of service targets act as a surrogate for customer choice. (HM Treasury, 1992, 12–13)

The PAC's report was in its classical, somewhat admonitory, style and concentrated on potential improvements in three main areas which had been identified as being of particular importance: quality of service, delegation of responsibilities and monitoring of performance. It generally endorsed the NAO's findings and concluded, for example, that the

Inspectorate's own efficiency index had 'significant weaknesses of design and coverage' which had led to misleading impressions of increased efficiency, and that the index needed to be refined in order to eradicate such weaknesses. 'Until this is done we consider that the evidence is as yet inconclusive on the extent to which the Inspectorate have improved their performance'. Concern was expressed at the NAO's finding that only 30% of the Inspectorate's staff thought that the organisation was characterised by efficient working practices and the Inspectorate was told that 'we expect them to secure practical improvements in efficiency by working closely with their staff'.

Concern was also expressed at the lack of knowledge among vehicle operators about the availability of some of the Inspectorate's services and at the views of 60% of the Inspectorate's staff that two new initiatives were unsuccessful. Similarly, nearly a quarter of the staff thought that standards of enforcement activity had deteriorated and it was recommended that the Inspectorate 'should investigate this matter to obtain hard evidence on the current quality of such work'. (PAC, 1993a)

The report endorsed the NAO's scepticism about whether agency status as such was necessarily a source of improved performance in a way which might be seen as an explicit challenge to the rationale behind the Next Steps Initiative:

We welcome the management improvements that the Inspectorate have introduced since becoming an Agency, although the Department were unable to explain convincingly why such beneficial changes could not have been made while the Inspectorate was still part of the Department of Transport. (Summary of Conclusions and Recommendations, para. 2(vi))

The report did not refer to the NAO's other qualifying observation about the limits to what agency status might ultimately achieve but it did in effect question some of the other basic assumptions on which the relationship between the Department and the Inspectorate was based. Some of the constraints imposed by the Department were questioned, particularly when they led to under-utilisation of assets. The role of the performance targets laid down by the Department and how they related to the Inspectorate's internal targets were considered in some detail:

We endorse the Department of Transport's stated approach of setting out its requirements, establishing targets and monitoring performance, and leaving the Inspectorate to get on with the job. However, we are surprised that in practice customer service targets have not been set out in terms of outputs at all, and that these were established without reference to whether customers want a particular level of service. We recommend that in future the Department should express performance measures in relation to outputs, and the targets should reflect the expressed needs of the Inspectorate's customers. (para. 25)

Some of the Department's targets were seen as insufficiently challenging for the Inspectorate and the Department was criticised for failing to monitor the Inspectorate's performance throughout the year, as well as for not investigating why some targets had not been met. In addition, it was concluded that the Department was trying to draw an irrelevant distinction between targets set by Ministers and monitored by the Department and those indicators which the Inspectorate monitored itself, particularly as both were included in the Inspectorate's Business Plan. 'We recommend that the Department should monitor performance against all the performance indicators and targets set out in the Business Plan'. (para. 28)

The PAC's questioning of the rationale behind the Next Steps was clearly seen by the Treasury as a challenge which could not be ignored. The subsequent Treasury Minute (Cm 2175) went to unusual lengths to defend the position of the Department and Inspectorate and to counter many of the PAC's specific criticisms. It refuted point-blank the contention of both the NAO and PAC that agency status as such was not essential in order to improve performance:

> The Inspectorate is still a part of the Department of Transport. What has changed is its status within the Department. The transfer to Agency status for the Inspectorate provided powerful impetus for change. The process of producing a framework document defining the Agency's parameters led to a much clearer definition of the Inspectorate's objectives and of management responsibility and accountability. The Department welcomes the Committee's recognition that improvements have been made. (para 6)

There was a similar reaction to the PAC's comments on the constraints imposed on the Inspectorate by its Framework Document:

All Executive Agencies operate within an agreed framework which is subject to review within an agreed timescale. A formal framework document sets out the operational constraints. This is kept under constant scrutiny. The Inspectorate's framework document is currently being reassessed in the wider review of the Inspectorate. As part of this the relevance and adequacy of the operational constraint set out in the document will be examined. (para 8)

The PAC's criticisms of some of the Inspectorate's performance measures and how they had been monitored by the Department were countered in equally blunt language, starting with a statement of how the Treasury (and presumably the Department and the Inspectorate) saw the position, particularly in relation to the role of the agency chief executive as accounting officer:

11. Clarity of roles, managerial authority and accountability go hand in hand with the establishment of Executive Agencies. The strategic direction of an agency is a matter for the responsible Minister. This includes the setting of published key targets for the Agency, performance against which is reported in the Agency's annual report.

12. The Agency Accounting Officer, who is the Chief Executive, is accountable for the Agency's performance against these key targets. In working to meet these, the Agency Accounting Officer may develop a wider range of internal performance indicators, and set internal targets, for management purposes. The level at which these are set is a matter for the Agency Accounting Officer's judgement, paying due regard to the Agency's customers.

And:

14. There is a clear difference between key targets set by Ministers and lower level internal targets. In the case of the Inspectorate, key targets are monitored by the central Department on the basis of quarterly reports, which are carefully analysed and used when agreeing future targets. The Department agrees that these targets should be challenging and that is the basis on which they have been set in the past ...

18. It would be inappropriate to set the Agency Accounting Officer formal targets for the Inspectorate's internal performance indicators in

the same way as is done for the key targets. That would detract from
the general principle embodied in the Next Steps initiative of greater
devolution of managerial responsibility ... But in these areas it is
nevertheless important to monitor performance against suitable
indicators so as to spot unusual trends and to seek explanations for
them.

The NAO and PAC have always had to walk a tightrope in order to
avoid commenting on the merits of government policy and both bodies
must find that constraint inhibiting on occasion. It could be argued that the
NAO's comments about the effects of agency status should be seen more
as an implied rebuke to the Department of Transport for earlier failures
to improve the Vehicle Inspectorate's performance than as a challenge to
the rationale behind the Next Steps. It is certainly exceptional for either
body openly to question a central plank of government strategy, as they
appear to have done over the benefits of agency status, and it is unusual
for Treasury Minutes so openly to refute criticisms by the PAC. That
particular development may have wider long-term repercussions which
cannot be discussed here.

The more specific argument which has emerged between the NAO and
the PAC, on one side, and the Treasury, Department of Transport and
Vehicle Inspectorate on the other, over responsibility for establishing and
monitoring performance measures is being widely repeated elsewhere in
the public sector. It is also a new aspect of the more traditional and
inevitable tension between the NAO/PAC and government departments. In
the particular context of the Next Steps agencies, its existence shows that
even in relatively straightforward cases such as the Vehicle Inspectorate,
different perspectives can lead to very different perceptions of who should
be responsible for what, who should be accountable for what—and how far
the NAO and PAC can legitimately intervene in an area where the NAO
can justifiably lay claim to professional expertise.

As the NAO itself has acknowledged, the Vehicle Inspectorate cannot
necessarily be regarded as a typical agency (as Sir Peter Kemp has
frequently contended, it is anyway doubtful if such a creature can exist).
The Inspectorate is medium-sized, with specific and relatively limited
functions, clearly defined in its framework document, and a
well-understood financial framework. It is part of a department which has
been recognised, unlike some, as being willing to make considerable
delegations of authority to chief executives in agencies (see the Balme
Efficiency Scrutiny Report on the Department of Transport, quoted in

para. 1.8 of the NAO report on the Vehicle Inspectorate), an approach which must help in achieving clear divisions of responsibility.

It is also evident that the Inspectorate has been willing to work with the NAO from the start so that the NAO may well have been, in effect, preaching to the converted in its dealings with the Inspectorate. It would be mistaken to assume either that all the other agencies present such straightforward tasks for the NAO or that the other agencies will be so willing to work with the NAO in the way that the Inspectorate has. A precedent has nevertheless been set and it is possible that the other agencies will find that they increasingly have to justify their position if they want to resist pressure to conform with the NAO's standards in relation to performance measures. The PAC's endorsement of the approach embodied in the NAO's report suggests that other agencies may well be expected to follow the pattern set by the Vehicle Inspectorate.

The NAO's second value for money report on the work of an individual agency—on the Department of Social Security's Resettlement Agency (NAO, 1993a)—had not by July 1993 been followed by a PAC report. It was not specifically concerned with the effects of agency status as such but otherwise adopted a very similar approach to the one on the Vehicle Inspectorate, although in relation to a very different type of organisation. The report analysed how far the Resettlement Agency had succeeded in providing appropriate standards of care for the residents of its units and its effectiveness in resettling residents. It also examined the controls over the Agency's costs, measures taken to improve efficiency and the Agency's progress in developing replacement facilities.

The report concluded that the establishment of the Agency had led to the clarification of objectives and to the setting of performance targets, as well as to the creation of a reporting system on performance against plan and in relation to performance targets. It identified areas where action was needed, such as improved collection of board and lodging charges, the development of more challenging efficiency targets, and of a clear strategy for replacing resettlement units inherited by the Agency. The report recognised that the Agency faced real difficulties in balancing the requirement for economy and efficiency with the needs of a particularly vulnerable group of people but argued that further improvements in the quality of service provided to residents should be achieved, although 'significant management attention' would be required for that purpose.

Quality of service reports

The Resettlement Agency report illustrated the NAO's more general concern with the quality of service provided by the Next Steps agencies, particularly those in the areas of social security and social services. That is an obvious growth area, especially in view of the size of the agencies involved, the extent of their dealings with the public and the scale of the expenditure for which they are responsible. Two reports have been explicitly concerned with the topic, one published in June 1992 (NAO, 1993b) which was followed up by the PAC (PAC, 1993b); and one published in April 1993 on *Quality of Service: Income Support for Self-Employed and Formerly Self-Employed People.* (NAO, 1993d) A third published in January 1993 dealt with *Statutory Sick Pay and Statutory Maternity Pay.* (NAO, 1993e) By July 1993, the PAC had not followed up the latter two reports.

The first of the three reports—on the payment of the four allowances—criticised many aspects of the performance of both the Department of Social Security and the Benefits Agency, although it did acknowledge the magnitude of the task involved and that there had been some improvements as a result of strenuous efforts, partly by the Department before the Agency came into operation. The PAC, not surprisingly, endorsed the criticisms and the lack of the type of information, particularly about costs, which would enable management to evaluate the efficiency and quality of the services being provided.

The report on income support also acknowledged the efforts which had been made since 1991 by the Benefits Agency to develop and improve its services 'but there remains room for further improvement'. There had been particular problems over the payment of income support by Agency offices in southern England, where the numbers eligible had been seriously underestimated, but 'strong remedial action' had been taken to improve the situation. Neither of those reports considered the way in which the Benefits Agency's performance measures were established or applied, but both looked at such aspects of quality of service as delays in assessment and payment of benefits, and how the existence of specific benefits was publicised to potential claimants.

The report on statutory sick pay and statutory maternity pay was partly concerned with another agency—the Contributions Agency—and, again, did not consider specific performance measures. It did, however, reach damning conclusions about how badly the system was working:

the Department's monitoring of the schemes was insufficient for the effective supervision of a programme costing more than £1 billion a year. There was little assurance that the schemes' objectives were being achieved, that the public funds spent were adequately controlled, and that employees who were incapacitated by sickness or taking maternity leave could expect to receive their correct entitlements. The Department and their Agencies are working hard to improve their monitoring and oversight of the schemes. But their plans will need to be pursued vigorously, and supplemented by further action, if the interests of the Exchequer and employees are to be fully safeguarded. (NAO, 1993e, para. 27)

Conclusions

It is difficult to foresee the consequences of the apparently confrontational approach on policy issues adopted by the NAO in the Vehicle Inspectorate report or, indeed, whether such an approach will be repeated in future and endorsed again by the PAC. The friction undoubtedly generated by the Vehicle Inspectorate report could well affect the NAO's general credibility and possibly undermine the long-established tacit alliance between the NAO and the Treasury. The NAO's value for money work, including its more recent preoccupations with performance measures and quality of service, is nevertheless in many respects a logical extension of its traditional certification audit functions and, as its reports on the agencies have already shown, can be carried well beyond the strictly financial aspects of the agencies' performance. It has yet to be shown how effective the NAO's involvement can be in improving the performance of the really large agencies.

The NAO's approach could well have more ultimate impact on the agencies than the earlier somewhat arid debate about the division of responsibility between accounting officers—important though that debate may be in formal constitutional terms. The classic route of financial accountability to Parliament is through the NAO and PAC and the evidence so far is that both bodies are determined that that route should remain open, whatever efforts there may be by the agencies, probably aided and abetted by their parent departments and the Treasury, to construct obstacles across it. As the arguments over performance measures which arose over on the Vehicle Inspectorate report show, the NAO's relationships with both departments and agencies form a complex web which is still evolving.

Success—however measured—is by no means guaranteed. Despite reservations about the need for the Next Steps Initiative, both the NAO and PAC have explicitly endorsed agency status as a practical means of improving public sector performance and they have commended the agencies' efforts in that direction, while recognising the limitations of what agency status by itself can be expected to do. Such an attitude may encourage the agencies to think that the NAO at least understands what they are trying to achieve—but such understanding alone cannot resolve the widely recognised conflict between the freedom of operation which agency status is intended to confer and the need to ensure proper accountability to Parliament.

References

Cm 2175:   *Treasury Minute on the 19th, 20th, 23rd and 25th Reports from the Committee of Public Account*, April 1993.

Efficiency Unit,   *Making the Most of Next Steps: the Management*
1991:   *of Ministers' Departments and their Executive Agencies*, Cabinet Office Efficiency Unit, May 1991.

HM Treasury,   *Executive Agencies: A Guide to Setting Targets*
1992:   *and Measuring Performance*, HMSO, 1992.

NAO, 1989:   National Audit Office, *The Next Steps Initiative*, HC 410, 1988-89.

NAO, 1991:   National Audit Office, *HM Land Registry: Review of Performance*, HC 350, 1990-91.

NAO, 1992:   National Audit Office, *The Vehicle Inspectorate: Progress as the First Executive Agency*, HC 249, 1991-92.

NAO, 1993a: National Audit Office, *Department of Social Security: Resettlement Agency*, HC 22, 1992–93.

NAO, 1993b: National Audit Office, *Quality of Service: War Pensions, Mobility Allowance, Attendance Allowance, Invalid Care Allowance*, HC 24, 1992–93.

NAO, 1993c: National Audit Office, *Manpower Planning in the Home Office: the Passport Agency and the Nationality Division*, HC 535, 1992–93.

NAO, 1993d: National Audit Office, *Quality of Service: Income Support for Self-Employed and formerly Self-Employed People*, HC 602, 1992–93.

NAO, 1993e: National Audit Office, *Statutory Sick Pay and Statutory Maternity Pay*, HC 384, 1992–93.

PAC, 1989a: Fourth Report from the Public Accounts Committee, Session 1988–89, HC 93, *National Audit Office Estimates, 1989–90 and Corporate Plan 1989–90 to 1993–94*.

PAC, 1989b: Thirty-eighth Report from the Public Accounts Committee, Session 1988–89, HC 420, *The Next Steps Initiative*.

PAC, 1990a: Second Report from the Public Accounts Committee, Session 1989–90, HC 527, *Accounting Officers' Memorandum*.

PAC, 1990b: Tenth Report from the Public Accounts Committee, Session 1989–90, HC 42, *National Audit Office Estimates 1990–91 and Corporate Plan 1990–91 to 1994–95*, Evidence, Appendix I, para. 1.13.

PAC, 1991a: Twenty-fourth Report from the Public Accounts Committee, Session 1990-91, HC 479, *The Social Fund*.

PAC, 1991b: Twenty-sixth Report from the Public Accounts Committee, Session 1990-91, HC 216, *Support for Low Income Families*.

PAC, 1991c: Twenty-ninth Report from the Public Accounts Committee, Session 1990-91, HC 413, *National Audit Office Corporate Plan 1991-92 to 1995-96 and Estimates for 1991-92*.

PAC, 1991d: Thirty-third Report of the Public Accounts Committee, Session 1990-91, HC 435, *HM Land Registry: Review of Performance*.

PAC, 1992:   Tenth Report from the Public Accounts Committee, Session 1991-92, HC 207, *National Audit Office Estimates, 1992-93*.

PAC, 1993a: Nineteenth Report from the Public Accounts Committee, *The Vehicle Inspectorate: Progress as the First Executive Agency*, HC 118, 1992-93.

PAC, 1993b: Twenty-seventh Report from the Public Accounts Committee, Session 1992, *Quality of Service: War Pensions; Mobility Allowance; Attendance Allowance; Invalid Care Allowance*, HC 339, 1992-93.

PAC, 1993c: Minutes of Evidence to the Public Accounts Committee, 25 January 1993, HC 425i, 1992-93.

TCSC, 1991   Seventh Report from the Treasury and Civil
                      Service Committee, Session 1990–91, *The Next
                      Steps Initiative*, HC 496, 1990–91.

7

Members of Parliament and Agencies: Parliamentary Questions

Paul Evans

This chapter seeks to illuminate the debate over the implications for 'accountability' of the Next Steps Initiative by an examination of the debate in Parliament over the delegation, by Ministers, of responsibility for answering certain parliamentary questions for written answer to the chief executives of executive agencies. In doing so, it seeks to separate the two issues of accessibility and accountability which have often been conflated, both accidentally and deliberately, in debates on this issue. It also seeks an explanation for the prominence of this issue in parliamentary debate given the relative insignificance of the questions involved both in terms of content and number. The explanation proposed is that the debate has, apparently unintentionally, for conflicting reasons and against the express wishes of many Members of Parliament from all parties, resulted in a constitutionally radical redefinition of a form of direct accountability to parliament which by-passes traditional notions of ministerial, as opposed to parliamentary, accountability.

Introduction

As we have seen from earlier chapters, a central concern of the House of Commons from the very beginning of the Next Steps Initiative has been the extent to which the executive agencies would remain accountable to Parliament through the medium of parliamentary questions. It was upon this issue that most parliamentary debate over accountability was focused and has been sustained.

In terms of parliamentary time consumed, debate over this aspect of accountability has far exceeded any on the wider questions of the implications of the establishment of executive agencies for the constitutional relationship between the civil service and Parliament. Those broader issues, as earlier chapters have indicated, have been largely left to the deliberations of select committees, and in particular the Treasury and Civil Service Committee.

This phenomenon may appear paradoxical in view of the doubts expressed over the efficacy of parliamentary questions as an instrument of accountability, as for example in the work recently published by the Study of Parliament Group on *Parliamentary Questions*. (Franklin and Norton, 1993) The authors of one chapter described as 'sobering' the finding that 85% of respondents to their survey of MPs did not judge parliamentary questions as performing well their supposedly central task of influencing the policies and actions of Government.

Nonetheless, the editors emphasised the continuing symbolic, as well as practical, importance of parliamentary questions both to individual backbench MPs and, from the other side, to ministers themselves. One reason for the importance attached by Members to parliamentary questions was adduced by Tony Prosser in his discussion of parliamentary accountability of the nationalised industries, where he suggested that:

> In Britain the parliamentary question plays a peculiarly central role in arrangements for accountability, largely due to the lack of an effective system of administrative law or of a more sophisticated means of audit of government. (Prosser, 1986)

This significance was explored in Chapter 4 of *Parliamentary Questions*, where evidence from Members of Parliament was analysed. The authors sought to discover some causes of the inexorable growth in the last 10–20 years in the number of questions tabled for written answer. One factor identified was that the potential for publicity attaching to parliamentary questions had, to an extent, displaced the earlier practice among MPs of writing to ministers to raise particular constituency issues. This was despite the finding that only 8% of MPs surveyed believed that a written parliamentary question would be more effective than a letter to the relevant minister. It is clear that for many MPs the tabling of a parliamentary question had become the line of first (rather than, as previously, last) resort. (Franklin and Norton 1993, 108–113) Nonetheless, a recent survey by Philip Giddings found that for a representative sample of agencies, in the period between September 1992 and March 1993, 51% of agency cases raised by Members of Parliament came direct from the Members themselves and 49% had been referred via departments. In the case of the Benefits Agency, the proportion of cases coming direct from Members was 63%. Questions themselves represented well under 10% of the Benefits

Agency communications with Members of Parliament. (Giddings, 1994)

When the Prime Minister made her statement to the House on 18 February 1988 announcing the Next Steps Initiative, several of the supplementary questions which followed touched on whether Members of Parliament would continue to be able to question the work of agencies through the medium of parliamentary questions. Mr Alan Beith MP claimed that the House 'would be strongly opposed to any attempt to prevent members ... from tabling questions that affected the fundamental rights of their constituents'. In response, the Prime Minister repeated her claim that 'there will be no change in the arrangements for accountability'. The Prime Minister's reply, of course, begs the question of just what were the pre-existing 'arrangements for accountability'. (HC Deb 127, 1151)

The theoretical thrust of the Ibbs report was that genuine accountability could be improved if a clear distinction could be drawn between those matters for which ministers should properly be held personally responsible and the area, which has come to be described as that of 'operational matters', for which officials (i.e. chief executives) themselves should be held to account. The authors of the report had concluded that 'we believe it is possible for Parliament, through Ministers, to regard managers as directly responsible for operational matters ...' (Efficiency Unit, 1988, para. 23) In Chapter 3, Barry Winetrobe quoted Jordan's comment that:

> ... in reality it is now accountability to the Minister by the chief executive rather than accountability of the Minister to the House of Commons that is now on offer ... (Jordan, 1992)

However, the choice may not be quite so limited as Jordan suggests. The apparent confusion in the Ibbs report between the notion of managers being *directly* responsible to Parliament and the insertion of the phrase 'through Ministers' is indicative of an unresolved tension between a new notion of direct parliamentary accountability and traditional notions of ministerial accountability. The causes of the subsequent three-year wrangle over this issue in Parliament may lie in the failure to resolve this contradiction.

In the event, the parliamentary debate on executive agencies and parliamentary questions has centred around the apparently rather narrow question of the form of publication of answers—rather than the nature of the questions which can be asked or the content of answers. At the outset of the Initiative the formal position, as described for example in April 1991 by the Prime Minister in a written answer, was that while questions on executive agencies would not be blocked 'Ministers may arrange for chief executives to write to Members on matters which have been delegated to an Agency in its framework document'. (HC Deb, 189, 294w) When this occurred, the only answer which appeared in *Hansard* was 'I have referred the question to Mrs X, Chief Executive of the Y agency, who will write to the hon Member'. The first appearance of such answers provoked a small flurry of complaints from Members and the Prime Minister's exhortation to Members 'to approach Chief Executives in the first instance on such matters' does not appear to have been heeded by those Members of Parliament who have most frequent recourse to parliamentary questions.

The first discussion of any length in Parliament on this particular issue was an Adjournment debate initiated by Henry McLeish MP in May 1990 prompted by the establishment of the Employment Service Agency in April 1990. He argued that the practice of referring answers to the chief executive for answer deprived Parliament of the 'ability to obtain the information necessary to ensure proper public debate of specific issues ...' This, he believed, represented a diminution of the accountability of ministers to the House of Commons. The minister responding enunciated the Government's view that this procedure was part of a policy of *enhancing* accountability. (HC Deb, 173, 145ff)

The prolongation of this particular debate over the succeeding three years appears, at first glance, rather curious in view of the very small proportion of questions involved in the early period of the initiative. For example, in the 1991–92 session of Parliament, probably less than 300 parliamentary questions were answered by means of a chief executive's letter out of a total of around 16,500 questions for written answer tabled in the session, or some 1.5–2.0% of the total. In the 11 issues of *Open Lines* published between June 1991 and November 1992 (see below), around 420 letters from chief executives were published out of approximately 540 deposited in the Library of the House of Commons. In the same period roughly 38,000 questions for written answer were tabled. Even as recently as March 1994, questions to all departments from Martin Redmond MP revealed the very small numbers involved in most departments in the fourth year of the initiative, though they demonstrate the significant proportions of questions answered by chief executives in the Department of Employment, the Home Office and the Department of Social Security.

Table 7.1
Questions delegated to chief executives for answer
April 1993 to March 1994

Department	No.	Per cent*	Department	No.	Per cent*
Agriculture	13	0.54	Home	492	12
Attorney General	0	0	National Heritage	20	2
Defence	46†	1.5†	Northern Ireland	71	4.7
Duchy of Lancaster	0	0	Scotland	20	<1
Education	0	0	Social Security	463	17
Employment	202	10.1	Trade and Industry	31	1.1
Environment	4	0.075	Transport	14	0.84
FCO	1	<0.01	Treasury	0	0
Health	0	0	Wales	6	0.2

* Percentage of all written questions to that department
† Declined to answer on the grounds that it was 'a matter of public record'. The figures inserted are from *POLIS:* they may not be exactly comparable with the others because a single entry on *POLIS* may refer to several questions answered together.
Source: HC Deb., vol. 139, c. 880w, vol. 140, cc. 10w, 57-8w, 74w, 122w, 136w, 192-3w, 249w, 281w, 297w, 342w, 354w, 357w, 366w, 430w, 460w, 652w.

However, despite the misgivings cited earlier about the effectiveness of parliamentary questions as tools of accountability, and despite the small numbers involved, it is clear that significant issues were at stake in this debate. It was this same issue—the treatment of parliamentary questions—that had been at the heart of the somewhat confused and confusing struggle in Parliament over the accountability of the nationalised industries some forty years earlier. That earlier debate is discussed in some detail below. However, the clearest lesson to be drawn is that parliamentary questions were, and remain, a highly significant symbolic battleground in the struggle between Parliament and the executive.

Learning Resources
Centre

Procedural background

Before entering on a fuller description of the history of these debates it is important to draw a clear procedural distinction, which has not always been grasped in discussions of this issue. At no point has the Government sought to 'block' answers to questions about operational matters relating to agencies. A block was commonly invoked by an answer along the lines of 'it has been the practice of successive administrations not to answer questions on ...' (e.g. 'matters of national security', 'forecasts of unemployment', 'interest rates'). As the Select Committee on Nationalised Industries put it in 1967:

> To put it bluntly, if a Minister has previously shown himself willing to answer Questions of a certain type, ie. to accept responsibility, then further Questions of that type will be in order; if a Minister denies responsibility in a certain area and refuses to answer, the further Questions in that area would appear to be out of order. (SCNI, 1967, para. 850)

In contrast questions on the work of agencies *do* continue to receive answers, but in a different style and explicitly (though probably not effectively) from a different source, that is, by means of letters from chief executives.

Previous Governments had been determined to uphold the 'arms-length' status of ministers' relationships with the boards of nationalised industries embodied in statute, and questions about their 'day-to-day management' had received the reply 'This is a matter for the Chairman of the Board ...' an answer which in parliamentary terms constituted a 'block'. The nationalised industries 'block' became so well-established that it was in due course incorporated into successive editions of *Erskine May*. In the current edition, it is explained as follows:

> Questions relating to nationalised industries, i.e. industries or services placed by Parliament under the control of statutory bodies, are restricted to those matters for which a Minister is made responsible by the Statute concerned or by other legislation and to those matters in which Ministers are known to be involved. In general Ministers have powers, under the statutes, to make regulations concerning (or otherwise deal with) certain specific matters such as safety and to give

directions to the industry, or part of it. They can therefore be asked about the use of these powers.

The statutes also confer on Minsters power to obtain information from the Boards or governing bodies concerned, but successive governments have refused, on grounds of public policy, to answer questions seeking information on the day-to-day administration of the industries or on administrative matters contained in the annual reports of the industries. *Since the refusal to answer a class of questions prevents further questions dealing with the class of matters most questions asking for information on the working of the Boards are in practice inadmissible* [emphasis added]. (Erskine May, 290)

Thus, a Member who had missed the opportunity to table oral questions because of a traffic jam on the M1 could immediately demand an explanation from the Secretary of State for Transport by means of a parliamentary question, while one who had suffered the same fate because his train was late could not. The refusal of questions which were deemed to touch upon the 'day-to-day' responsibilities of the boards of nationalised industries was a common cause of dispute between the Clerks in the Table Office and Members. The 'arms-length' relationship of nationalised industries to ministers was, for many years, a jealousy guarded constitutional distinction.

The debate over nationalised industries

Clearly, the parallels between nationalised industries and agencies are by no means exact. Perhaps most importantly, the debate over parliamentary scrutiny of the newly nationalised industries in the 1950s was concerned with establishing some form of accountability where none had before existed: with the Next Steps Initiative the issue is a fear among some Members of Parliament of the reduction of accountability in areas where Parliament's rights have never before been challenged. However, while approached from a different direction, the issue is at heart the same in the 1990s as it was in the 1950s—how can accountability be reconciled with freedom of action within a statutory (in the case of the nationalised industries) or a non-statutory (in the case of executive agencies) framework of targets and controls?

The opposing anxieties provoked in both government and Parliament either by proposals to relinquish any apparent degree of control or proposals to acquire any apparent degree of oversight produced a confused debate in the 1950s, and have done so again in the more recent debates. David Coombes summarised this confusion over Questions on nationalised industries in 1966:

> This issue is one of the most interesting and confusing in the field of public administration in this century, and it still has not been resolved. Basically, however, those Members of Parliament who wanted to subject the industries to full scrutiny like a government department could not, at the same time, claim that the industries should be run by public corporations. The difficulty was that many Members of Parliament claimed *both* that the industries should be run by public corporations rather than state departments *and* that they should be subject to the same level of scrutiny as a government department. (Coombes, 1966, 44–5)

The issue that was unresolved in 1966 remains unresolved in 1994. A reading of the debates and reports of the early 1950s on the nationalised industries (conducted with, it must be said, a great deal more passion than those on executive agencies of the 1990s) demonstrates how, although the site of battle has shifted, its terms remain remarkably similar. In particular, the warning given to the Select Committee on the Nationalised Industries in 1952–53 by Sir Geoffrey Heyworth of the National Coal Board that:

> The mere fact ... that I felt someone was looking over my shoulder all the time the less I would be inclined to take action on a decision, and the less would be the results. (SCNI, 1953, QQ739–742)

would find a ready echo in the conviction among many civil servants (and perhaps some chief executives) that direct accountability to Parliament and commercial or quasi-commercial effectiveness were incompatible aims.

Evidence of the decline in political sensitivities about the independence of the nationalised industries can be adduced from the rapid widening of the interpretation of the proviso, recorded in *Erskine May*, permitting parliamentary questions to be tabled about nationalised industries that raised 'matters of urgent public importance'. This became increasingly permissive as, in the era of privatisation in the 1980s, ministers of all ranks were willing to demonstrate to Parliament their close knowledge of the 'day-to-day' workings of various soon-to-be-denationalised industries. They thereby opened themselves to questions which, for obvious political reasons, they were increasingly ready to answer. However, such progress was always in the direction of more apparent willingness by ministers to answer from a zero baseline and therefore provoked little resistance in Parliament.

In contrast, during the continuing debate over executive agencies and parliamentary questions, the House of Commons Table Office has never been required to make the attempt (which would surely, in any event, be hopeless) to define 'operational matters' and prevent the *tabling* of questions on such areas as it has had to in respect of 'day-to-day' management of nationalised industries. In this, they have acted in accordance with the Government's declared position that in some way ministers remain responsible for every aspect of an agency's work, and that the process of delegation to chief executives is renewed on a case-by-case basis. Such a notion of delegation is quite distinct from that which operated with the nationalised industries—it does not raise the prospect of there emerging among chief executives someone such as Sir Dennis Rooke who was prepared publicly to criticise the resources given to him by Government to run British Gas, or to invoke the aid of a select committee to counter what was seen as an attempt by ministers to trammel his freedom.

There is conflicting evidence on the extent of delegation of responsibility for the contents of chief executives' letters. The relatively provisional nature of this delegation and its cancellability is illustrated by the changing nature of its description by the Government. For example, in October 1991 Paul Flynn MP asked the Secretary of State for Social Security:

(1) whether, and at what stage, copies of letters from the chief executive of the Benefits Agency in response to parliamentary questions are submitted to his office; (2) whether, and at what stage, drafts and copies of letters from the chief executive of the Benefits Agency in response to parliamentary questions are submitted to his office.

To which he received the reply:

Ministers generally see a copy of the letter which the chief executive proposes to send in response to a parliamentary question at the time at which the proposed answer to that question is submitted to the Minister for approval. A copy of the final reply is submitted to the Minister's office on the day the letter is despatched.

In February 1993, all Secretaries of State were asked the following question:

> ... at what stage (a) drafts and (b) copies of letters from chief executives of agencies within his responsibility, in response to parliamentary questions, are submitted to Ministers.

On this occasion the DSS took the line of the other departments in dismissing (with a diversity of subtle disclaimers) any suggestion that chief executives' letters were in any way *approved* by Ministers in draft, stating:

> The chief executives of our agencies reply direct on the operational matters which have been delegated to them. Ministers receive a courtesy copy of replies on the day before they are answered.

Ironically, this produced an Early Day Motion, tabled by Paul Flynn MP, in the following terms:

> ... this House deplores the practice adopted by chief executives of Next Steps agencies within the responsibilities of the Secretary of State for Social Security of delaying letters to honourable Members in reply to Parliamentary Questions so that drafts can be submitted to Ministers; notes that letters from [other] agencies are not subject to similar delays; and calls on the Secretary of State for Social Security to instruct the chief executives concerned to discontinue this practice.

The debate over executive agencies

The Treasury and Civil Service Committee took up the issue of parliamentary questions and answers in their July 1990 report *Progress in Next Steps Initiative.* (TCSC, 1990, paras. 63–70) On the whole, they supported the aim of the arrangements for answering parliamentary questions by means of letters from chief executives which, in the view of Minister responsible for the Employment Service Agency replying to the adjournment debate in May 1990, were 'designed to ensure that hon Members deal directly with the person ... who is best placed to answer the matter on hand'. (HC Deb. 173, 145ff) But the Committee picked up on a concern among Members that access to these replies was limited and their status uncertain (since they were not proceedings in Parliament). They recommended that some way be found to publish them, adding in an unemphatic aside the startling presumption of a wholly new doctrine of direct parliamentary accountability, saying that 'if an acceptable convention is not established, there is a danger that, despite the wholly laudable intention *of making those responsible for carrying out the service wholly accountable to Parliament*, [emphasis added] much information currently available to Parliament and the public will no longer be readily accessible ...' This focus on the issue of *accessibility*, rather than *accountability*, was the one which was also taken up by the Procedure Committee in its 1991 report on parliamentary questions. (Procedure Committee, 1991) The Committee accepted it as a legitimate use of parliamentary questions by Members to act as agents to obtain information on behalf of pressure groups and other lobbyists whose aims they support. *Hansard* (especially the columns of written answers) was acknowledged to be a resource for outside researchers as much as for Members of Parliament. It was clear then that most of the concern about the non-publication of chief executives' replies was aroused by the difficulty of access to answers by such groups rather than by Members of Parliament.

We have already seen, in earlier chapters, the lack of clarity about the precise meaning of *ministerial* 'accountability' and how, if at all, it differs from *parliamentary* accountability. The compression (and possibly confusion) of the two essentially separate issues of accountability and accessibility by both the Treasury Committee and the Procedure Committee has tended to further obscure the key question of what, essentially, ministerial accountability means. The debate has instead been carried down the line, which it continues to follow, of the narrow issue of accessibility.

For example, in its response to the Treasury Committee's report the Government ignored the Committee's radical, if understated, redefinition of the doctrine of *parliamentary* accountability as being something quite separate from *ministerial* accountability which, in their words, would make 'those responsible for carrying out the service *wholly* accountable to Parliament'. Instead, the Government, disregarding the question of whether this had been its intention, also seized on the question of accessibility and undertook to place chief executives' replies in the House of Commons Library and its Public Information Office where they would 'thus be in the public domain and available to the public on request'. (Cm

1263, 1990) The declared rationale for accepting that these answers should be placed 'in the public domain' was that they might sometimes raise issues of policy broader than the immediate circumstances relating to the 'operational' issue under discussion. This concession would appear to be an acknowledgement that 'policy' and 'operational matters' are not so clearly distinguishable as the authors of the Ibbs report had so confidently asserted. However, the implications were not further pursued. The change of practice was formally announced in a written answer by the then Leader of the House in 1990:

> **Sir Geoffrey Howe:** I refer the hon Member to the White Paper (Cm 1263) which the Government have published today in response to the eighth report of the Treasury and Civil Service Committee, 'Progress in the Next Steps Initiative'. In its supportive report, the Committee made some observations about the procedure for dealing with Members' questions on matters delegated to executive agencies. The Government's reply makes clear that it is for the Minister responsible for an executive agency to decide the most helpful and appropriate way to respond to such a question: normally, he or she will ask the chief executive to respond by letter. In future, a copy of all such letters (save only for personal or confidential cases) will automatically be placed in the Library and in its Public Information Office ... We shall keep these arrangements under review. As the White Paper says, the Government's intention is that the establishment of Next Steps Agencies should improve the flow and quality of information to Parliament and the public and help to ensure that replies about management and delivery of Government services are full, prompt and as helpful as possible. (HC Deb, 178, 586w)

We see again here, that the emphasis is on the 'flow and quality of information to Parliament' rather than the issue of the location of accountability to Parliament. It was this aspect of accessibility rather than accountability about which the MP Paul Flynn, together with the academic Tony Lynes, sought to do something. Partly in an attempt to force the government's hand, they co-operated (with the help of funds from the Rowntree Trust) in producing a 'samizdat' Hansard entitled *Open Lines* which contained edited highlights of chief executives' letters which had been deposited in the Library in the previous month. The publication concentrated on the answers relating to the Employment Service and Benefits Agencies, and was available on subscription. It ran for 11 issues between June 1991 and July 1992 and published the texts of some 420 chief executives' letters out of the 540 or so deposited to the Library. In the brief editorials which prefaced each issue Mr Flynn kept up a constant attack on what he depicted as an evasion of accountability by the Government, remarking in what he announced as the last issue that the Government 'continue to use the Next Steps Agencies as a means of undermining the constitutional role of parliamentary questions'. Nonetheless, the argument was still focused on accessibility rather than on the broader issues raised by distinction between policy and operational matters.

Meanwhile, in response to a submission from Dave Nellist MP, the Procedure Committee of the House of Commons had examined the issue of chief executives' letters as part of its wider inquiry into parliamentary questions. In its report published in May 1991 the Committee joined the forces demanding the full publication of such replies. It commented:

> So long as questions relating the Executive Agencies remain in order, as we trust they will, Members should be entitled to receive a reply in the normal way by written answer. We therefore recommend that, in future, replies from agency chief executives in response to parliamentary questions referred to them by Ministers should appear in the *Official Report*. (Procedure Committee, 1991, paras. 122-6)

When the Treasury Committee returned to the issue in its 1991 report on the Next Steps Initiative it sought to support the recommendation from the Procedure Committee, while at the same time attempting to keep hold of the issue of the location of accountability, saying:

> We wish to make clear that although some Members are, with justice, dissatisfied with current arrangements for answering parliamentary questions, their dissatisfaction is with the arrangements for *publishing* the replies they receive. There is no reason for departments to use this dissatisfaction as an excuse for increased intervention in agency operations. (TCSC, 1991)

This conclusion, however, seems somewhat at odds with the immediately preceding paragraphs of the report which took the government to task for inconsistency in its definition of 'operational matters', which the Committee found had 'been so unexpectedly wide in their scope', and recommended central guidance to redress this problem. It seemed that the debate over chief executives' replies had succeeded in muddying the purity of the Committee's line on separation of accountability.

In its response to this report, the Government undertook to keep the application of the delegation criteria under review. On the question of accessibility, the Government accepted that there had been practical difficulties, and agreed that access to agency replies to parliamentary questions should be improved and proposed a system where the House itself would publish all replies regularly and frequently, so that the information was current, and available to outsiders. (Cm 1761, 1991) However, the Government did not accept that the letters should be published as ministerial written answers in *Hansard* but suggested 'a separate weekly publication'. The proposal was announced in a written answer from the Leader of the House in November 1991:

> ... The arrangement whereby chief executives reply direct by letter to written questions on operational matters is intended to recognise their direct responsibility for matters which have been delegated to them by Ministers to ensure that replies about the carrying out of Government business are full, prompt and as helpful as possible. The arrangement has worked well in those respects. However, it has become apparent that there have been some practical difficulties with the procedure ... The Government have therefore decided to propose to the House authorities that the House should publish all replies from chief executives which are placed in the Library. The Government consider that the replies should be published regularly and frequently, so that the information they contain is current and useful; that the publication should be available to individuals and organisations outside the House on a similar basis to the *Official Report*; but that the replies should not be published as ministerial written answers in the *Official Report*. A separate weekly publication for the replies would meet these criteria, although the precise form of publication and the resource implications will be a matter for the appropriate Committee of the House, to which the Government, will put their proposals at the earliest opportunity ... (HC Deb, 198, 558–9w)

Paul Flynn MP attacked this proposal as inadequate in the next issue of *Open Lines*, not least because it failed to address the questions of the application of parliamentary privilege or the practical problems of publication and dissemination. These were the issues which swayed the Administration Committee (to which the issue was remitted) in its considerations. As the Principal Clerk of the Table Office pointed out to that Committee in an unpublished memorandum:

> There were considerable difficulties for the House authorities in Mr MacGregor's original answer which, while proposing that the House should publish the replies from Chief Executives, firmly ruled out the recommendations of both the Procedure Committee and the Treasury and Civil Service Committee that the replies should form part of the Ministerial written answer in the Official Report. He suggested instead a separate weekly publication, but left it to the appropriate Committee to decide on the form of such publications. Had the Government persisted in such proposal, the Committee would have been faced with some very real problems, since in effect the House was being asked to publish, at its own expense, a freestanding document containing letters from strangers to Members of Parliament without any Ministerial authority. Quite apart from the cost involved, there would have been difficulties over such matters as copyright and the privileged status of such a document, since it would not have been a proceeding in Parliament.

The pressure was thus maintained for chief executives' letters to be published in *Hansard*. The first Early Day Motion tabled after the 1992 general election was on this subject:

> that this House deplores the denial of public access to a large amount of information of public interest supplied in letters from Next Steps agencies to honourable Members in reply to parliamentary questions; notes that such information would in the past have been given by Ministers in written answers published in the *Official Report*, and is now available only in the monthly booklet Open Lines, published with the financial support of the Joseph Rowntree Reform Trust; and calls for urgent action to ensure that this information, whether supplied by Ministers or by agencies, is in future published in the *Official Report* and not in a separate publication, whether official or not.

On the day the House rose for the summer adjournment in 1992, the Chairman of the Administration Committee announced in a written answer:

> At its meeting on 8 July the Committee resolved that, from the first sitting day after the summer recess, letters sent to Members by agency

chief executives in response to parliamentary questions should be printed among the written answers in the daily *Official Report*, beneath a standard form of reply given by the Minister with responsibility. The Cabinet Office has been advised of this decision and is understood to be considering its implications. (HC Deb, 211, 941w)

In the following Autumn, when the House resumed, the Leader of the House announced that the Government had acceded to the multiple recommendations of these select committees:

The Government welcome the Administration Committee's decision ... The decision meets the Government's aim that replies from agency chief executives should be more readily accessible while recognising the direct operational responsibilities of chief executives ... Guidance has been issued to allow the new arrangements to come into effect as from the beginning of the new term ... The arrangements apply to questions tabled on operational matters for which responsibility has been delegated by Ministers to agency chief executives. It remains open to hon Members to write to chief executives direct on such matters and I would encourage them to do so wherever they judge it appropriate. (HC Deb, 212, 287-8w)

The system came into operation in November 1992, and continues as a now unremarkable part of parliamentary procedure.

Conclusion

Writing in 1966 about the establishment, some ten years previously, of the Select Committee on Nationalised Industries in its final form, David Coombes commented:

There were two remarkable features about the birth of the ... Committee ... first, after offering resistance for about three years, the Government finally gave way to back-bench pressure ... secondly ... one would not normally have expected the Opposition to deplore the prospect of such Government embarrassment ... yet the Labour Opposition ... fought the possibility with relentless force ... (Coombes, 1966, 62-3)

There are some intriguing parallels in the upshot of the two controversies as there were in their origins. The Government, in 1992, did accede (after some three years) to back bench pressure on the publication of chief executives' answers in *Hansard*. The Opposition has manifested contradictory and conflicting reactions, coming to no clear official line on the question of accountability. As recently as January 1993 Gerald Kaufman MP, speaking as a backbencher, declared in an adjournment debate that:

> the Government are diminishing parliamentary democracy ... more and more Ministers are washing their hands of responsibilities for which, until recently, they were fully accountable to the House ... what is more ... the Government are eroding the rights of parliamentarians in another sense because until now only Ministers, as Members of Parliament had access to *Hansard*. Now, non-parliamentarians have access to it. (HC Deb, 236, 1289–90)

This last point certainly records an extraordinary constitutional event (though whether it has eroded the rights of parliamentarians is more controversial). The resolution of this long dispute by the publication of chief executives' letters in *Hansard* represents an intriguing if accidental constitutional advance, and potentially a very fundamental one. It means that the words of someone other than a formal witness before a Committee of the House or one of its Members have now become proceedings in parliament on an everyday basis. The establishment of the Select Committee on Nationalised Industries opened up a new perspective on what accountability to Parliament could mean in practice and in many ways paved the way to the establishment of the modern departmentally-related select committee system. After its initial reluctance, Parliament seized effectively the opportunity to draw aside the veil of ministerial accountability, and developed a taste for what it saw. In a different way, the recent innovation of the publication of chief executives' letters in *Hansard* may have opened a new area for Parliament to explore and exploit. It raises the intriguing vision of a Table Office of the future receiving questions from Members of Parliament addressed directly to chief executives for answer.

Were that vision ever to materialise, the possibility of a consequent public debate between ministers and chief executives over the boundaries of 'policy' and 'operational matters' could certainly bring a new transparency to the conduct of the public service. Into that debate

Parliament would no doubt be as ready to enter as it was into the gap between boards of the nationalised industries and their ministers. Such a version of accountability might be very different from the unresolved confusion of roles and definitions that currently exists, and which is described in Chapters 2 and 3 of this work. The almost accidental outcome of this debate may well have paved the way to the notion of the 'direct accountability to Parliament' talked about in the Next Steps Initiative becoming a reality, rather than the convenient administrative fiction it has been perceived as by many Members of Parliament. Whether this would reinvigorate or diminish the democratic control of the executive, only experience could show.

References

Cm 1761, 1991:   *The Next Steps Initiative*, HMSO, November 1991.

Cm 1263, 1990:   *Progress in the Next Steps Initiative*, HMSO, October 1990.

Coombes, 1966:   David Coombes, *The Member of Parliament and the Administration: the Case of the Select Committee on the Nationalised Industries*, Allen and Unwin, London, 1989.

Efficiency Unit, 1988:   Cabinet Office Efficiency Unit, *Improving Management in Government: the Next Steps*, Report to the Prime Minister, HMSO.

Erskine May: *Treatise on the Law, Privilege, and Proceedings of Parliament*, (21e), Butterworths, London, 1989.

Franklin and Norton, 1993:   Mark Franklin and Philip Norton, eds, *Parliamentary Questions*, Clarendon Press, Oxford.

Giddings, 1994:   Philip Giddings, *Agencies and Parliamentary Questions*, Reading, 1994.

Jordan, 1992:   'Next Steps Agencies: from management by
                          command to management by contract?', *Aberdeen
                          Papers in Accountancy, Finance and Management*,
                          W6, 1992.

Procedure   Third Report from the Procedure Committee,
Committee, 1991:   *Parliamentary Questions*, HC 178, 1990–91.

Prosser, 1986:   Tony Prosser, *Nationalised Industries and Public
                          Control: Legal, Constitutional and Political
                          Issues*, Blackwell, Oxford.

SCNI, 1967:   First Report of the Select Committee on
                          Nationalised Industries, *Ministerial Control of the
                          Nationalised Industries*, HC 371, 1967–68, cited
                          in Prosser, 1986.

TCSC, 1990:   Eighth Report of the Treasury and Civil Service
                          Committee, *Progress in the Next Steps Initiative*,
                          HC 481, 1989–90.

TCSC, 1991:   Seventh Report of the Treasury and Civil Service
                          Committee, *The Next Steps Initiative*, HC 496,
                          1990–91.

8

Agencies and the Ombudsman

Philip Giddings

Introduction: the Theory

The implications of the executive agency concept for the work of the Parliamentary Commissioner for Administration (PCA)—Britain's Parliamentary Ombudsman—and his associated Commons Select Committee have not loomed large in the development of the Next Steps programme. In the Ibbs Report it rates a single sentence in the Annex dealing with *Accountability to Ministers and Parliament on Operational Matters*, a sentence which says simply, 'the powers of the Parliamentary Commissioner for Administration could continue to apply to agencies'. (Efficiency Unit, 1988, 19) In the Prime Minister's statement to Parliament in February 1988, the matter was dealt with only in response to a more general supplementary question from Terence Higgins about implications for the relationship between ministers, civil servants and select committees: Mrs Thatcher simply said, 'The new approach does not affect the work of the Parliamentary Commissioner for Administration'. (HC Deb, Vol 127, 1151)

There should have been no surprise at this. Agencies were intended to be about operational matters; so is the PCA with his statutory remit based on maladministration. (Gregory and Hutchesson, 1975) The 1967 Parliamentary Commissioner Act authorises the PCA to 'investigate any action taken by or on behalf of a government department or other authority to which the Act applies' where a member of the public 'claims to have sustained injustice in consequence of maladministration'. [s.5(1)(a)] The Act goes on explicitly to declare that nothing in the Act 'authorises or requires the Commissioner to question the merits of a decision taken without maladministration by a government department or other authority in the exercise of a discretion vested in that department or authority'. [s.12(3)] Executive agencies are either part of departments or exercise their functions on behalf of departments. On the face of it they are firmly within the PCA's jurisdiction.

However, what is true 'on the face of it' does not always apply in practice. The rationale of the Ibbs report was to separate managerial responsibility for 'operational matters' from ministerial responsibility for policy. (Efficiency Unit, 1988, 10) The rationale of the PCA is based on ministerial responsibility: the 1965 White Paper spoke of Parliament as the place for ventilating the grievances of the citizen and of building on the existing systems and procedures based on ministerial responsibility:

> It is one of the functions of the elected Member of Parliament to try to secure that his constituents do not suffer injustice at the hand of Government ... We do not want to create any new institution which would erode the functions of Members of Parliament in this respect nor to replace remedies which the British Constitution already provides. Our proposal is to develop those remedies still further. We shall give Members of Parliament a better instrument which they can use to protect the citizen, namely the services of a Parliamentary Commissioner for Administration. (Cmnd 2767, 1965, para. 4)

In short, the test for the PCA's jurisdiction was ministerial responsibility, as demonstrated by parliamentary accountability, particularly in the form of questions. If part of the object of setting up executive agencies was to persuade MPs taking up a constituent's case not to use parliamentary mechanisms and ask questions of the minister about operational matters but to write direct to the chief executive, would there be a similar discouragement to taking cases to the PCA?

Formally, the answer is certainly 'no'. Chapter 9.5 of the May 1992 edition of the Civil Service Management Code, which deals with the PCA, is explicit:

Next Steps Agencies

9.5.14 The Parliamentary Commissioner Act 1967 ... places on the PCA certain obligations in respect of the 'principal officer' of the department which is the subject of investigation. For these purposes, the principal officer in charge of the department is the Permanent Secretary ...

9.5.15 In most cases Next Steps agencies legally remain part of a department: they are not listed separately in Schedule 2 (which lists administrative authorities subject to the jurisdiction of the PCA)—and their principal officer is therefore the Permanent Secretary of the department rather than the Chief Executive. (A number of agencies *are* listed separately in Schedule 2 because they were formally non-Ministerial departments in their own right. In those cases, the Chief Executive is the principal officer.)

9.5.16 Permanent Secretaries may delegate to the Chief Executive of an Agency the day-to-day responsibility for handling PCA investigations concerning matters delegated to the Agency in its Framework document ...

9.5.17 The kind of cases in which Permanent Secretaries will wish to retain some oversight will vary but they are likely to include all cases where significant ex-gratia payment is proposed. Where an apology is to be given, in cases where the matter for complaint is entirely within the discretion of the agency, it will normally be appropriate for the apology to come from the Chief Executive.

The PCA's position was similarly made clear in agency framework documents, if in slightly varying language. For example, the Queen Elizabeth II Conference Centre document states, in its 1989 version, 'There will no change in the role of the Parliamentary Commissioner for Administration in relation to the work of the Centre'. (DoE, 1989, para. 13) The Ordnance Survey's framework document says, 'there is no change to the jurisdiction of the Parliamentary Commissioner for Administration' (DoE, 1990, para. 3.1) and the Planning Inspectorate's says 'the Inspectorate is subject to the scrutiny of the Parliamentary Commissioner for Administration'. (DoE, 1992, para. 2.6)

The Practice—the Commissioners' Perspective

However clear the formal provisions may seem, what matters is what occurs operationally and on this the best witnesses are the Commissioners themselves. Before the agency programme got under way, the then PCA, Sir Anthony Barrowclough, was expressing his concern to the Select Committee that the Next Steps Initiative should not lead to a reduction in accountability for maladministration. (Select Committee, 1989, 8) The Select Committee, noting that the Driver and Vehicle Licensing Centre and the Land Registry as well as social security benefits operations had been mooted as candidates for agency status, commented, 'While it appears that the activities of these agencies will continue to constitute actions taken by or on behalf of a department, and therefore within jurisdiction, we would wish to be reassured that they will remain within the ambit of the PCA even though they would be that much further from the centre of government'. (Select Committee, 1989, ix)

In his Annual Report for the following year, the PCA (now William Reid) explained more fully how he saw the position. 'Legally ... agencies are either departments in their own right or part of their parent departments and one way or another come within my investigative remit.' He pointed out that the intention was that agencies which remained within departments should operate 'quasi-independently' and that the chief executive of an agency would be 'charged with its control and responsibility for its day to day affairs'. He commented:

In support of those arrangements it has been claimed that, through the devolution of responsibility in that way, a greater accountability for the operations which the agencies carry out will be achieved with corresponding benefits in practice for those who use their services. If that aim is attained, I shall welcome the achievement. The goal of every Ombudsman should be to be put out of work for lack of business. The alternative view, however, with human errors occurring as they do, is that administrative faults will continue to arise and that members of the public will complain in much the same way as before. If so, my jurisdiction is unaffected by transition to Agency status. (PCA, 1991, 2)

Accordingly, since much of his work relates to executive functions of central government, Mr Reid proposed to discuss with the Principal Officers (i.e. the Permanent Secretaries concerned) how the contacts between the PCA's office and their Next Steps Agencies could be made 'as efficient and streamlined as possible'. (PCA, 1991, 2) The successful outcome of this process was reported the following year when Mr Reid pointed out that, already, 'as many of the cases which I investigate involve the administrative actions of departments' agencies as they do the actions of the departments themselves'. (PCA, 1992a, 2)

In the same Annual Report Mr Reid recorded that the setting up of the Benefits and Contributions Agencies had not had an adverse effect on his work and that the responses of the two Agencies in the case of complaints against them investigated by him continued to be 'marked by the same co-operative spirit' as had characterised the responses of their parent

Department. Nevertheless, he commented that it remained to be seen what longer term impact the setting up of these Agencies would have on the administration of the services concerned and the number of complaints coming to him. He noted that the agencies had produced Charters, the listed aims in which—if achieved—should help to eliminate many of the complaints levelled against the Department in the past. However, the higher expectations engendered by Charters might bring more complaints if those expectations were not in fact met. (PCA, 1992a, 11)

The Department of Social Security is usually the PCA's 'best provider of work'. (Select Committee, 1993, xii) Another good customer is the Inland Revenue. In his 1992 Annual Report the PCA noted that the Revenue had reorganised its activities on Next Steps lines, setting up 34 Executive Offices which, together with the Valuation Office (an executive agency since September 1991) would account for 96 per cent of the Inland Revenue's total staff. 'I shall watch with their development with interest', commented Mr Reid. (PCA, 1993a, 22) That same report included Mr Reid's comments on several cases he had investigated concerning the Valuation Office, in one of which he had been critical of the agency's maladministration. (PCA, 1993a, paras. 57 and 58)

Thus in practice the Commissioners have kept a watching brief on 'developments', which has proved highly appropriate. The Government's policies for the civil service have not stood still. The number of agencies has grown and Charters have multiplied with them. The introduction of market testing, the *Competing for Quality* White Paper, 'prior options' reviews and in some instances privatisation (Cm 2430, 1993, 9–11) have taken those policies further. But the foresight of the drafters of the 1967 Parliamentary Commissioner Act, with its provision that not just the administrative actions carried out by but also those carried out on behalf of departments should be within the PCA's remit, has come into its own: the PCA continues in place as a necessary external mechanism for redressing complaints for all these activities. (PCA, 1993a, 2)

In their watching brief the Commissioners have been greatly assisted by the support they received from the Select Committee and it is to the Committee's role that we now turn.[1]

---

1 The author gratefully acknowledges the help of Colin Lee, former Clerk to the Select Committee, in preparation of this section.

The Role of the Select Committee

The fact that the involvement of the Select Committee on the Parliamentary Commissioner for Administration with Next Steps Agencies has so far been limited is a reflection of its role. The Committee is concerned, not with policy development, but with administration. Much of its work is reactive: it responds to matters raised in the reports of the Parliamentary Commissioner for Administration. Nevertheless, the Committee has shown interest in the Next Steps programme and, as the agencies came to represent a greater proportion of the civil service, the Committee's concern for their work grew correspondingly.

It has been said that the Select Committee has three functions: direct supervision of the work of the Parliamentary Commissioner, reinforcing his recommendations; acting as a focus for enlarging his jurisdiction; and giving his work greater political significance. (Bates, 1988, 198; Gregory, 1982) Each of these aspects of the Committee's work has led it to examine the Next Steps process.

As we have seen, the Committee has sought and received reassurance from the present Parliamentary Commissioner, William Reid, that the development of Next Steps agencies will leave his jurisdiction unimpaired. They remain part of the civil service and of government departments and are thus clearly within his jurisdiction. (Select Committee, 1991, para. 24)

In written evidence to the Committee in February 1991 the Commissioner explained that he had discussed with Peter Kemp, then Next Steps project manager, how the increase in the number of agencies would affect the method of his investigations. Mr Reid told the Committee that the 1967 Act governing his work required his contact during an investigation to be with the principal officer of a department, in most cases a permanent secretary, but he felt that where the complaint concerned a Next Steps agency the remedy would normally be initiated by the chief executive. Finally, he noted that the Committee would have to decide, on those occasions when oral evidence from departments was required, whether to invite the permanent secretary or the chief executive. (Select Committee, 1991, 30) Traditionally, the Select Committee had seen it as important that permanent secretaries should appear before it to account for the conduct of civil servants within their departments. However, following the pattern of the appearance before the Public Accounts Committee of chief executives (as agency accounting officers) with their permanent secretaries, the PCA Select Committee has clearly accepted that the normal practice will be for agency chief executives to appear with their permanent secretaries when their agency is under scrutiny by the Committee.

The Committee pursued some of these points in oral evidence from Mr Reid, demonstrating concern that Next Steps agencies prove as responsive to the Commissioner as government departments. The Committee, as part of a wider interest, also welcomed efforts to ensure awareness of the Commissioner's role among the staff of the Next Steps agencies.

The Committee has noted the stress placed by the Treasury and Civil Service Committee on the need to maintain the accountability of Next Steps agencies to Parliament and the public. It has argued that the Parliamentary Commissioner can provide one element of this accountability. The Committee has also stated: 'we believe that the trends in the level of complaints made to the Commissioner, investigated by him and upheld will be important indicators of how effectively these new agencies are performing'. (Select Committee, 1991, paras. 23–24)

As we have noted, the Department of Social Security generates more complaints to the Parliamentary Commissioner for Administration than any other Government department. By 1993 over 97 per cent of the Department's 80,000 staff were operating in one of its executive agencies. It is thus not surprising that the Committee's examination of the practical effects of the Next Steps programme has so far concentrated on this Department. In June 1991 the Committee took evidence from Michael Bichard, Chief Executive of the Benefits Agency, along with the Department's Permanent Secretary. (Select Committee, 1991, paras. 25 and 26)

In a report the following month the Committee welcomed the general direction of the Benefits Agency's policies regarding customer service. The Committee noted that 'an improved working atmosphere will help staff and customers alike; responsiveness to customers and to their initial complaints should reduce the level of complaints coming to Member of Parliament. If they, in turn, are responded to effectively, there should be a welcome reduction in the Commissioner's workload'. (Select Committee, 1991, para. 28)

The Committee's work—on Next Steps agencies as generally—has been reactive but progressive. While it might appear on occasion to have responded slowly to innovations in public administration, it has returned persistently to examine the effects of their implementation. In this way, prompted no doubt by successive Commissioners, the Committee is able to provide the Commissioners with significant parliamentary backing in their pursuit of remedies for injustice suffered by individual members of the public and, more significantly in our present context, in maintaining an effective external system for dealing with complaints about the operations of central government, whether organised in departments or their agencies. The Select Committee has helped to ensure that the PCA's remit has continued to cover executive agencies.

The Commissioner in Action

The heart of the PCA scheme is case-work: the investigation by the Commissioner of complaints of injustice in consequence of maladministration referred to him by MPs. The acid test of the various assertions about the PCA scheme not being affected by Next Steps is whether the PCA has continued to be able to obtain redress of such injustices caused by maladministration in the agencies. To demonstrate this we shall examine a selection of PCA cases, which we will draw from two agencies—the Driver and Vehicle Licensing Agency (DVLA), the first to be established; and the Benefits Agency (BA), the largest. We shall also consider one of the most significant cases which the PCA has dealt with, the *Disability Living Allowance* case concerning which he issued a Special Report. (PCA, 1993b) It is worth at the outset noting that a high proportion of the PCA's cases concern agencies: Mr Reid recorded in his 1993 Annual Report that most of the thirteen investigations involving the Department of Employment which he had completed had concerned their executive agency, the Employment Service, and that eight of fourteen cases involving the Department of Transport were DVLA cases. (PCA, 1994, paras. 42 and 61)

The first case we consider is an example of a BA case taken up from pre-agency days. A woman teacher complained that maladministration by the Department of Social Security (DSS) over several years had caused her to lose over five years' entitlement to incapacity benefits. The PCA's investigation began in May 1991 when he obtained the comments of the Chief Executive of the BA on the case. The crux of the complaint was that the DSS had been at fault in failing to notify the woman, until November 1989, of her possible entitlement to benefit resulting from a change of legislation in April 1983. The woman contended the DSS had had sufficient evidence of her entitlement from her claims for other allowances. She believed the DSS had lost her file, but the Commissioner's investigation revealed that she was omitted from a notification exercise which was specially targeted at those submitting medical evidence of incapacity for work. Whilst the Commissioner accepted that it was not unreasonable for the DSS to target notifications in the way it did, bearing in mind the costs involved and likely effectiveness, he considered it would be inequitable for an individual who had not been caught up in that exercise because her injury was permanent to be debarred from receiving the benefit available to others who had been alerted by that exercise. When the Commissioner put this point to the BA Chief Executive, he accepted that it was unfair and accordingly agreed that the Department should provide a remedy for the complainant by meeting her losses in full (£5,626) on an extra-statutory basis, an outcome which the Commissioner considered very satisfactory. (PCA, 1993c)

Our second BA case concerns a man's complaint that, on the basis of incorrect advice given to him by the DSS, he decided to emigrate to Dominica and as a result lost his entitlement to invalidity benefit. The Commissioner began his investigation in February 1991 following a reference from the complainant's MP, who had taken up the case with the local DSS office manager without success and then with the Secretary of State, also without success. Following the Commissioner's intervention, the BA Chief Executive had decided to look into the matter again and three months later concluded that the balance of probabilities was in the complainant's favour and the Department was prepared to accept that misdirection might have taken place. Accordingly, the Department agreed to make to the complainant statutory, extra-statutory and *ex gratia* payments to compensate him for the losses incurred, including those resulting from delays in the Department's handling of the case, which the Commissioner had strongly criticised. This was a satisfactory outcome to a case in which a Member of Parliament had enlisted the Commissioner's assistance in gaining redress for his constituent's complaint about incorrect advice from, and excessive delay from, an executive agency. (PCA, 1992b, 102–104)

Delay was the central feature in our third case in which a woman sought financial redress for the fact that, because of unnecessary delay by the DSS in dealing with her claim for income support, her home had been re-possessed and she had incurred substantial costs. The Commissioner found that there was excessive delay not only in the handling of the woman's claim for income support, but also in dealing with her claim for compensation. He found it 'devious and reprehensible' that the local office's report on the case failed to point out that the initial delay was a direct result of a mistake by the local office. He also found that that office's reply to the Citizen's Advice Bureau when it took up the complainant's case, was 'wholly unsatisfactory' and that the office's handling of the claim for an *ex gratia* payment 'revealed a lamentably poor grasp of the issue'. That it then took the Department almost ten months to resolve the case after the Commissioner had taken it up was 'not good enough'. The eventual outcome achieved by the Commissioner was the payment of the benefit arrears, plus *ex gratia* payments totalling £2,616. (PCA, 1992b, 105-107)

Turning now to the DVLA cases, the first again concerns delayed handling of a complainant's case—on this occasion in dealing with an application for restoration of a heavy goods vehicle licence which had deprived the man concerned of an opportunity to work in his normal occupation. The Commissioner found that the Agency's handling of the complainant's application had been flawed and this had led to avoidable delay in issuing a replacement licence. The Commissioner did not accept the complainant's claim for compensation since it turned on the unknowable outcome of a court appeal to reduce the period of his disqualification and concluded that the *ex gratia* payment offered by the Agency to cover the complainant's direct costs in pursuing his application was suitable recompense. (PCA, 1992b, 124-127) This was a case in which the complainant's use of his solicitor had failed to achieve what he sought. When the case was then taken up with the complainant's Member of Parliament, he referred it immediately to the PCA. A somewhat similar case of the mistaken revocation of licence to drive a heavy goods vehicle causing loss of employment occurred in the following year and was made a Special Report because of its wide implications. (PCA, 1993e) Unusually, this case, which resulted from a mistake in the drafting of a statutory instrument, was followed up by the Committee of Public Accounts as part of its inquiry into the DVLA's quality of service. The PAC were concerned to establish how the drafting error had occurred and who was responsible. The Committee noted that both the department and the agency were prepared to accept a share of responsibility for the lapse. (PAC, 1994, paras. 27-28, 34)

But perhaps the most celebrated of the PCA's agency cases to date has been that concerned with the delays by the DSS/BA in handling disability living allowance claims. Complaints about this began reaching the Commissioner in June 1992 and by the end of that year he had received complaints from 55 MPs and accepted 30 cases for investigation. He published a special report on the outcome in May 1993. The problems arose from the Government's decision, announced in January 1990, to introduce two new disability benefits, one of which was disability living allowance (DLA). As the Commissioner concluded, the implementation of DLA represented a very challenging logistical and administrative task for the DSS and it went badly wrong. Higher than expected workloads, inexperienced staff and an over-estimate of staff productivity 'pushed the organisation beyond the point at which it could cope' so that special measures were need to deal with the large backlogs and long delays which had built up. Before those special measures could take effect, 'it appeared to claimants, welfare rights organisations and the Members of Parliament who referred complaints to me that chaos, and I do not use that word lightly, reigned for a time'.

In the circumstances, the Commissioner considered that the DSS compensation scheme, which was available only to those whose payments had been delayed for over a year through departmental error, was inadequate. In response to the Commissioner's views, the Secretary of State agreed to change those arrangements so that compensation could be paid on delays (due to official error) of six months or more. The Department also agreed to the Commissioner's request for special compensation to be paid to those caught up in the DLA delays. (PCA, 1993d)

There are two significant aspects of this case for our purposes. First, it was not an isolated instance of individual error or maladministration. It involved a large number of complaints—from some of the most vulnerable members of the community—and many Members of Parliament. Second, as was clear from the PCA's account of the case, the problems involved both the agency and the core department and, by implication, ministers (one key decision made by ministers which aggravated the problem was not to phase the introduction of the new allowances). (PCA, 1993b, 5–6) But the Commissioner seems to have experienced no difficulty—there is none apparent in his report—in dealing with both the department and the agency and this was reflected in the joint appearance of the Permanent Secretary and Chief Executive before the Select Committee. (Select Committee, 1993, 14–29) This represents very clear evidence that the introduction of agency status has not adversely affected the operation of the PCA scheme. The theory has been borne out in practice.

References

Cm 2430, 1993:   *Next Steps: Agencies in Government: Review, 1993*, HMSO, December 1993.

Cmnd 2767, 1965:   *The Parliamentary Commissioner for Administration*, HMSO, October 1965.

DoE, 1989:   Department of the Environment, *Queen Elizabeth II Conference Centre: Framework Document*, July 1989.

DoE, 1990:   Department of the Environment, *Ordnance Survey: Executive Agency Framework Document*, May 1990.

DoE, 1992:   Department of the Environment, *Planning Inspectorate: Framework Document*, October 1992.

Efficiency Unit,   *Improving Management in Government: the Next
1988:   Steps—Report to the Prime Minister*, Cabinet Office Efficiency Unit, 1988.

Gregory, 1982:   Roy Gregory, 'The Select Committee on the Parliamentary Commissioner for Administration, 1967–80', *Public Law*, Spring 1982.

Gregory and   Roy Gregory and Peter Hutchesson, *The
Hutchesson, 1975:   Parliamentary Ombudsman: a Study in the Control of Administrative Action*, Allen and Unwin, 1975.

PAC, 1994:   Committee of Public Accounts, Thirty-fourth Report, 1993–94, *Driver and Vehicle Licensing Agency: Quality of Service to Customers*, HC 279, June 1994.

PCA, 1991:   Parliamentary Commissioner for Administration, *Annual Report for 1990*, HC 299, 1990–91, March 1991.

PCA, 1992a: Parliamentary Commissioner for Administration, *Annual Report for 1991*, HC 347, 1991–92, March 1992.

PCA, 1992b: Parliamentary Commissioner for Administration, *Selected Cases 1992—Volume 3*, Case No C.577/90, HC 202, 1992–93, October 1992.

PCA, 1993a: Parliamentary Commissioner for Administration, *Annual Report for 1992*, HC 569, 1992–93, March 1993.

PCA, 1993b: Sixth Report of the Parliamentary Commissioner for Administration, 1992–93, *Delays in Handling Disability Living Allowance Claims*, HC 652, May 1993.

PCA, 1993c: Parliamentary Commissioner for Administration, *Selected Cases, 1993,* Volume 1, Case No C.702/90, pp 48–54, January 1993.

PCA, 1993d: Parliamentary Commissioner for Administration, *Press Notice*, 11 May 1993.

PCA, 1993e: Parliamentary Commissioner for Administration, First (Special) Report Session 1993–94, HC 13, 1993/94.

PCA, 1994: Parliamentary Commissioner for Administration, *Annual Report for 1993*, HC 290, 1993–94, March 1994.

Bates, 1988: 'The Scrutiny of Administration' in M Ryle and P G Richards, (eds), *The Commons Under Scrutiny*, Routledge, 1988.

Select Committee, 1989: Third Report from the Select Committee on the Parliamentary Commissioner for Administration, 1988–89, *Report of the Parliamentary Commissioner for Administration for 1988*, HC 480, July 1989.

Select Committee,
1991:

Fourth Report from the Select Committee on the Parliamentary Commissioner for Administration, 1990–91, *Report of the Parliamentary Commissioner for Administration for 1990*, HC 368, July 1991.

Select Committee,
1993:

First Report from the Select Committee on the Parliamentary Commissioner for Administration, 1992–93, *Report of the Parliamentary Commissioner for Administration for 1991*, HC 387, April 1993.

PART III

Case Studies

9

The Environment Agencies

George Jones and June Burnham, with Robert Elgie

Introduction

This chapter examines the Next Steps Agencies under the responsibility of the Secretary of State for the Environment between 1989 and July 1992. Its objective is to reveal the impact of the establishment of these agencies on parliamentary accountability. It seeks to show the extent to which civil servants working in the agencies were more, or less, accountable to Parliament after their agencies were established. The question explored is whether agencies increase or reduce the parliamentary accountability of Government.

First, the chapter explains the agencies within the responsibility of the Secretary of State for the Environment (SoS): not a simple exercise. Second, it analyses the roles of the agencies. Third, it discusses the theory of accountability embodied in the Next Steps programme. Fourth, it analyses the formal statements about parliamentary accountability contained in the framework documents that guide the work of the Environment agencies. Fifth, it presents the results of a research project analysing in detail the ways the work of agencies within the responsibility of the SoS were dealt with before and after they became agencies. Sixth, it draws conclusions about the parliamentary accountability of the Environment agencies. Seventh, it makes general conclusions about agencies and parliamentary accountability. It concludes with policy recommendations.

The Agencies

The Secretary of State for the Environment was accountable to Parliament in July 1992 for the work of five Executive Agencies: in order of creation, the *Queen Elizabeth II Conference Centre* (QECC), set up 6th July 1989; the *Building Research Establishment* (BRE), set up 2nd April 1990; Ordnance Survey (OS), set up 1st May 1990; *The Buying Agency* (TBA), set up 31st October 1991; and the *Planning Inspectorate* (PI), set up 1st April 1992.

A sixth agency, *Historic Royal Palaces* (HRP), set up 2nd October 1989, was transferred from the SoS to the Secretary of State for National Heritage after the general election of April 1992, when John Major reallocated ministerial responsibilities.

The SoS was also responsible for the *Fuel Suppliers Branch* (FSB)—sometimes referred to as Fuel Procurement Branch or Fuel Branch—which has been a candidate for agency status since July 1988 and *Property Holdings Portfolio Management* (PHPM), a candidate since October 1989. In October 1992 the *Transport and Security Services Division* (TSSD) was announced as a candidate for agency status and became the *Security Facilities Executive* in October 1993.

There is ambiguity, even in official statistics, about the proportion of staff in the Department of the Environment (DoE) organised into agencies, stemming from the difficulty of defining the DoE. Its Annual Report for 1992 divided the SoS's responsibilities between: (1) the Department of the Environment; (2) PSA Services—the major part of the former Property Services Agency (PSA) 'which operates *as if* a separate department', and (3) Ordnance Survey 'which *is* a separate Government department' [our emphases]. (DoE, 1992a, 1) QECC, TBA, and the candidates, FSB and PHPM, are sponsored by or (for the candidates) are divisions of Property Holdings, Central and Support Services Command (PH), now a separate section within the DoE with its own parliamentary vote (annual funding) and additional accounting officer. Until April 1990 Property Holdings was a small part of the PSA. QECC became a Next Steps Agency while still part of PSA. Taking the department to include PSA Services, as did *Civil Service Statistics 1991*, the percentage of DoE civil servants working in agencies (HRP, BRE, QECC) in April 1991 was 4.7% (HM Treasury, 1991, 3-4); by April 1992 with five agencies it was 8.7%; but if the DoE is interpreted more narrowly to be the central divisions, as *Civil Service Statistics 1992* seems to have done, the percentage of DoE staff serving in agencies in April 1991 was 13.7%, rising by April 1992 to 22.0%. (HM Treasury, 1992, 3 and 5) Since then the Government has sold part of the PSA Services (PSA Projects, comprising about 15% of PSA Services staff) and plans gradually to privatise the rest. Until this disposal is complete these larger figures for DoE's agencies are hard to justify, particularly since four of its five current and candidate agencies were part of PSA or PSA Services (and not part of DoE's central divisions) until after or shortly before their new status was announced.

Table 9.1

Agencies responsible to the Secretary of State for the Environment

Staff (a) at launch (b) in 1992 [1]	*Operating costs (£m)* [2]	*Financial regime*	*Chief executive: grade; method of appointment; origin*
Queen Elizabeth II Conference Centre (QECC) (launched 6.7.89)			
(a) 50	6	net running	Grade 5; open competition;
(b) 60		cost control	direct entrant
Historic Royal Palaces (HRP) (launched 2.10.89)[3]			
(a) 350	27	net running	Grade 3; open competition;
(b) 340		cost control	direct entrant
Building Research Establishment (BRE) (launched 2.4.90)			
(a) 680	31	net running	Grade 3; internal appointment;
(b) 710		cost control	civil servant
Ordnance Survey (OS) (launched 1.5.90)			
(a) 2,550	70	net running	Grade 3; open competition;
(b) 2,340		cost control	direct entrant
The Buying Agency (TBA) (launched 31.10.91)			
(a) 110	4	trading fund	Grade 5; open competition;
(b) 80			direct entrant
Planning Inspectorate (PI) (launched 1.4.92)			
(a) 605	26	gross running	Grade 3; open competition;
(b) 605		cost control	civil servant

Candidates announced by November 1992 (with numbers of staff)
Fuel Suppliers Branch (FSB) (20)
Property Holdings Portfolio Management (PHPM) (460)
Transport and Security Services Division (TSSD) (1,235)

1. Numbers of civil servants: part-time staff counted as half units.
2. Costs for PI are 1992–93; for the others, 1991. TBA's annual attributed sales in 1991 were about £100m.
3. Responsibility for HRP transferred to the Secretary of State for National Heritage in April 1992.
Sources: Staff numbers: HC Deb, 214, cc. 314–15w, 515–16w; financial regime: HC Deb, 209, cc. 667–8w; chief executives' status: HC Deb, 210, cc. 103–6w; operating costs for QECC, HRP, BRE, OS: *Improving Management in Government: The Next Steps Agencies, Review 1991* (London: HMSO, Cm 1760, 1991) and for TBA from DoE; costs for PI and attributed sales for TBA from their framework documents.

The Ordnance Survey is the largest executive agency, measured by staffing, for which the SoS is responsible. Combining all three responsibilities together (DoE, PSA Services and OS), in April 1991 the percentage of the minister's officials serving in agencies was 13.9%; in April 1992 it was 17.9%. Table 9.1 presents key data about the agencies and candidates responsible to the SoS in July 1992, drawn from the two Government White Papers issued in November 1991 (Cm 1760 and Cm 1761) and the framework documents for the Buying Agency (DoE, 1991) and the Planning Inspectorate. (DoE, 1992b) The number of staff in each agency is that cited in a Written Answer in November 1992. (HC Deb, Vol 214, 314–5w)

Royal Parks (RP) was a candidate for agency status from February 1988 while it was within the DoE, but it never became one, and after the general election of 1992 was transferred to the Department of National Heritage, from where it was launched as an agency in April 1993. Entities in the DoE like PSA Services and the Pollution Inspectorate are not counted as Next Steps agencies, nor even as candidates, although they are discrete entities with some devolved functions. The Pollution Inspectorate was included in lists of candidates given to MPs in 1990 and 1991. It was deleted from lists of candidate agencies once ministers had announced it was to form part of the proposed Environment Agency, but no formal statement of its change of status appears to have been made to MPs.

Roles

The role of *The Queen Elizabeth II Conference Centre* is 'to provide and manage fully secure conference facilities for national and international Government meetings and to market the Centre commercially for both private sector and government use'. It is described by the Department of the Environment as a trading agency, that is, it provides services on a full commercial basis to both governmental and private customers. In 1991 it employed about 60 staff (full-time equivalents) and its operating costs were £6.2m. Its financial goal for 1991–92 was to reduce its operating deficit to £1.73m (it achieved a deficit of £0.84m).

The role of the *Building Research Establishment* is to provide guidance and carry out 'research on the design and performance of buildings and their constituent materials, and on the prevention and control of fire'. In 1991 it had 700 staff. Dunleavy and Francis classified it as a delivery agency, that is, carrying out functions and implementing programmes directly, using its own personnel and resources. But it could be regarded as a servicing agency, that is, providing services to other government bodies. (Dunleavy and Francis have eight categories: delivery, transfer, control, contract, regulatory, taxing, trading and service. They allocated RP to the delivery category; PI to the regulatory category; and PH and FSB to the trading category—Dunleavy and Francis, 1990.) BRE's financial regime is a trading account. Its operating costs in 1991 were £31m. In its first year its net cost to the Exchequer was £1.1m. One of its financial goals for 1991–92 was to break even on its trading account and reduce its cost to the Exchequer to £200,000.

The role of the *Ordnance Survey* is to survey and map Great Britain. It is a trading agency. In 1991 it employed about 2,380 staff. In 1991 its operating costs were £70m. One of its key targets for 1991–92 was to recover at least 70% of its total costs.

The role of *The Buying Agency* is to help government departments and other public bodies obtain better value for money in purchasing a range of engineering, building, maintenance and domestic services through this central agency. In 1991 it employed 110 staff. It arranges about £100 million of business each year. It has trading fund status: that is, it was initially established with an issue of funds from the DoE, and must subsequently attract sufficient receipts, primarily from providing goods and services, to meet its outgoings. One non-financial target is for delivery times quoted to be met in 90% of cases.

The role of the *Planning Inspectorate* is to receive and process planning appeals and other casework under legislation about planning, housing, the environment and highways, acting on behalf of the Secretaries of State for the Environment and for Wales. It is one of the few executive agencies to cover two departments. The DoE takes the lead on general matters. In 1991 it employed about 630 staff, and in addition used the services of about 250 other inspectors on a consultancy basis. In 1992–93 its operating costs were expected to be about £26m. The PI operated in 1992–93 under gross running cost control within DoE's running cost limit. The Welsh Office pays for the service provided by the PI in Wales. The Agency's performance measures include a requirement to demonstrate 2% overall efficiency savings each year, and indicators for timeliness in deciding appeals and the proportion of justified complaints received.

The role of *Historic Royal Palaces* is to preserve, manage and display to the public the five royal palaces of the Tower of London, Hampton Court, the Banqueting House, Kensington Palace and Kew Palace. In 1991 it employed about 330 staff. It is a trading agency. Its commercial operations produced a surplus of £4.3m in 1990–91 and £3.2m in 1991–92, and the Exchequer contributes around £9m a year to the cost of maintaining the palaces. Its operating costs in 1991 were £27m. Its key financial target for 1991–92, revised because of the reduction in tourism following the Gulf War, was to achieve a commercial surplus of £1.6m.

At present executive agencies do not loom large in the work of the department. Their work seems peripheral to the central department: it is not highly political and makes little impact on the department's mainstream work. The BRE, and the five agencies and candidates once within the PSA, have long been semi-autonomous in practice from central divisions. The Department has other more pressing and politically important matters to tackle, including the finance, structure and functions of local government, strategic land-use planning, housing, inner cities, waste disposal and environmental pollution. The agencies are concerned with execution and have little impact on high-level policy-making. However, its newest agency, the Planning Inspectorate, is much more the focus of MPs' and pressure groups' attention than are the older siblings. If the Pollution Inspectorate too becomes an agency, the department may need to pay them more attention. The department also seems to take a long time to turn candidate agencies into real ones—PI was a candidate from July 1988 to April 1992. In April 1991 the department had a lower proportion of staff working in agencies than had eleven other departments (in a list of 14), and in 1992 on a definition of DoE which discounted PSA Services it was in ninth place. (HM Treasury, 1991, 4 and 1992, 5) The DoE is not at the forefront of pressing for agencies.

Parliamentary Accountability

The work of civil servants in a department is under the responsibility of the Secretary of State. This minister in principle accounts to Parliament for everything civil servants in the department do, whether it is high policy, executive action or operational detail. MPs can use all the procedures of the House of Commons to call ministers to answer for the work of their civil servants. As we have seen in Part I, the Government has repeatedly stated that this traditional doctrine of ministerial responsibility will not be affected by the establishment of executive agencies under the Next Steps programme.

However the logic of the programme seems intrinsically to diminish traditional ministerial accountability to Parliament for the work of civil servants in agencies. It seeks to devolve responsibility for defined segments of departmental work to civil servants called chief executives, who are given a clear framework of objectives for their agencies, their own budgets, and some discretion over use of their resources of money, personnel, property and material. The point of the venture is to reduce central controls over day-to-day policy implementation by ministers and their closest official advisers at the top of departments, and by the Treasury. If ministers' responsibilities are reduced, so correspondingly is their accountability to Parliament, since they can be accountable only for what they are responsible for.

Since Parliament calls ministers to account and since ministers should under the Next Steps programme be excluded from detailed responsibility for the work of the agencies, then once an agency is set up there should be less parliamentary accountability by the minister for the day-to-day work of civil servants in agencies. Yet because some MPs are alarmed at the prospect of this reduced accountability, the Government has stated that the full rigours of ministerial responsibility still apply. This paradox is at the heart of the Next Steps programme and presents it with the fundamental challenge of making the work of civil servants in the agencies accountable through ministers to Parliament while its objective appears to be to reduce that accountability.

A way of resolving the paradox is for the Government to make clear that a major advantage from the setting up of agencies is not just increased efficiency and effectiveness of civil servants' executive operations but an enhanced accountability of civil servants to ministers and of ministers to Parliament over what is important. Civil servants are being given greater discretion by the Next Steps programme to achieve objectives determined by ministers and expressed in framework documents. Ministers should account to Parliament for the objectives they have set, and chief executives of agencies should account to ministers for the performance of their agencies in the day-to-day operations of meeting those objectives. Ministers will be rid of the impossible burden of pretending they were responsible and could be accountable for every minor detail of the work of their civil servants.

Having been relieved of these minor matters they could, so the advocates of Next Steps might argue, concentrate on setting objectives and giving policy guidelines, for which they should be accountable to Parliament. Ministers lose responsibility and accountability for the small items but retain and could gain in responsibility for the big matters. They can be held accountable for setting broad policy, while day-to-day executive operations carried out by civil servants in agencies can be controlled by the published objectives determined by ministers.

Indeed ministers' control over the civil service can be enhanced by strengthening ministerial management control over the work of agencies through the setting of clear and measurable objectives. The civil service is being reorganised to make it do what ministers want: it is being made more accountable to ministers, and in turn ministers can account more sensibly to Parliament for something important. Since agency objectives are published, accountability is enhanced even more. Both Parliament and the public can examine the objectives when established, and judge the ministers' choice of objectives and standards more easily than in the past. They can check on performance against those objectives afterwards, and hold civil servants to account for their management of their agency. Accountability, both before and after agency action, is increased.

This model will work only if MPs are prepared to give up their concern for day-to-day matters and focus on broad policy issues. They would have to appreciate they could benefit from losing the ability to insist on ministers being accountable to them for minutiae in return for an increased capacity to concentrate on policy. Ministers in turn will have to play their part by ensuring MPs are kept informed and given the opportunity to comment before framework documents and annual objectives are set out or amended. When the Minister responsible for executive agencies, William Waldegrave, was asked by an MP in June 1992 which agencies had had their framework document amended, he said it was primarily a matter for ministers and chief executives, and did not even give the names of the four agencies affected. (HC Deb, Vol 209, 685) If the framework document is to be the basis of accountability of ministers to MPs about the agencies, laying down overall objectives, then MPs should be told about changes in the responsibilities or objectives laid down in them.

The problem is that constituents tend to contact MPs about the implementation of policy rather than about policy itself, and MPs as representatives of their voters and potential voters reflect their concerns, as is clear with the Planning Inspectorate. MPs want to show their constituents they have done something. A letter from a chief executive may not be enough: MPs will want an answer from a minister. Ministers in turn have to respond to the pressures from MPs, and if what MPs want is attention paid to day-to-day operations then ministers will find it politically and personally difficult to refuse to answer their questions and to deal with the problems they raise. Therefore accountability to

Parliament on day-to-day operations will continue to be exercised by ministers.

One way around the problem of accountability is for select committees to drop from their terms of reference a concern with policy and concentrate their attention on administration. They can then question civil servants about the administration of policy, including chief executives of agencies, who should be implementing ministers' policies. Ministers can then account for policy to the House as a whole and to their party committees, and not to select committees, which are in our view inappropriate as a means to hold ministers to account for policy. (See Jones, 1990)

Another problem is that ministers as politicians are reluctant to set clear policy objectives. To avoid and fend off possible attacks which might alienate some voters, they prefer unclear, vague, ambiguous and even contradictory objectives, or not to express them at all. The champions of Next Steps agencies argue that part of their value is that they force ministers to set out in a public document the objectives for which they will be held accountable, while civil servants will be held responsible for failures to implement the objectives. However, the setting of clear objectives may be appropriate for business managers: it is little help for politicians. Indeed 'fudging', which is part of the politician's repertoire of techniques, is apparent in the paradoxes and confusions of the Next Steps programme.

Formal responsibilities and accountability

The framework documents for the agencies contain sections on ministerial responsibility and accountability to Parliament. Their provisions are similar, although the wording often varies. Their substance is substantially the same but ingenuity has been exercised to vary the words used so that they are phrased slightly differently. The extracts are from the relevant framework documents.

Who is Accountable?

QECC 'The Chief Executive of the PSA will retain overall responsibilities as Accounting Officer for the Department and the Secretary of State will as such remain accountable to Parliament'.

(DoE, 1989a, para. 12): 'The Secretary of State is answerable to Parliament for the Agency's policy and operations'. (DoE, 1992c, para. 2.1)

BRE   'The Secretary of State is answerable to Parliament for the Agency's operations and its policy and resources framework'. (DoE, 1990a, para. 4.2)

OS   'The responsible Minister is the Secretary of State for the Environment' and 'The Director General will continue to report to the Secretary of State for the Environment who is answerable to Parliament'. (DoE, 1990b, paras. 1.1 and 3.1)

TBA   'The Secretary of State is answerable to Parliament for all aspects of the Agency's operations and the policy and resources framework within which it operates'. (DoE, 1991, para. 2.2)

PI   'The Secretaries of State [for the Environment and for Wales] are answerable to Parliament for the Agency's policy and operations but the Secretary of State for the Environment will, in the first instance, deal with parliamentary matters concerning the Agency as a whole'. (DoE, 1992b, para. 1.4)

HRP   'The Secretary of State is answerable to Parliament for the Agency's policy and operations'. (DoE, 1989b, para. 1.4)

Ministerial responsibilities

QECC   'The Secretary of State for the Environment, with departmental ministers, will determine the policy and financial framework within which the Centre operates'. They will not 'be involved in the day-to-day running of the Centre.' (DoE, 1989a, para. 11): 'The Minister responsible for the Agency is the Secretary of State for the Environment, who determines the policy and financial framework within which it operates. He does not normally become involved in its day-to-day management'. (DoE, 1992c, para. 1.3)

BRE 'The Secretary of State for the Environment determines the policy and financial framework within which the Agency operates but is not normally involved in its day to day management. He is responsible for the Agency but may designate another Minister in the Department to assist him'. (DoE, 1990a, para. 4.1)

OS 'The Secretary of State will determine financial and other performance targets' and 'The Secretary of State will review policy and trading guidelines, set financial targets and approve the Corporate Plan, but will not be involved in the day-to-day management of Ordnance Survey'. (DoE, 1990b, paras. 1.4, and 3.1)

TBA 'The Secretary of State determines the policy and financial framework within which it operates, but is not normally involved in its day-to-day management ... Each year the Secretary of State sets the key performance targets the Agency is to achieve'. (DoE, 1991, para. 2.1)

PI 'The Secretaries of State determine the policy and resources for the Agency in England and Wales respectively but do not normally become involved in its day-to-day management'. (DoE, 1992b, para. 1.3)

HRP 'The Minister responsible for the Agency is the Secretary of State for the Environment'. But he 'may designate another Minister in the Department to assist him. The Secretary of State will determine the policy and financial framework within which the Agency operates but will not normally become involved in day-to-day management'. (DoE, 1989b, para. 1.3)

Appearing Before Select Committees

QECC 'While it will continue to be for Ministers to decide who should represent them at departmental select committee hearings, in practice, where a Committee's interest is confined to day-to-day operations of the Centre, Ministers will normally regard the Chief Executive as the person best placed to appear on their behalf'. (DoE, 1989a, para. 13): 'It is for the Secretary of State to decide who should represent him at departmental select committee hearings. In practice, where a committee's interest is confined to day-to-day operations of the Agency, he will normally regard the Chief Executive as the person best placed to appear on his behalf'. (DoE, 1992c, para. 2.2)

HRP as for QECC. (DoE, 1989b, para. 1.5)

BRE 'Ministers decide who should represent them at departmental select committee hearings. In practice, where a committee's interest is confined to day-to-day operations of the Agency, Ministers will normally regard the Chief Executive as the person best placed to appear on their behalf'. (DoE, 1990a, para. 4.3)

OS 'It will be for the Secretary of State to decide who should represent him at departmental select committee hearings. In practice, where a committee's interest is confined to the day-to-day operations of the Agency, he will normally regard the Chief Executive as the best person to answer on his behalf'. (DoE, 1990b, para. 3.1)

PI as for OS. (DoE, 1992b, para. 3.9)

TBA 'The Secretary of State will consider who should appear at departmental select committee hearings. In practice, where the committee's interest is confined to the day-to-day operations of the Agency, the Secretary of State will normally regard the Chief Executive as the person best placed to appear on his behalf'. (DoE, 1991, para. 2.4)

Dealing with Correspondence

QECC 'The Secretary of State has invited Members of Parliament to address to its Chief Executive correspondence concerning the day-to-day work of the Centre. If such a letter is received in the Department, it will be referred to the Chief Executive of the Centre for direct reply. Ministers will reply to letters dealing with questions of policy or received from a Member of Parliament who specifically seeks a reply from a Minister'. (DoE, 1989a, para. 14): 'He [SoS] will deal with any matters which raise questions of policy direction or resource allocation and with any cases where a Member of Parliament specifically seeks a Ministerial reply. Members of Parliament are encouraged to deal directly with the Chief Executive on matters concerning the day-to-day management of the Agency'. (DoE, 1992c, para. 2.1)

BRE 'Members of Parliament are invited to deal directly with the Chief Executive of the Agency on operational matters. DOE Ministers will normally ask the Chief Executive to reply on their behalf to correspondence concerning the Agency from Members of Parliament and others which does not raise policy or resource issues'. (DoE, 1990a, para. 4.2)

OS 'The Secretary of State will deal with questions of policy and enquiries from Members of Parliament who specifically seek a Ministerial response. MPs will be encouraged to communicate directly with the Director-General on day-to-day operational matters'. (DoE, 1990b, para. 3.1)

TBA 'The Secretary of State encourages Members of Parliament and the public to approach the Chief Executive direct in the first instance when they have an enquiry about a matter which has been delegated to the Agency'. (DoE, 1991, para. 2.2) 'If a Parliamentary Question about a matter delegated to the Agency is tabled, the Secretary of State or other Minister will normally ask the Chief Executive to reply direct to the MP.' (DoE, 1991, para. 2.3)

PI 'Members of Parliament ... are encouraged to deal directly with the Chief Planning Inspector, who is also the Chief Executive of the Agency, on matters of day-to-day management which have been delegated to the Agency'. (DoE, 1992b, para. 1.4) 'Appropriate arrangements are made to put the Chief Planning Inspector's replies in the public domain'. (DoE, 1992b, para. 1.5)

HRP 'Members of Parliament, however, will be invited to deal directly with the Chief Executive on matters of day-to-day management affecting the palaces which have been delegated to him. The Secretary of State will deal with any cases which raise questions of policy direction or resource allocation, and with any cases where a Member of Parliament specifically seeks a reply from a Minister'. (DoE, 1989b, para. 1.4)

The Parliamentary Commissioner for Administration

QECC 'There will be no change in the role of the Parliamentary Commissioner for Administration in relation to the work of the Centre'. (DoE, 1989a, para. 13) 'The Agency's operations remain within the jurisdiction of the Parliamentary Commissioner for Administration'. (DoE, 1992c, para. 2.3)

BRE as for QECC. (DoE, 1990a, para. 4.3)

HRP as for QECC. (DoE, 1989b, para. 1.5)

OS 'There is no change to the jurisdiction of the Parliamentary Commissioner for Administration'. (DoE, 1990b, para. 3.1)

TBA 'The Agency remains within the jurisdiction of the Parliamentary Commissioner for Administration'. (DoE, 1991, para. 2.5)

PI 'The Inspectorate ... is subject to the scrutiny of ... the Parliamentary Commissioner for Administration'. (DoE, 1992b, para. 2.6)

The Research Project

The objective of the research was to discover whether the establishment of executive agencies responsible to the Secretary of State for the Environment increased or decreased, or had no effect on, the accountability for their activities to the House of Commons. Examination was made of references in the Commons to the work carried out by the agencies during the parliamentary sessions between June 1987 and July 1992. It covered their work both in the years before they were set up and in the years afterwards, the periods varying between agencies depending on their launch dates. The Planning Inspectorate was launched only in April 1992 but its importance to MPs means that as much data were obtained for it by July 1992 in the short period after launch as for other agencies in their post-launch periods. The Buying Agency was separated from its parent organisation, the Crown Suppliers, just before its launch date so that references to its work before it became an agency cannot be easily identified, and it was therefore omitted from this project. (There were 18 references in the Commons to The Buying Agency in the nine months following its launch. Three items related specifically to this agency: an announcement of its launch; one probing question from an MP; and one answer by a minister which included a reference to the agency. The remaining fifteen items were all questions seeking information on all, or all DoE, executive agencies). The Historic Royal Palaces agency had left DoE by July 1992, but references to this agency while in DoE's charge are included as a useful example of the effect of agencification.

The project examined references to agencies, and to their work before agencification, in written questions, oral questions, statements and debates. References to agencies in which there was an element of accountability were then distinguished from those where the reference was incidental. The survey also examined the number of questions referred by ministers to the chief executives of the agencies.

Agencies have been discussed in debates and statements, and referred to in questions, both written and oral: all the usual modes for making departments accountable to Parliament through ministers.

The Treasury and Civil Service Committee (TCSC) has produced regular annual wide-ranging surveys on the process of establishing agencies and on their early progress. As we have seen in Chapter 4, its reports contain much data about agencies in general, including the five environment agencies. Civil servants from agencies and departments have appeared before the committee to give evidence about agencies. So the committee's investigations are an important means by which agencies give an account to Parliament. But it has not made any special inquiry into the five agencies responsible to the Environment Secretary, nor has the DoE submitted to it a memorandum about its agencies. The TCSC is mainly concerned with the concept of agencies not with the operations of any particular ones.

As Chapter 5 shows, some other departmental select committees have examined the work of agencies within the department they scrutinise. The Select Committee on the Environment, whose terms of reference enjoin it to have regard to the policy, administration and expenditure of the department and of its associated bodies, can inquire into the DoE and OS executive agencies.

By July 1992 it had dealt with the work of only one agency, the QECC, during its examination of DoE Property Holdings Estimates 1990-91 and 1991-92. (Environment Committee, 1990, viii-x, 24-6, 35-6; and 1991, 65-70) In May 1990 the Committee asked DoE Property Holdings officials about the financial objectives set for the agency and suggested that targets were set too low. In April 1991 the Committee followed up its inquiry when the QECC's chief executive appeared before it. He was able to explain the Centre's special problems and costs, sustaining the Government's argument that MPs should direct questions to chief executives with first-hand experience instead of submitting PQs for answer by ministers. There was a strong difference in tone and content between the questions to officials in 1990, which stressed their advice to ministers, and the questions in 1991 to the chief executive, which emphasised the problems 'you' have and 'your' aims to bring down costs. The contrast suggested how accountability to Parliament for services provided by executive agencies could shift towards personal responsibility by appointed officials and away from elected government ministers, even if the Government continues to claim that ministers exercise full responsibility.

As is explained in Chapter 6, chief executives are Accounting Officers for the use of resources allocated to their agencies by their departments: they thus come under the scrutiny of the National Audit Office and have to answer to the Public Accounts Committee, although Permanent Secretaries remain Accounting Officers for their departments, including the allocation of resources to the agencies. The Comptroller and Auditor General, the National Audit Office and the Public Accounts Committee have not conducted any inquiries into the DoE agencies, probably because they are so new, and until the Planning Inspectorate joined them their work attracted little public interest.

Departmental select committees report on individual agencies almost by chance, when some particular issue catches their attention. More frequent accounting mechanisms are the annual reports required from agencies. In principle they do not provide more accountability than previous arrangements where departments reported on the work of their divisions, but singling out agencies for separate regular comment, combined with monitoring published objectives, may in practice produce more effective accounting to Parliament. MPs outside the limited group specialising in Environment affairs are more likely to note the activities of the agencies when they are presented more explicitly and attractively in annual reports from the DoE and OS, or in the annual Next Steps reports summing up the achievements of each agency.

Agencies have started to produce corporate and business plans, but not all are published. Of the five executive agencies responsible to the SoS, the OS and the PI have made such plans freely available to MPs and the public and they could become the focus of attention by MPs though so far appear not to have done so. The plans of the QECC, BRE and TBA are commercially sensitive; their circulation is restricted because their contents are judged confidential.

The House of Lords has paid little attention to the five Environment agencies. Four questions were asked over the three years 1988 to 1991 specifically about the OS and DoE's agencies, which seemed to be mainly to allow the minister to announce the establishment of agencies and their targets. As an example nine references in all were made to these agencies in the year November 1990–November 1991. One announced the Planning Inspectorate was to become an agency: six references were made by peers to the work of planning inspectors, and a question on planning asked how long the SoS would take to decide a particular appeal. The ninth reference was to the Tower of London, a responsibility of the Historic Royal Palaces agency. Parliamentary concern about agencies is overwhelmingly expressed through the House of Commons.

The accountability of individual agencies to Parliament has been carried out not primarily through select committees but through debates and statements, and written and oral questions, where ministers are held responsible. This research focuses on those procedures for the Environment agencies.

Table 9.2 (page 173) analyses parliamentary references to each agency which seem to involve a significant level of accountability. More detailed agency-by-agency tables are provided in the Appendix. Tables 9A.1–A.5 give examples of the types of items categorised as providing accountability. The first section (A) of Table 9.2 shows how many items—written or oral questions, or references in debate—occurred before and after agencification. Because the periods 'before and after' vary for each agency the most important comparative figures are the 'items per month' (in bold in the (B) Appendix tables).

The second section (B) of Table 9.2 is an analysis of the contents of the references—more details are given in the Appendix tables. They fall into three categories. the first (a) covers questions on the process of agencification, especially how the Next Steps scheme is progressing, and/or seek information about agencies in general. The second (b) includes questions involving some accountability as a by-product, often by chance, of information given to MPs about some other topic or the department in general, for instance about departmental money spent on publicity. The third (c) groups questions focusing directly on the work of the agency.

The final section (C) of Table 9.2 covers questions referred by ministers to chief executives, which over the period examined always fell into the third category of questions, those focusing directly on the work of the agency. In all three sections of Table 9.2 two figures are given for references in the post-launch period: first for the early period of the agencification process (between launch date and October 1991) and second for the whole period since agencification (between launch date and July 1992). For the four agencies in place by October 1991 it is possible by reading down the columns of figures to see the initial effect of agencification, and then any longer-term effect.

Findings

1. At present the *main channel for accountability for all five agencies is through written questions*, as it was for their work before agencification.

2. From the number of items calling to account per month (see especially section A of Table 9.2) *there was a significant increase in references after agencification for QECC, HRP and the PI*, which continued even after two years of the new regime. *There was no significant change in the frequency of references in the Commons to BRE or initially to OS: references to OS seem later to have become more frequent.*

One explanation for this variation between agencies relates to MPs' interest in agencies or agency candidates. The smaller and less publicly-known organisations such as QECC have fewer questions asked or comments made about their normal day-to-day work than those providing a more widely-used service, e.g. HRP's Hampton Court Palace, or BRE's research on concrete houses or OS's land-use plans. The new questions MPs are prompted to ask as a result of the agencification process have a greater proportional effect on total references for the less-frequently named agencies than for agencies already the subject of many questions. (see section B(a) of Table 9.2) There is less contrast between 'before' and 'after' for the better-known organisations.

Table 9.2
Comparisons across Environment Agencies, 1987–92

Agency Launch date	QECC 6.7.89	HRP 2.10.89	BRE 2.4.90	OS 1.5.90	PI 1.4.92

A. Parliamentary questions, answers or speeches providing accountability (before and after agencification)

	QECC	HRP	BRE	OS	PI
Numbers of items					
Before launch	7	22	52	47	192
Launch to October 1991	22	31	25	22	–
Launch to July 1992*	41	44	41	45	16
Items per month					
Before launch	0.3	0.8	1.5	1.3	3.3
Launch to October 1991	0.8	1.2	1.4	1.3	–
Launch to July 1992*	1.1	1.5	1.5	1.7	5.3

B. Subject of Item: the percentage of each agency's items which (a) refer to its agencification or privatisation; (b) refer to agency only as a side issue; (c) focus directly on agency

	QECC	HRP	BRE	OS	PI
(a) Agencification or privatisation					
Before launch	57	27	13	15	7
Launch to October 1991	64	26	28	50	–
Launch to July 1992*	54	23	32	38	37
(b) Agency as a side-issue					
Before launch	29	50	60	19	32
Launch to October 1991	23	45	60	18	–
Launch to July 1992*	12	36	39	13	6
(c) Directly on work of agency					
Before launch	14	23	27	66	61
Launch to October 1991	13	29	12	32	–
Launch to July 1992*	34	41	29	49	56

C. Questions referred to chief executive

	QECC	HRP	BRE	OS	PI
Number of items directly on the work of agency					
Launch to October 1991	3	9	3	7	–
Launch to July 1992*	14	18	12	22	9
Number of questions referred to chief executive					
Launch to October 1991	1	1	1	3	–
Launch to July 1992*	5	5	5	10	1
Percentage of items directly on work of agency referred					
Launch to October 1991	33	10	33	43	–
Launch to July 1992*	36	28	45	45	11

*April 1992 for HRP

The PI in character is more like the OS than the QECC—MPs and ministers were already asking and answering large numbers of questions about its work; yet items calling it to account increased significantly after agencification. The period after agencification is very short and atypical (immediately following the election of a new Parliament), so no firm conclusions can be drawn. But the data given in table 9.2(B)—and in 9A.5(B) in the Appendix—show MPs have asked more of PI's relatively few questions about the general progress of agencification (for clarification, these questions are relatively few in comparison with other types of reference to the PI: in comparison with other DoE agencies their number is large). MPs have asked more of the already large proportion of direct questions about the work of inspectors and delays in planning appeals. MPs and ministers have made fewer indirect references to the PI, notably in oral questions and debate. But the special circumstances of an opening session of Parliament may have affected all these post-launch findings for the PI; a longer period of research would be needed to confirm (or deny) this apparent increase of interest by MPs.

3. *The frequency of questions about the process of agencification has increased.* There are more references to the Next Steps process after than before agencification. MPs are continuing to ask about the progress of Next Steps for all agencies (the five DoE agencies are included in replies). In 1991 MPs were asking about the possibilities of privatisation for these agencies in the future, although there are fewer of these questions now. *Thus, although the frequency of questions about agencies has not declined, more of those questions are about the process of agencification rather than the agencies' work.*

4. *In the early period after agencification (up to October 1991) the proportion of references focusing directly on the work of the agency, rather than about the process of agencification, or incidental to some related topic in which an MP was interested, decreased significantly for two agencies, OS and BRE (the PI shows a similar decrease). For the QECC and HRP there was no change or a slight increase.* The pattern for this period immediately following agencification is similar when considered in absolute terms, that is, the number of questions asked a month. Direct questions were asked much less frequently on the work of BRE and OS after agencification than before; for QECC and HRP numbers were about the same or slightly higher. Over the longer period, between launch date and July 1992, questions focused more frequently on

the agencies' work than before agencification on average (though still well down on previous levels for OS).

But this increase in references to the agencies' work after agencification does not reflect necessarily any long-term real increase in accountability. Between October 1991 and July 1992, as in the previous period, the change in the focus of questions was caused by the attention MPs paid to the process of agencification itself, rather than by a particular interest in the work of the agencies. However, some MPs seemed in this second phase to be testing the Government's position on the issue of referring questions to chief executives (would ministers refer the question to the chief executive, would departments take a consistent view on referral, would ministers themselves answer a certain question about the core department but refer it to the chief executive if it concerned an agency?). These questions are more probing than those asked earlier about the process of agencification and have the effect of calling the minister to account for the structure and working of the agency; so they must be classified in this research project as 'direct questions about the agency' even though perhaps the prime motive for a question was a research project by an MP (John McAllion), probably on behalf of a civil service trade union, into the effect of agencification. These questions could be regarded as artificial—not the result of spontaneous interest by MPs and their constituents or favourite local pressure groups. *Yet the process of agencification has in practice been effective in attracting MPs' attention to sections of the administration and calling ministers to account for their work.* It remains to be seen whether this interest will continue if and when 75% of civil servants work in agencies.

5. *Until November 1992 (when chief executives' replies began to be published in Hansard), there was a decrease in accountability by the practice of referring questions to the chief executive for answer, a practice which became more frequent over time.* Though only a small proportion of questions that in some way impinge on the agency was referred to chief executives (from 6% to 22% of questions, depending on the agency), these questions were always among those concentrating directly on the agencies' work, and were the most important for accountability. Over a third of this important category of questions, and nearly half for two agencies, were referred to chief executives.

This practice represented a substantial decrease in accountability. Answers that once were exposed to all MPs and the public were limited to deposits in the House of Commons Library, likely in practice to be accessible only to the MP who asked the original question, and shut away from outside interested groups and the public. But for agencies responsible to the Secretary of State for the Environment the decline in accountability was even more evident. For only one of the six questions referred to the chief executive before October 1991 did the minister explicitly promise to place a copy of the chief executive's response in the Library. It is curious the same minister did not offer such a copy to the same MP when he asked the same question about other DoE agencies, answered on the same day, an inconsistency that continued into 1992.

As we have seen in Chapter 7, in response to MPs' persistent criticism of the lack of accountability to other MPs and to the public where a single private response is made to a parliamentary question by an agency's chief executive, the government in November 1991 proposed to the House that chief executives' replies to MPs should be published in a weekly publication, not Hansard. (HC Deb, Vol 199, 552w) The House Administration Committee resolved on 8th July 1992 to accept instead the Procedure Committee's recommendation that answers to PQs by chief executives be published in the daily Hansard, preceded by a standard introduction by the relevant minister with responsibility. (Procedure Committee, 1991) The House Administration Committee's resolution that this form of accountability should begin on the first day after the summer recess of 1992 ended was forwarded to the Cabinet Office for its consideration, and implemented at the end of October 1992. (HC Deb, Vol 211, 941w)

The appearance of chief executives' replies in Hansard is an example of the paradox of the Next Steps programme: that while responsibility is devolved to chief executives, ministers continue to claim they are responsible. Although the formal words express ministerial responsibility and authority, the account to MPs is visibly rendered by a named civil servant. Answers to PQs in the past were prepared for ministers by their officials, but these civil servants remained anonymous, and ministers took full public responsibility for replies. Now the continuous drip-feed of letters in Hansard from, for example, Mr Kendrick, Mr Courtney, Mr Powell, Mr Crow and Professor Rhind (the chief executives of DoE agencies and OS), may in the end transfer by association personal responsibility to those civil servants, whatever the form of words used by ministers asserting their responsibility. Printing chief executives' letters in Hansard has solved one problem of accountability—restoring to written answers their former wide distribution—but it has not solved the paradox.

And it will be intensified by such practices as having photographs of chief executives adorn agency reports.

General Conclusions

1. Overall the process of agencification has led to a decline in ministerial accountability for the work of the civil service to Parliament, which is surely the main objective of the Next Steps exercise. It is supposed to lead to devolution of responsibility to hived-away agencies, which will not be so closely scrutinised by MPs. That is happening, but it is incompatible with repeated claims by the Government that the establishment of Next Steps agencies does not affect ministerial responsibility to Parliament. The constitutional convention is that civil servants are responsible to Parliament through ministers. The setting up of agencies has challenged that convention. Ministers account less to Parliament about the work of their civil servants: civil servants account more directly themselves.

2. There may be less accountability of civil servants to ministers, since accountability is being transferred from ministers to civil servants, e.g. in select committees and PQs, despite the Government's contention that the constitutional position is being maintained.

3. Agencification may make both ministers and civil servants more accountable to Parliament than in the past, because both have to commit themselves to setting and trying to achieve objectives openly announced to Parliament and capable of being monitored by Parliament.

4. Our research has shown increasing parliamentary interest in agencies, but this early interest was mainly in the process of agencification, its effects on the working conditions and career prospects of civil servants, and later with arrangements for dealing with PQs. It is likely that when nearly all civil servants are in agencies and these issues have been settled, most of these types of question will cease. MPs may deal directly with agencies about matters of administration affecting constituents, if only because they are likely to receive answers more quickly from them than from departments.

Policy Recommendations

If there is to be more and effective accountability to Parliament, the Government should switch the focus of its justification for setting up agencies. It should emphasise they increase the capacity of ministers to control the work of civil servants where it most matters, in the setting of policy guidelines and standards of performance. It should also emphasise that they therefore increase the potential accountability of ministers to Parliament for policy and performance, but only if MPs give up their concern to raise with ministers the minutiae of implementation. For their part ministers must recognise the relevance of framework documents, annual reports, and quality-of-service and performance targets as crucial links in the chain of accountability between civil servants, ministers and Parliament, and be prepared to answer openly about them and keep MPs up-to-date. Except for individual matters which concern their own constituents, MPs can now, probably with more confidence than in the past, leave the day-to-day running of programmes to the agencies, but only if they are reassured about the overall guidelines governing the conduct of the agencies.

The terms of reference of departmental select committees should be revised by deleting policy and concentrating their attention on administration, so that the main parliamentary arenas for holding chief executives to account for the work of their agencies in implementing ministerial policies would be select committees.

The establishment of agencies should not be presented as if it does not affect accountability to Parliament. In one sense agencies reduce it, by allowing ministers to abandon their constitutional duty to answer for every official act. In another sense agencies have the potential to make it more effective, by clarifying the respective responsibilities of civil servants and ministers. Ministers would be responsible for policy and civil servants for implementation, and each would be accountable to MPs for his/her respective responsibility. However, that distinction has been found to be unsustainable in practice. Policy is made by taking into account its consequences in implementation; policy is often made in the process of implementation; and implementation needs to be driven by policy.

References

Cm 1760:	*Improving Management in Government: the Next Steps Agencies Review 1991*, November 1991.
Cm 1761:	*The Next Steps Initiative: Government Reply to the Seventh Report from the Treasury and Civil Service Committee*, HMSO, November 1991.
DoE, 1989a:	Department of the Environment, *Queen Elizabeth II Conference Centre: Framework Document*, July 1989.
DoE, 1989b:	Department of the Environment, *Historic Royal Palaces: Framework Document*, October 1989.
DoE, 1990a:	Department of the Environment, *Buildings Research Establishment Framework Document*, April 1990.
DoE, 1990b:	Department of the Environment, *Ordnance Survey: Executive Agency Framework Document*, May 1990.
DoE, 1991:	Department of the Environment, *Buying Agency: Framework Document*, October 1991.
DoE, 1992a:	Department of the Environment, *Annual Report 1992*, Cm 1908, HMSO, 1992.
DoE, 1992b:	Department of the Environment, *Planning Inspectorate: Framework Document*, 1992.

DoE, 1992c: Department of the Environment, *Queen Elizabeth
                           II Conference Centre: Framework Document*,
                           January 1992.

Dunleavy and   P Dunleavy and A Francis, 'The Development of
Francis, 1990:   the Next Steps Programme, 1988-90' in the
                           Eighth Report from the Treasury and Civil Service
                           Committee, HC 481, 1989-90, *Progress in the
                           Next Steps Initiative.*

Environment   Fifth Report from the Environment Committee,
Committee, 1990:   Session 1989-90, *PSA Services and DoE Property
                           Holdings Main Estimates, 1990-91*, HC 414,
                           1989-90.

Environment   Fourth Report from the Environment Committee,
Committee, 1991:   Session 1990-91, *DoE Property Holding and PSA
                           Services Estimates, 1991-92 and DoE Annual
                           Report 1991*, HC 389, 1990-91.

HM Treasury,   *Civil Service Statistics, 1991*, HM Treasury,
1991:   1992.

HM Treasury,   *Civil Service Statistics, 1992*, HM Treasury,
1992:   1993.

Jones, 1990:   G W Jones in Procedure Committee, *The Working
                           of the Select Committee System*, HC 19-II,
                           1989-90, 195-202.

Procedure   Third Report from the Procedure Committee,
Committee, 1991:   Session 1990-91, *Parliamentary Questions*, HC
                           178, May 1991.

APPENDIX

Table 9A.1 (A)
Queen Elizabeth II Conference Centre: all references

	June 1987–July 1989	July 1989–July 1992
Written PQs		
(a) Accountability		
MP asks specifically about this agency	1	5
MP asks more general question: Minister's reply makes direct reference to agency	<u>4</u>	<u>33</u>
	5	38
(b) Not accountability: MP or Minister refers to agency incidentally (PM attended CSCE at QEII CC)	1	0
Oral PQs		
(a) Accountability		
MP asks specifically about this agency	1	0
MP asks more general question: Minister's reply makes direct reference to agency	<u>0</u>	<u>0</u>
	1	0
(b) Not accountability: MP or Minister refers to agency incidentally (PM attended CSCE at QEII CC)	1	0
Debate in House		
(a) Accountability		
MP refers specifically to this agency	0	1
MP makes more general point: Minister's reply makes direct reference to agency	<u>1</u>	<u>2</u>
	1	3
(b) Not accountability: MP or Minister refers to agency incidentally (events at QEII CC)	1	1
Summary agency from 6.7.89		
Total written PQs	6	38
Total oral PQs	2	0
Total speeches in debate	<u>2</u>	<u>4</u>
Speeches or PQs in which agency is mentioned	10	42
Speeches or PQs which provide accountability	7	41

(The items which provide accountability are analysed in Table 9A.1 (B))

Table 9A.1 (B)
Queen Elizabeth II Conference Centre: items of accountability

	June 1987–July 1989	*July 1989–July 1992*
A. References to agency		
written PQs	5	38
oral PQs	1	0
speeches in debate	1	3
total speeches or PQs providing accountability	7	41
number of items calling to account per month	**0.3**	**1.1**
B. Subject of item		
1. Process of agencification/privatisation		
(a) simple query about process	4	14
(about future of agency or privatisation)		
(b) substantive inquiry about process	0	8
(how chief executives appointed)		
Total for process of agencification	4 (57%)	22 (54%)
2. Agency a side issue: PQ not principally about agency		
but produces information on agency		
(a) about agency in relation to another issue	0	0
(b) about another topic: agency is one item in the		
answer (usually money)	2	5
(c) about organisation related to agency	0	0
(d) when did Minister see ...	0	0
Total where agency a side issue	2 (29%)	5 (12%)
3. Directly about work, structure, finance of agency		
(a) enquiry on cost or quality of a product (cost		
of hiring, restrictions on service offered)	1	1
(b) finances, efficiency, accounts of agency	0	13
Total for work of agency	1 (14%)	14 (34%)
	(N=7)	(N=41)

C. Questions referred to Chief Executive: 5 (12% of post-agency PQs)
   These questions were all in section 3 (36% post agency PQs in this section were referred). They asked about the agency's annual report, budget and staff costs, bonus payments, working patterns and staff welfare facilities.
   Note: One PQ in section 3(b) was not answered at all, probably being omitted by mistake.

Table 9A.2 (A)
Historic Royal Palaces: all references

	June 1987– Oct 1989	*Oct 1989– Apr 1992**
Written PQs		
(a) Accountability		
MP asks specifically about this agency	1	8
MP asks more general question: Minister's reply makes direct reference to agency	<u>16</u>	<u>31</u>
	17	39
(b) Not accountability: MP or Minister refers to agency incidentally	0	0
Oral PQs		
(a) Accountability		
MP asks specifically about this agency	1	1
MP asks more general question: Minister's reply makes direct reference to agency	<u>0</u>	<u>0</u>
	1	1
(b) Not accountability: MP or Minister refers to agency incidentally (Henry VIII at Hampton Court)	0	1
Debate in House		
(a) Accountability		
MP refers specifically to this agency	4	3
MP makes more general point: Minister's reply makes direct reference to agency	<u>1</u>	<u>1</u>
	4	4
(b) Not accountability: MP or Minister refers to agency incidentally (taxi-drivers at the Tower)	0	1
Summary agency from 2.10.89		
Total written PQs	17	39
Total oral PQs	1	2
Total speeches in debate	<u>4</u>	<u>5</u>
Speeches or PQs in which agency is mentioned	22	46
Speeches or PQs which provide accountability	22	44

(The items which provide accountability are analysed in Table 9A.2(B))

* Responsibility for Historic Royal Palace was transferred to the Secretary of State for National Heritage in April 1992.

Table 9A.2 (B)
Historic Royal Palaces: items of accountability

	June 1987– Oct 1989	Oct 1989– Apr 1992*
A. References to agency		
written PQs	17	39
oral PQs	1	1
speeches in debate	<u>4</u>	<u>4</u>
total speeches or PQs providing accountability	22	44
number of items calling to account per month	**0.8**	**1.5**
B. Subject of item		
1. Process of agencification/privatisation		
(a) simple query about process	5	4
(would minister make a statement about future of agency or privatisation)		
(b) substantive inquiry about process	<u>1</u>	<u>6</u>
(cost of launch publicity)		
Total for process of agencification	6 (27%)	10 (23%)
2. Agency a side issue: PQ not principally about agency but produces information on agency		
(a) about agency in relation to another issue (govt aid for historical sites, parks)	1	4
(b) about another topic: agency is one item in the answer (usually money)	10	11
(c) about organisation related to agency (palace security if PSA privatised)	0	1
(d) when did Minister see ...	<u>0</u>	<u>0</u>
Total where agency a side issue	11 (50%)	16 (36%)
3. Directly about work, structure, finance of agency		
(a) enquiry on cost or quality of a product (Hampton Court, Armouries collection at Tower)	5	5
(b) finances, efficiency, accounts of agency	<u>0</u>	<u>13</u>
Total for work of agency	5 (23%)	18 (41%)
	(N=2)	(N=44)

C. Questions referred to Chief Executive: 5 (11% of post-agency PQs)

These questions were all in section 3 (28% post agency PQs in this section were referred). They asked about the agency's annual report, budget and staff costs, bonus payments, working patterns and staff welfare facilities.

*Responsibility for Historic Royal Palaces was transferred to the Secretary of State for National Heritage in April 1992.

Table 9A.3 (A)
Building Research Establishment: all references

	June 1987– *Apr 1990*	*Apr 1990–* *July 1992*
Written PQs		
(a) Accountability		
MP asks specifically about this agency	14	13
MP asks more general question: Minister's reply makes		
direct reference to agency	<u>32</u>	<u>25</u>
	46	38
(b) Not accountability: MP or Minister refers to agency		
incidentally (playgroup-nursery at BRE)	1	0
Oral PQs		
(a) Accountability		
MP asks specifically about this agency	0	0
MP asks more general question: Minister's reply makes		
direct reference to agency	<u>3</u>	<u>0</u>
	3	0
(b) Not accountability: MP or Minister refers to agency		
incidentally	0	0
Debate in House		
(a) Accountability		
MP refers specifically to this agency		
(Reference to BRE research plumbing)	0	2
MP makes more general point: Minister's reply makes		
direct reference to agency		
(Minister pays BRE's research in aid)	<u>3</u>	<u>1</u>
	3	3
(b) Not accountability: MP or Minister refers to agency		
incidentally	0	0
Summary agency from 2.4.90		
Total written PQs	47	38
Total oral PQs	3	0
Total speeches in debate	<u>3</u>	<u>3</u>
Speeches or PQs in which agency is mentioned	53	41
Speeches or PQs which provide accountability	52	41

(The items which provide accountability are analysed in Table 9A.3(B))

Table 9A.3 (B)
Building Research Establishment: items of accountability

	June 1987– Apr 1989	Apr 1990– July 1992*
A. References to agency		
written PQs	46	38
oral PQs	3	0
speeches in debate	<u>3</u>	<u>3</u>
total speeches or PQs providing accountability	52	41
number of items calling to account per month	**1.5**	**1.5**
B. Subject of item		
1. Process of agencification/privatisation		
(a) simple query about process		
(about future of agency or privatisation)	7	9
(b) substantive inquiry about process		
(financial regimes, cost of launch)	<u>0</u>	<u>4</u>
Total for process of agencification	7 (13%)	13 (32%)
2. Agency a side issue: PQ not principally about agency		
but produces information on agency		
(a) about agency in relation to another issue		
(building rules, energy efficiency)	19	8
(b) about another topic: (agency is prayed in aid		
by minister)	10	8
(c) about organisation related to agency		
(BRE panel, advisory committee)	2	0
(d) when did Minister see ...	<u>0</u>	<u>0</u>
Total where agency a side issue	31 (60%)	16 (39%)
3. Directly about work, structure, finance of agency		
(a) enquiry on cost or quality of a product (what		
research is BRE doing on ...)	3	1
(b) finances, efficiency, accounts of agency	<u>11</u>	<u>11</u>
Total for work of agency	14 (27%)	12 (29%)
	(*N*=52)	(*N*=41)

C. Questions referred to Chief Executive: 5 (12% of post-agency PQs)

These questions were all in section 3 (45% post agency PQs in this section were referred). They asked about the agency's annual report, budget and staff costs, bonus payments, working patterns and staff welfare facilities.

Table 9A.4 (A)
Ordnance Survey: all references

	June 1987– May 1990	May 1990– July 1992
Written PQs		
(a) Accountability		
MP asks specifically about this agency	20	19
MP asks more general question: Minister's reply makes		
direct reference to agency	<u>26</u>	<u>23</u>
	46	42
(b) Not accountability: MP or Minister refers to agency		
incidentally (e.g. gives or asks for OS map reference)	7	2
Oral PQs		
(a) Accountability		
MP asks specifically about this agency	1	0
MP asks more general question: Minister's reply makes		
direct reference to agency	<u>0</u>	<u>0</u>
	1	0
(b) Not accountability: MP or Minister refers to agency		
incidentally	1	0
Debate in House		
(a) Accountability		
MP refers specifically to this agency	0	3
MP makes more general point: Minister's reply makes		
direct reference to agency	<u>0</u>	<u>0</u>
	0	3
(b) Not accountability: MP or Minister refers to agency		
incidentally (e.g. in querying right of way)	3	0
Summary agency from 1.5.90		
Total written PQs	53	44
Total oral PQs	2	0
Total speeches in debate	<u>3</u>	<u>3</u>
Speeches or PQs in which agency is mentioned	58	47
Speeches or PQs which provide accountability	47	45

(The items which provide accountability are analysed in Table 9A.4(B))

Note: Written PQs before May 1990 included 22 written PQs answered in 5 batches to 2 MPs. One MP asked 20 of these PQs.

Table 9A.4 (B)
Ordnance Survey: items of accountability

	June 1987– *May 1990*	*May 1990–* *July 1992*
A. References to agency		
written PQs	46	42
oral PQs	1	0
speeches in debate	0	3
total speeches or PQs providing accountability	47	45
number of items calling to account per month	**1.3**	**1.7**
B. Subject of item		
1. Process of agencification/privatisation		
(a) simple query about process		
(about future of agency or privatisation)	4	8
(b) substantive inquiry about process		
(has minister talked to unions?)	3	9
Total for process of agencification	7 (15%)	17 (38%)
2. Agency a side issue: PQ not principally about agency		
but produces information on agency		
(a) about agency in relation to another issue		
(will OS make maps of afforestation?)	2	3
(b) about another topic: (govt computer network)	5	3
(c) about organisation related to agency		
(body now incorporated into OS)	1	0
(d) when did Minister see ...	1	0
Total where agency a side issue	9 (19%)	6 (13%)
3. Directly about work, structure, finance of agency		
(a) enquiry on cost or quality of a product (cost		
of a map; item omitted from map)	5	1
(b) finances, efficiency, accounts of agency	26	21
Total for work of agency	31 (66%)	22 (49%)
	(*N*=47)	(*N*=45)

C. Questions referred to Chief Executive: 10 (22% of post-agency PQs)
These questions were all in section 3 (45% post agency PQs in this section were referred).
These PQs asked about policy on maps, expenditure on management and consultancy, computer contracts, annual reports, budget and staff costs, bonus payments, working patterns and staff welfare facilities.

Table 9A.5 (A)
Planning Inspectorate: all references

	June 1987– *Apr 1992*	*Apr 1992–* *July 1992*
Written PQs		
(a) Accountability		
MP asks specifically about this agency	91	11
MP asks more general question: Minister's reply makes		
direct reference to agency	<u>34</u>	<u>5</u>
	125	16
(b) Not accountability: MP or Minister refers to agency		
incidentally (list of all DoE divisions)	1	0
Oral PQs		
(a) Accountability		
MP asks specifically about this agency	6	0
MP asks more general question: Minister's reply makes		
direct reference to agency	<u>5</u>	<u>0</u>
	11	0
(b) Not accountability: (inspection used as reason not to		
reply on another issue)	1	0
Debate in House		
(a) Accountability		
MP refers specifically to this agency	17	0
MP makes more general point: Minister's reply makes		
direct reference to agency	<u>39</u>	<u>0</u>
	56	0
(b) Not accountability: MP or Minister refers to agency		
incidentally	0	0
Summary agency from 1.4.92		
Total written PQs	126	16
Total oral PQs	12	0
Total speeches in debate	<u>56</u>	<u>0</u>
Speeches or PQs in which agency is mentioned	194	16
Speeches or PQs which provide accountability	192	16

(The items which provide accountability are analysed in Table 9A.5(B))

Table 9A.5 (B)
Planning Inspectorate: items of accountability

	June 1987– Apr 1992	*Apr 1992– July 1992*
A. References to agency		
written PQs	125	16
oral PQs	11	0
speeches in debate	<u>56</u>	<u>0</u>
total speeches or PQs providing accountability	192	16
number of items calling to account per month	**3.3**	**5.3**
B. Subject of item		
1. Process of agencification/privatisation		
(a) simple query about process	13	3
(about future of agency or privatisation)		
(b) substantive inquiry about process	<u>0</u>	<u>3</u>
(who will reply to PQs)		
Total for process of agencification	13 (7%)	6 (38%)
2. Agency a side issue: PQ not principally about agency		
but produces information on agency		
(a) about agency in relation to another issue	1	0
(b) about another topic: agency is one item in the		
answer (mostly inspector's report prayed in aid)	40	1
(c) about planning process in general	19	0
(d) when will Minister decide ...	<u>1</u>	<u>0</u>
Total where agency a side issue	61 (32%)	1 (6%)
3. Directly about work, structure, finance of agency		
(a) enquiry on cost or quality of a product		
(individual planning application)	50	4
(role of inspector in more general terms)	16	3
(b) efficiency/effectiveness of agency/		
appeal system	<u>52</u>	<u>2</u>
Total for work of agency	118 (61%)	9 (56%)
	(*N*=192)	(*N*=16)

C. Questions referred to Chief Executive: 1 (6% of post-agency PQs)

This question was in section 3 (11% post agency PQs in this section were referred). The PQ asked about an individual planning application (when the minister expected to determine a particular appeal).

10

The Department of Social Security and its Agencies

Patricia Greer

Introduction

In many ways the Department of Social Security is the most interesting case study of Next Steps. The establishment of agencies within the Department of Social Security is the greatest test of Next Steps principles and their effect on parliamentary accountability. It is by far the most important department in expenditure terms with a programme expenditure of some £86 billion a year (nearly a third of all public expenditure) and running costs of over £2.5 billion a year. It has a total staff of around 85,000, a sixth of the entire civil service. All citizens will have at least some contact with the Department at various points in their lives. The Department has the highest public and parliamentary profile—there are more parliamentary questions on social security than on any other subject. The Department of Social Security has established six agencies to date.

The Benefits Agency: The Benefits Agency is the benefits paying arm of the Department of Social Security and is responsible for paying a wide range of benefits from income support and social fund payments, through to child benefit, family credit, pensions, war and widows pensions through to industrial injuries, disability benefits and invalid care allowance. The Benefits Agency is also responsible for providing relevant information to other bodies to assist in determining entitlement to other benefits such as Statutory Maternity Pay and Sick Pay, Unemployment Benefit, Housing Benefit and Legal Aid. The staff are situated in the centralised sites or in the network of local social security offices based throughout Britain.

The Contributions Agency: The Contributions Agency has two main roles: to ensure that individuals and employers pay the due National Insurance Contributions, and to maintain the National Insurance Contribution records, making this information available to the Benefits Agency when claims are made for contributory benefits such as Retirement Pensions, Unemployment and Invalidity Benefits. The Inland Revenue collect the bulk of National Insurance Contributions on behalf of the Contributions Agency. Most of the Agency's staff now work in the central Newcastle upon Tyne site.

The Information Technology Services Agency: The Information Technology Services provides a wide range of information technology services to the Department of Social Security and to others. Its main aims are to maintain and operate existing systems, to develop new systems and provide consultancy services to the Department of Social Security and its other Agencies.

The Resettlement Agency: The Resettlement Agency was established to fulfil two apparently conflicting purposes: to manage the facilities for temporary board and lodging provided by the Secretary of State for people without a settled way of life with the aim of influencing them to lead a more settled life, and to implement the Government's policy of closing Resettlement Units and handing over responsibility for providing alternative facilities to local authorities and voluntary organisations. In effect the agency has the role of running itself down—once it has succeeded in closing down all the resettlement units it ceases to exist.

The Child Support Agency: The Child Support Agency is an example of an agency starting almost from scratch. It inherited an Act of Parliament but few extant organisational structures. The Benefits Agency did hold responsibility for collecting maintenance from the liable relatives of those claiming benefit but this will only be one aspect of the new agency's work. It is responsible for implementing the collection of maintenance from all liable relatives in accordance with the new legislation.

The War Pensions Agency: The War Pensions Agency was launched in April 1994. Its roots were in the Blackpool branch of the Benefits Agency responsible for administering war pensions.

Typology of Social Security Agencies

The Department of Social Security's Agencies have been established at different times. This is an important consideration in a case study as different issues emerge at different stages in the development of agencies. The Department's agencies also range across the spectrum of 'types'. This is also significant because there are marked differences between the different agencies in the issues raised and in their effect on parliamentary accountability. Table 10.1 shows how these agencies range across the spectrum of agency 'types'.

Those agencies raising revenue from receipts and competing for their 'markets' clearly have more scope to develop as autonomous arms of government than those agencies which are entirely dependent on vote funding and provide a monopoly service close to the core of Government. The following section uses the case study of the different 'types' of agencies within the Department of Social Security to consider the differences in the main issues facing these agencies and the wider implications of these issues for parliamentary accountability.

Table 10.1
Typology of Department of Social Security Agencies

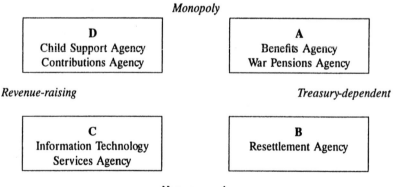

Box A, *Vote Funded Monopoly Agencies*: Table 10.1 also points to some of the issues facing the Department of Social Security's agencies. The Agencies in box A, the Benefits Agency and the War Pensions Agency, are clearly close to the core of government. There are limitations in the extent to which these agencies in particular can follow the path of becoming 'business like' as they provide fundamental public services which spend rather than generate income. They also provide services which attract a high degree of political interest. The core issue facing these agencies in particular is the extent to which they are able to become distinct entities at arms length from headquarters and from ministers. How far is it possible to detach the political nature of these services from their day to day operations? How far can the agency chief executives be left to get on with day to day operation of their agencies, operations which could prove to be political dynamite? This is also an issue for other 'types' of agencies but less so as they are generally not so close to the core of government and less politically sensitive.

General characteristics of agencies: In theory, with executive agencies being delegated certain freedoms, responsibilities and accountabilities, they have the freedom to run the day to day operations with no outside interference from parent departments or ministers. Agency chief executives are designated as Accounting Officers and as such are directly accountable to Parliament for the day to day operations of their agencies. The theoretical difficulties with this arrangement have been well documented (for example, see Greer, 1992) and are discussed at greater length in Chapter 6. The main difficulty is that the lack of a clear dividing line between 'policy matters' and 'day to day operations' results in an obfuscation of responsibilities and a means for departmental headquarters and ministers to become involved in agency operations. The scope for those with a reluctance to 'let go' to interfere under such a regime is highlighted by Robert Maclennan MP who when debating the National Audit Bill in 1983 stated:

> I believe that it is possible to go right through the decision making process in any Department, Authority or body which could be subject to examination and at almost any point seek to cover the subject under investigation by the claim that it is an issue of policy'. (HC Deb, 23 March 1983)

Agency and departmental accounting officers do not know where their respective responsibilities begin and end.

Similarly, as we have seen in Chapter 7, on the issue of parliamentary questions the theory is that Ministers should reply on matters concerning 'policy' or where Members of Parliament specifically seek a ministerial reply (these answers are usually prepared by departmental headquarters) and that chief executives should reply on matters concerning the 'day-to-day operations' of the agency. Again, this theory fails to distinguish clearly respective responsibilities.

As has been illustrated by the furore surrounding the Child Support Agency, there is the danger that departmental headquarters and ministers will resist allowing politically sensitive agencies autonomy because if the agency fails to handle an issue 'well', this could leave the agency, the department and ministers open to political and public scandal. (Greer, 1993)

The experience of the Benefits Agency has, in part, also reflected these theoretical concerns, but none of the difficulties raised have been nearly so fundamental as was the case with the Child Support Agency. First, with regard to the respective roles of the agency and departmental Accounting Officers, the Benefits Agency was the only executive agency examined by the Treasury and Civil Service Committee in 1991 for which a Departmental spokesman (a Deputy Secretary) accompanied the agency chief executive. (TCSC, 1991) This could be taken to suggest that the Department of Social Security is more concerned with the affairs of its politically sensitive agencies than other departments are with their less sensitive agencies. Indeed, Mr Montagu who attended the TCSC hearing on behalf of the Department was asked by the committee Chairman whether he was in attendance in order 'to mind the Agency'. He of course answered that this was 'absolutely not' the case. (TCSC, 1991)

The Fraser report (Efficiency Unit, 1991), which recommended that Departments should allow their agencies greater autonomy, was generally unpopular amongst some senior staff within the Department of Social Security's headquarters, who argued that social security's political sensitivity coupled with the sheer size of the Benefits Agency make it imperative that the agency and the department work closer together than may be necessary for other departments and agencies. (Greer, 1994) Indeed, Michael Bichard, the Chief Executive of the Benefits Agency sees that one of his main roles is to be politically 'tuned in' and to ensure that his managers are also politically aware and ready to judge which issues are or could be significant and should be reported to departmental headquarters and ministers. So long as ministers and departmental Accounting Officers are to be held ultimately accountable for all the work of their departments this process of agency managers reporting up and departments and ministers looking down will continue, particularly for those agencies and departments working in politically sensitive areas.

The revised system for parliamentary questions raised concerns that policy issues would be defined downwards into operational matters, particularly on sensitive subjects, so as to avoid having the answers aired in the House or published in Hansard. (Greer, 1992) As we have seen in

Chapter 7, there are two issues here: the first is that is that these concerns have resulted in a change to these arrangements. Chief executive's replies to 'operational questions' are now published in Hansard. The second is that there is little evidence that policy issues have been defined as operational issues so as to prevent such questions from appearing in Hansard. Analysis of the Benefits Agency's replies to questions published by Paul Flynn MP in *Open Lines* (see Chapter 7) shows that, on the whole, the questions have divided quite clearly between 'policy' and 'operational' issues.

Table 10.2 below shows the break down of parliamentary questions relating to the Department of Social Security in the parliamentary session 1991–92. Overall the table shows that the majority of questions were referred to agency chief executives. A main effect of this is to raise the level of questions aired in the House and published in Hansard from the particular (MPs asking parliamentary questions about the experiences of their individual constituents or MPs asking questions about specific officers) to the more strategic.

Table 10.2
**Department of Social Security Parliamentary Questions
between 15 April 1991 and 16 March 1992**

	Parliamentary Questions
Answered in full by Ministers	2,118
Answered by Benefits Agency Chief Executive	189
Answered by other chief executives	32
Total	2,339

Box B, Vote Funded Non Monopoly Agencies: Overall there are few agencies in the Box B category in general and returning to the example of the Department of Social Security, there is only one agency in this category. It is clear however, that agencies in this category are non-essential (as there are others in their line of business) but mostly government funded activities. This explains why the present drive to reduce the size of government falls heavily on those activities falling within Box B.

In Box B we have the Resettlement Agency. The two main aims of the resettlement agency are to run the resettlement units as effectively and efficiently as possible and to run to timetable the programmed closure of the units. Responsibility for resettlement is to be passed to local authorities. The money for local authorities to provide this service is to be included in the block grant from central government to local authorities. This transferring of functions will impact on parliamentary accountability as Parliament will lose its rights of scrutiny of resettlement units once they are no longer run (even if they continue to be indirectly financed) by central government.

As an aside, a further example of where this transfer of responsibility has already taken place is the Department of Employment's Training and Enterprise Councils. These are now run by private businesses but continue to be largely financed by government money. Parliament, through the National Audit Office and the Public Accounts Committee, has the right to scrutiny of the amount of money paid over to the Training and Enterprise Councils but has no right to look at how that money is being spent.

Parliamentary interest has not focused directly on the continuance of its rights of scrutiny to agencies in this category. Instead, parliamentary questions have focused primarily on the timetable for closures of Resettlement Units and on the effect of the closures in particular areas—for example, there were some parliamentary questions about the programme of closures when the closure of one Resettlement Unit resulted in a sit in by its residents. In addition, a National Audit Office report focused on the efficiency and effectiveness of the resettlement units and the extent to which the programme for closures was being met. (NAO, 1992) At the time of writing this report had not yet been considered by the Public Accounts Committee.

Box C, Revenue Raising Non Monopoly Agencies: In Box C we have the Information Technology Services Agency (ITSA). The main issue facing this agency (and the other agencies in this category) is the fact that it is increasingly having to compete for much of its work with other computer specialists. Indeed, ITSA has recently announced the outsourcing of a main part of its core function, the provision of IT service delivery. It is also increasingly using private sector management consultants both to work alongside staff performing day to day functions and to carry out discrete blocks of work as well as to advise on organisational growth. Again this raises issues about parliamentary scrutiny. First, with regard to those areas of work that are contracted out, Parliament will be able to look at the amount of money spent on the work but will not be able to look at how that money is spent. Second, with regard to the work contracted out to management consultants, Parliament is in theory able to look at the amount paid to consultants but in practice the information appears to be difficult to obtain. Parliamentary questions on this issue have been side-stepped or narrowed down to amounts spent in particular areas. The consultancy firms themselves, although they are gaining an increasing amount of public money, do not have to publish accounts or make public their turnover.

Box D, Revenue Raising Monopolies: In Box D, we have the Department of Social Security's revenue raising monopoly agencies. The Contributions Agency and the Child Support Agency fall into this category. One of the main issues facing these agencies is how they can increase their yields of revenue to ensure full compliance with the law.

There have been few parliamentary questions relating to the Contributions Agency. The National Audit Office produced a report examining:

(a)   The Department's procedures (i) for seeking to ensure that the correct amounts of national insurance contributions are received from all those required to contribute, and (ii) for crediting the amounts received to each individual's contributions record; and

(b)   the arrangements being established by the Department for the overall management of national insurance contributions work. (NAO, 1991, para. 1.9)

The report found that 'work on the collection and recording of national insurance contributions lacked clear purpose and direction'; but the fieldwork was carried out prior to the establishment of the Contributions Agency and the Department commented that the Contributions Agency had been established to provide a clear management focus for addressing the problems identified in the NAO report. (NAO, 1991) To date there has been little parliamentary interest in the success of the Contributions Agency in overcoming these difficulties.

By contrast, the experiences of the Child Support Agency have been very different. The change to its work priorities in order to maximise the amounts of maintenance paid by focusing on those already paying some maintenance rather than on those not paying anything, as originally planned, stirred considerable public and parliamentary interest, including Commons debates on 31 March and 4 July 1994. The furore prompted the social security committee to conduct an extensive enquiry into the CSA and its chief executive, Ros Hepplewhite, gave evidence to the committee on 6 July 1994, followed by the Secretary of State for Social Security, Peter Lilley, a week later. Both in her evidence to the social security committee and in the CSA's Annual Report the chief executive admitted that there had been very serious shortcomings in the service provided by the agency to its clients and to MPs raising constituents' cases. At the time of writing the Committee has yet to report but there was considerable support for the view that changes should be made to the formula for calculating the amounts of maintenance to be paid and that the agency should recognise earlier 'clean-break' agreements. Pressure on the agency has continued to build and in early September 1994 Ros Hepplewhite, the chief executive, resigned.

These examples of the experiences of the Department of Social Security therefore show how Next Steps is affecting parliamentary accountability to varying extents depending on the 'type' of agency. Essentially the main changes are to the arrangements for answering parliamentary questions, the appointment of chief executives as agency Accounting Officers and the consequences of component, semi or complete privatisation and contracting out. The section above has demonstrated how the degree of importance of each of these changes is contingent on agency type. The following section shows a further way in which Next Steps is affecting parliamentary scrutiny of the Department of Social Security and its agencies.

The Move to Management by Contract in the Department of Social Security

Central to the success of Next Steps is more explicit performance information. Parliament has traditionally monitored the performance of departments as a part of the annual expenditure round. Performance information was published in the Public Expenditure White Papers, which were replaced by Departmental Annual Reports.

Next Steps generates more information for Parliament to use in the course of the expenditure round but also for the purposes of general scrutiny. There is more documentation by which Parliament can scrutinise the performance of different arms of the department. In addition to the departmental report, there are the three-yearly agency framework agreements which set out the framework in which the agency must operate, the annual agency business plans which set out the agencies' plans for the following year and incorporate their resources and targets to be achieved, and the annual agency reports which report on what has happened within the year including the extent to which targets have been met.

Next Steps also results in more robust information being made available to Parliament. This is because performance measures are now a crucial tool for departments in monitoring and controlling their agencies. They are a tool which must be used to manage rather than as a sales pitch by departments to show the Treasury and Parliament how well they have been doing. The experience of the Department of Social Security's agencies illustrates how the new crucial role of performance measures in the move to management by contract is resulting in departments and agencies going back to first principles in reviewing their performance measures with a view to making them more coherent, meaningful and useful. (Carter and Greer, 1993) Surprisingly, this is particularly true for the Benefits Agency which, on the face of it, as earlier departmental measures covered much of this ground, should have less work to do than other agencies. The Benefits Agency has taken a fresh look at the way in which it measures and reports clearance times and accuracy rates. For example, the Benefits Agency has now replaced measures of average clearance times with actual end-to-end clearance times, that is, to sample measures of the numbers of days taken to clear certain types of cases for certain benefits. The new measures are expressed in terms of x % to be cleared in five days. The new measures develop the idea of a contractual agreement between the Benefits Agency and customers, parent departments, Treasury and Parliament.

The Citizen's Charter

Clearly, the Citizen's Charter is also influencing this re-think of performance measures. There is much in common with the Citizen's Charter aims and the Next Steps aims of improving quality of service to the 'customer'.

All this is resulting in more accessible and more usable performance information being available to Parliament. Parliament has more information on what is happening within departments and agencies. Such information is used by Parliament, Treasury and parent departments in the annual expenditure round but is also available for general scrutiny by select committees and by individual Members or their researchers.

Summary and Conclusions

This case study of the Department of Social Security's agencies illustrates how Next Steps is affecting the role of Parliament. A major change is that Parliament's role of scrutiny of the Executive is easier. Parliament is being provided with more and better information about the workings of Departments and their Agencies. Performance indicators and targets are becoming more meaningful and accessible. The key issue is now whether Parliament will rise to the opportunity and make full use of this information.

The other overt changes to Parliament's role in relation to the social security agencies are that parliamentary questions on operational issues are now answered by agency chief executives, that chief executives are now agency accounting officers and as such are answerable to Parliament for the workings of their agencies and that Parliament will lose its rights of scrutiny to agencies or parts of agencies which are privatised or contracted out. The experience of the Department of Social Security's agencies has been that certain of these changes present more difficulties in relation to some agencies than to others. For example, within the Benefits Agency and the Child Support Agency the appointment of an agency accounting officer and the delegation of responsibility for parliamentary questions to the chief executive is likely to be more problematic than for other agencies because of their high political profile and, in the case of the Benefits Agency, its proximity to the core of government. Political sensitivity makes it more difficult to differentiate between policy and operational issues and this results some ambiguity in who is answerable to Parliament for what and conversely, whom Parliament should hold accountable for what.

The transferring of responsibility, contracting out, and the part or complete privatisation of agencies are all being given added impetus by the 'prior options' reviews and the *Competing for Quality* white paper. (HM Treasury, 1991). Such measures will inevitably limit Parliament's rights of scrutiny. The issue is whether or not this matters. This chapter illustrates that those areas most likely to be privatised are those furthest away from the core of Government—agencies which raise revenue for services they perform or the goods they produce. But Parliament must take an increasingly active role in monitoring and debating the progress of Next Steps within the Department of Social Security if it wishes to ensure its future rights of scrutiny as the contracting out and privatisation programme develops.

References

Carter and Greer, 1993:	Neil Carter and Patricia Greer, 'Evaluating Agencies: Next Steps and Performance Indicators', *Public Administration*, Vol 71, No 3, Autumn 1993.
Efficiency Unit, 1991:	*Making the Most of Next Steps: the Management of Ministers' Departments and their Executive Agencies*, Cabinet Office, May 1991.
Greer, 1992:	Patricia Greer, 'The Next Steps Initiative: an Examination of the Agency Framework Documents', *Public Administration*, Vol 70, No 1, Spring 1992.
Greer, 1993:	Patricia Greer, 'Targets that Hit Home', *The Times*, 27 November 1993.
Greer, 1994:	Patricia Greer, *Transforming Central Government: the Next Steps Initiative*, Open University Press, 1994.
HM Treasury, 1992:	*Competing for Quality*, Cm 1730, HMSO, November 1991.
NAO, 1991:	National Audit Office, *National Insurance Contributions*, HC 655, 1990–91.
NAO, 1992:	National Audit Office, *Department of Social Security: Resettlement Agency*, HC 22, 1992–93.
TCSC, 1991:	Seventh Report from the Treasury and Civil Service Committee, Session 1990–91, *The Next Steps Initiative* HC 496, July 1991.

11

Accountability and the Employment Service Agency

Norman Lewis

A Brief History

The Employment Service was set up in the autumn of 1987 when the Government decided to bring together the separate Job Centre local office network, which was then run by the Manpower Services Commission, and the Department of Employment. What was created was a separate quasi-autonomous body. The policy thinking behind this reorganisation was to bring together the job placement services and the benefit payment services into one common structure so that a unified service could be offered to clients. Combining the two separate streams of activity effectively took two years and in December 1989 the Secretary of State announced that the Employment Service would be a candidate for agency status. Agency status as the Employment Service Agency (ESA) was acquired in April 1990. The ESA is then an agency within the Employment Department Group responsible for executing Government policies as agreed by ministers. Its main aim, to quote the Employment Service Operational Plan for 1992–93, is 'to help promote a competitive and efficient labour market particularly by giving positive help to unemployed people through its job placement service and other programmes and by the payments of benefits and allowances to those entitled to them'.

At the time the ESA was by some measure the largest of the agencies, though that accolade has since passed to the Benefits Agency. Even so, in the financial year 1991–2 ESA employed some 46,000, 9,000 more than the previous year on account of the sharp rise in unemployment, especially in the south of England. It operates over 1,300 local offices, of which 670 are Employment Service Job Centres offering the full range of ESA services. They operate through a network of 59 areas, formed into 7 English regions and the offices for Scotland and Wales. It accounts for around 70 per cent of all Department of Employment expenditure. Its

1992-3 budget was £1,162 million and it pays out in excess of £5 billion a year in benefits to unemployed people. It may be worth noting that agency status has given ESA certain flexibilities over and above those generally available to Vote-financed bodies. These flexibilities include virement and limited revenue generation. During 1991-2 for example it vired just over £10 million between subheads. It is also permitted to charge a fee for a limited range of services above those normally expected from a publicly funded employment service.

The Employment Service Agency and the New Conventionalism

The framework documents of agencies have been called 'mini-constitutions'. They lay down the terms of the relationship between an agency and its sponsoring department. Their primary interest is in laying down the responsibilities of the various partners and the description of operational objectives which will be supplemented annually by performance indicators and targets. That of the ESA expired in the autumn of 1993 and was expected to be the subject of a lengthy period of consultation between the ESA and the Department of Employment.

It is the performance indicators and targets which have become the dominant issue in the new set of emergent relationships between the agencies and their departments. The ESA is very representative of the Next Steps philosophy in expecting a regular tightening of targets to ensure their robustness. In its case the annual process begins with the Chief Executive, currently Mike Fogden, going to his field directors and seeking their views on the state of the employment market as it appears to them. This is supplemented by quarterly assessments on the state of the economy and the job market by the National Institute for Economic and Social Research. The figures are then sent to the Secretary of State, who examines them with his own financial advisers. In 1992-93 it is believed that the Department accepted Mr Fogden's own view of what was possible under the circumstances. At this point, of course, the hand of the Treasury looms large since the Chief Secretary to the Treasury has to be satisfied that the targets produced are stretching and 'robust'. This exercise is supposed to be conducted in a six-week period but has been known to take up to three months. After the British fashion, these exercises are conducted outwith the public gaze but, as may be expected, there is the occasional disagreement between the Secretary of State and the Treasury. Michael Howard, for example, when he was Employment Secretary, is believed to have stood extremely firm against Treasury pressure to sharpen the ESA's targets further at a time of rising unemployment. In any event, the performance targets agreed with the Secretary of State are included in the Annual Performance Agreement.

Perhaps the most important of the targets is placing into jobs. For the year 1992 the ESA's Operational Plan aimed to achieve some 1.425 million placings of unemployed people into jobs. This in turn was based upon an assumption that 2.1 to 2.2 million vacancies would be notified to the ESA. These placing estimates were further broken down into proportions of long term claimants, people with disabilities and the unemployed in the inner cities. During the year 1991-2 the Agency helped 1.33 million unemployed people back to work, representing 99.8 of the 1.335 million target set by the Department. It is impossible for an outsider to gauge how rigorous such a target is in the absence of all the information available to the various players and the firmness of the political positions adopted. However, on the face of things, the 1993 target does look sharp and robust when we consider that the economy, in the UK was, at the time, continuing to shrink.

There are, of course, other targets. These include 92 per cent of new claims to be input into the NUBS computer within six days of the claim being made, a minimum of 96 per cent of the total value of unemployment benefit payments to be correct, efficiency savings of over £17 million and at least a three per cent increase in client satisfaction rating for each type of Employment Service office. In each case the targets have been marginally tightened over the previous year's figures where the primary targets were, in fact, exceeded.

The purpose of the ESA's Operational Plan, again approved by the Secretary of State, is to describe the measures to be taken to achieve its performance targets, to indicate how services are to be improved in terms of value for money and to set out how ESA's business is expected to develop over a three year period within the policies agreed by the Secretary of State. Those policies and objectives are laid down in the Framework Document. As has been noted earlier in this volume, some discontent has been expressed over the level of information and public debate prior to the emergence of framework documents, not least by the relevant Select Committees. It will be interesting to monitor Parliament's concern with these matters as the framework documents of the more prominent agencies come up for revision.

One of the great advances of Next Steps is the amount of information made available to the general public which was previously inaccessible.

This information, as I have indicated, is by no means complete but it does afford some insight into the workings of our system of public administration. Together with the developments heralded by the Citizen's Charter there is real constitutional advance discernible. What is, however, perhaps more interesting is that by making so much information public we can look into the crevices of the constitution and see how much is still hidden. Next Steps is a clear advance and at the same time shows the Diceyan formula of conventional accountability to be bogus and a sham. Even in relation to the Citizen's Charter there are major deficiencies: a promise of great openness but no freedom of information legislation; improved complaints procedures but few of them given statutory force; and, above all, a commitment to consultation without the law playing any direct role. American experience has shown such developments to be capable of degenerating into a list of exceptions and exemptions which suit the executive purpose. A step forward then, in terms of open government, but also a step to the side.

The issue of tightening targets needs to be elaborated upon. It is clear that adjustment of targets represents an important method of departmental control, even though they will be the subject of extensive consultation with the chief executive. However, there may come a point where a minister either wishes to or is forced to change policies in circumstances where the targets will take the brunt of the new challenge. This may occur in circumstances where the agency's true interests are not properly represented. Interestingly, New Zealand after the 1989 reforms adopted a different approach. There the chief executive (formerly the Permanent Secretary equivalent) is responsible for outputs, and if he fails to achieve the requisite level of performance his contract is on the line. On the other hand, the minister is quite clearly made responsible for outcomes so that he will be surrounded by policy advisers subjected to close parliamentary scrutiny. Separating out responsibility for objectives against performance of those objectives makes for a more satisfactory balance of constitutional accountability than Next Steps appears to have produced. We shall have to wait for the emergence of any policy-implementation tensions and see how they are resolved. The suspicion remains, however, that the Next Steps line cannot hold as presently constituted.

Monitoring the Agency's Performance

The Agency's performance against the annual targets it has been set is monitored through performance returns submitted quarterly by the chief executive on a basis approved by the Secretary of State. However, Mike Fogden explained to the TCSC Sub-Committee that there were frequent and regular contacts both with ministers and with a few civil servants in the Department whose job it is to advise the Secretary of State on their activities and to observe those activities. (TCSC, 1991) Agency status is clearly intended to improve management in the Employment Service resulting in better value for money for taxpayers and customers. Of course resources are allocated by the Secretary of State in the context of overall Public Expenditure Survey and Estimates procedures. Given the centrality of the ESA to the Employment Department Group the chief executive is a member of the ministerial PES team, though he has no direct involvement with the Treasury on these matters. There are, however, other areas of financial activity where there are direct negotiations with the Treasury: such matters as capital bids for new buildings and computer systems.

A combination of the framework document, operational plan, performance indicators/targets and quarterly monitoring by the department represents a quiver of weapons to ensure the accountability of the chief executive and the agency to Parliament via the Secretary of State. That these processes are, in the British tradition, largely closed is no indictment of the agency development as such; indeed it can be argued with some cogency that the Next Steps programme has opened up much to the public that was previously submerged. This is not the place to rehearse the arguments for freedom of information or indeed other constitutional reform. They can perhaps be taken as read. What may be argued is that, within the confines of the British tradition, the procedures for monitoring and for value for money for the examination of inputs and outputs are, as far as the ESA is concerned, highly developed and appear managerially highly efficient.

Fogden has gone on record in his evidence to the Treasury Committee (TCSC, 1991) as saying that he feels he enjoys a strong degree of managerial autonomy while being accountable not only in the ways described but also in terms of the select committee system, not least the PAC through the NAO. This combination of methods of account and monitoring should be concerned to allow efficient management to emerge while ensuring some form of ministerial responsibility of policies adopted.

Whether, in addition, it provides the opportunity to endorse and expand on the agreed delegations and discretions within which the chief executive may, without further agreement, be able to change the balance between programmes or vary the scale of activities in any particular year is difficult to observe. Before addressing the question of monitoring by and accountability to the general public in the form of clients/customers a word might be added about the ESA's relations with the Benefits Agency and the DSS.

First, the Chief Executive of the ESA monitors adjudication on claims to benefit to the extent agreed between the Chief Adjudication Officer and the Secretary of State for Employment for the purposes of the Chief Adjudication Officer's Annual Report. (Agreement between the Secretary of State for Social Security and the Secretary of State for Employment on the Administration of Benefits for Unemployment, Annex 1, Framework Document) Secondly the ESA works alongside the Benefits Agency and has set up formal arrangements with the chief executive of the BA. Liaison includes exchange of information and advice on instructions, publicity and policy implementation as well as provision of procedural, policy or legal clarification and liaison between personnel involved in tackling social security fraud and abuse. Most of these arrangements are laid down in Annex 1 to the ESA's Framework Document. Similar arrangements exist with the ITSA, the DSS computer arm.

Relations with the Public

Learning from the public may also constitute a form of monitoring and the ESA has been an early leader in this field. Unlike a number of other agencies it does not have a steering committee or management board with outside representatives. Nevertheless, it runs customer satisfaction surveys, or rather it contracts the surveys out. So far they have run large national surveys of up to 1500 'clients' in a number of different locations around the country. Now they have taken to conducting surveys at the local office level as well which, among other things, might allow comparisons between areas to be made. The intention is to run the surveys at quarterly intervals, but financial restraints may not render this possible. The most recent national survey indicated that 88 per cent of their clients were satisfied with the standard of service offered and 72 per cent with the usefulness of advice received. Some interesting findings have emerged, such as the importance claimants place on privacy, not least among the disabled.

There is no doubt that customer satisfaction surveys can be highly valuable, especially where they are made public as is the case with the ESA. One way or another customer satisfaction is likely to be the constitutional flavour of the nineties, as witness the Citizen's Charter. The ESA has produced a Jobseeker's Charter which makes a series of promises to its public; a litany so to speak of what lawyers call 'legitimate expectations'. The monitoring of the several charters by Government had not been decided upon at the time of writing but the effectiveness of the whole enterprise will depend crucially on effective monitoring machinery. This applies of course to all the agencies.

Be that as it may, and aside from the customer satisfaction surveys, the ESA displays a leaflet in each office at the reception desk entitled 'Help us to get it right' which, in effect, asks 'clients' for their ideas on how to improve the service. The leaflet also tells clients how to make a complaint. The Service insists that 'Whenever anything goes wrong we will put it right, apologise and explain what happened'. The leaflet is in fact a model of its kind. It suggests at the first stage that a complainant speaks to the person who originally dealt with them. This is made easier these days by the fact that the desk staff now wear name badges. If the client is still not satisfied then they are advised to approach the supervisor or manager. The procedure for making written complaints is comprehensive and straightforward. The leaflet contains a detachable form on which the complaint can be written accompanied by an envelope addressed to the Employment Service Local Office Manager. In May 1992 the number of complaints received on this form was 761, of which 393 concerned the level of benefit payment and 123 were concerned with the standard of service. The totals are broken down into regions and analysed for the purposes of quality control. A reply will normally be received within a week and further information explains the availability of the chief executive, MP and Parliamentary Commissioner, who is also described as 'the ombudsman'. Admirable though the complaints literature is, I should personally be much happier if the requirement to provide forms of grievance redress was a statutory requirement, as has long been the case in the field of employment law.

The Service also runs internal staff surveys to find out what the staff think about the organisation and what might be improved. Between them, these feelers put out to several different publics have produced valuable information, not least in identifying shortcomings in ESA practice. As good an example as any is the identification of dissatisfaction at the speed with which job vacancy boards are cleared when the vacancies have in fact been filled. The Service is also concerned to let their clients know the practical effect of their services so that each office now displays its own targets, and the results it achieves. The Service is also investigating ways of supporting leaflets and posters in local offices with audio-visual information and is engaged in monitoring both local and national client suggestions and complaints to identify problems which need to be addressed to improve customer service.

There has been some criticism of customer satisfaction approaches to the provision of public services. This is seen as the replacement of politics by quasi-contract. I believe this view is mistaken and that customer care and customer satisfaction approaches are here to stay and quite rightly so. Yet a political balance has to be struck. Our failed political system, as I believe it to be, needs to be reformed and buttressed to operate alongside the kind of initiatives which bodies such as the ESA are concerned to foster. The select committee system does obviously play a very valuable role in highlighting matters of public interest even if the committees, the TCSC apart, have shown relatively little interest in the Next Steps developments. Of course the committees have not always been given the information they required and, in any event, they ordinarily operate after the event.

If we remind ourselves that Parliament as such has had precious little to say about the whole Next Steps initiative, the restrictions under which select committees operate become more important. Simply as a matter of fact, at the time of writing Mike Fogden has appeared twice before the TCSC and annually before the Employment Committee. He is known to regard the TCSC as more positive and constructive in its approach to the problems faced by agency chief executives. Needless to say, he will appear before the PAC on the back of a report from the NAO. Sometimes he will go with his Permanent Secretary, more often he will not. My own reading of select committee reports supports the view expressed by Mr Fogden informally. There is no doubt that the Employment Committee has given the ESA a very severe grilling from time to time. It would be no exaggeration to say that much of the cross-examination to which senior officials were subjected appears bad-tempered and a little spiteful. As well as party political points being scored, a great deal of the questioning appears to be pedantic and self-serving. (Employment Committee, 1993) The TCSC is undoubtedly more helpful and it is to be hoped that in future departmental select committees will see their role as to be constructively critical as well as seeking to hold agencies accountable to Parliament.

Complaints, Ombudsmen and Parliamentary Questions

I shall treat complaints, queries, questions and observations concerning the work of the ESA in a single section since they are all so closely bound up together. The general concern about the division of responsibilities for answering questions between the minister and the chief executive has been expressed elsewhere (see Chapter 7) and there is therefore little point in repeating it here. Suffice it to say that there has as yet been no obvious instance of responsibility for a mixed policy/implementation issue falling through a hole in the middle of the principal actors as far as the ESA is concerned.

For the record the volume of PQs received since the ESA was established is as follows:

Table 11.1
Department of Employment Parliamentary Questions
since the establishment of the Employment Service Agency

Financial year	1990–91	1991–92	Apr–June 1992
Chief Executive reply	90	107	16
Ministerial reply	40	32	–
Total	130	139	16

The 1992 figures cover too short a period to be of any assistance and at the time of writing Parliament was in recess. However, there does seem to be an emergent pattern of most questions falling into the operational rather than the policy arena.

The chief executive (CE) collects and monitors performance information in the form of complaints, comments, questions etc received on a monthly basis. They are divided into chief executive cases, private office (PO) cases, treat official (TO) and PQs. Private Office cases are those where MPs write to the Minister, perhaps seeking policy information. Here the reply is drafted by the agency but the minister handles it. 'Treat official' cases are where members of the public write to the Minister. These come back to the CE who replies on the minister's behalf. Direct complaints to the ESA from members of the public are, as we see, classified as CE cases. During August 1992, to take the latest figures available at the time of writing, the secretariat received and allocated 82 CE cases, 12 PO cases and 340 TOs. Out of the 82 CE cases, 28 were sent directly to the CE. Five new Parliamentary Commissioner cases were received and allocated. The main subjects of the correspondence were entitlement to unemployment benefit, adjudication, jobclubs and travel to interview scheme. Incidentally, such adverse findings as there have been of the Service by the PCA have been accepted with good grace and attendant apologies.

Ministerial acknowledgement letters (POs) are drafted by the secretariat and signed by ministers' private secretaries explaining that as the case is for the ES it has been passed to the CE for reply. The secretariat is required to send the draft letter to private office within 48 hours of the case being received. In August 1992, again the last date for which figures are presently available, the deadline was met in all cases. Ministers have set the ES a target for replying to 95% of all CE cases within three weeks of their receipt in the Secretariat. In August 1992, 10 deadlines were extended.

The procedures seem to have bedded down reasonably well at this time and replies of varying sorts are becoming speedier. It is also clearly apparent from discussions within the ESA that more and more MPs are writing directly to the chief executive.

As to ombudsman cases it is normally the permanent secretary who replies but under the agency concept the present PCA will write to the permanent secretary with a copy to the chief executive. The chief executive will reply with a copy to the Permanent Secretary where it is a matter clearly within his remit. Where an issue is part policy and part operational then either there will be a joint reply or two separate replies. Sometimes the issue is complicated by the contemporaneous involvement of the Benefits Agency.

It appears clear that at the present time complaints and suggestions from the general public are being taken seriously within the Employment Service Agency. Given that close monitoring of correspondence occurs it also seems likely that complaints are being successfully used as a form of quality control. This should feed into the quality of service being provided.

There is little distinctive to say about the role of the Parliamentary Commissioner for Administration as far as the ESA is concerned. A detailed treatment of the PCA's role in relation to agencies is given in Chapter 8 but here a jurisprudential point might be made. It is this. Both the appearance of framework documents and the advent of the Citizen's Charter extend the potential for the office of the PCA. This is because they either make promises about performance levels or raise expectations about standards of service to be met. With a little imagination the PCA should at a stroke thereby be able to extend the concept of maladministration accordingly. (PCA Select Committee, 1992) We shall have to wait and see. Furthermore, the responsibility for policing the *Open Government* guidelines under the terms of the 1993 White Paper (Cm 2290) poses an interesting challenge to the Office. For all the evident weaknesses of the proposed arrangements, there can be no doubt that the role of the PCA will be greatly extended. For my part, however, I remain convinced that the fact that we have a distinctly *Parliamentary* Commissioner is a great disadvantage. A true 'Citizen's Defender' not tied to Parliament would almost certainly be infinitely more effective in vindicating citizen complaints.

The Employment Service Agency and Policy

Next Steps has been trumpeted in many quarters as signalling the hiving off of the policy-making process from the administrative/ implementation/management side. As was discussed in the earlier chapters of this book, that sharp divide was never theoretically or practically sustainable and the ESA is as good an example as can be found of the fact that Next Steps has begun the process of identifying new policy communities within Government. In many instances the agencies and their client groups, more or less formalised, are part and parcel of those policy communities.

The framework document of the ESA is worth quoting in full on the issue of the relationship between the management of an agency and its policy priorities:

> The Chief Executive is a member of the appropriate senior Employment Department Group Committees and in that capacity participates in discussions about overall Employment Department Group policy. The Chief Executive may also make proposals to the Secretary of State for changes in the policies and programmes operated by the Agency which are designed to improve the effectiveness with which the Agency meets its overall objectives. In doing this the Chief Executive consults with the Permanent Secretary or with Employment Department head office officials, to ensure that any proposals submitted to the Secretary of State are consistent with the overall policy objectives of the Employment Department Group.

The Chief Executive is consulted before any policies affecting the Agency are put to the Secretary of State.

Mr Fogden has gone on record as saying that because of the nature of the business they are in, which is about labour markets, and their volatility and their variations, ESA obviously makes very important input into policy thinking, which does 'set us a little aside from the pure philosophy of Next Steps'. (TCSC, 1991) How set apart from other agencies is open to doubt, but it is clear that the chief executive of the Employment Service Agency is very much a policy insider. Not only does the agency influence policy but the department actively seeks information from it to enable policy formulation to proceed. The DE senior management group meets fortnightly and consists of half a dozen or so key players, of whom Mr Fogden is one. It also seems clear that his role is by no means restricted to being reactive since, for instance, he has been actively considering ways of preventing the growth of long-term unemployment. This is evident both from TCSC Reports and from observations within the ESA and the Department of Employment itself.

We have seen that the ESA does not have a Steering Group as such and seeks information and opinion in other ways. As might be expected, the chief executive and other senior officers hold a considerable number of *ad hoc* meetings with interested parties, not least with Full Employment UK. However, the most structured and regular arrangements are with the Citizen's Advice Bureau movement. It is clear that the ESA seeks the views of others in a genuine and structured fashion, quite apart from the customer surveys which are now a regular feature of its operation. Whether it is satisfactory for consultation to take place as a matter of administrative discretion rather than law is another matter. This is, however, an issue which should be directed at all the agencies and not just the ESA. The USA practice is more formal and ultimately enforceable through the courts. The UK has always shied away from such constraints; but in the age of consumer sovereignty it might well be opportune to reconsider the position.

Conclusions

It is difficult to draw lessons about either devolved government or improved managerial standards in government from a cursory examination of one agency, however important. Agencies differ in type as well as style; some are essentially regulatory, some concerned with relatively commercial-style delivery of services, others with the delivery of services which are accompanied by social responsibilities. It is easier to manage some services than others. It is easier to be restricted to commercial considerations in delivering some services than others. The Employment Service Agency is in the position of having a strong social responsibility mission combined with the need to deliver services efficiently and to account for a vast tranche of public expenditure.

On the whole the ESA's record, in all the circumstances, is good. Much of this credit must go to the chief executive, whose qualities are widely admired. However, at the end of the day, the Next Steps revolution has to come to terms with the relationships between inputs, outputs and outcomes. Up to now the concentration has largely been on inputs/outputs. What outputs do we get for what inputs? The Treasury is naturally the driving force in these matters and if reduced inputs can produce stable, or preferably improved, outputs then they are going to be delighted. And, after all, each of us must wish for value for money. But targets have to be chosen and there is, within the British system, an inadequate debate about desirable outcomes for public services. Targets have been too frequently concerned with outputs and too little concerned with qualitative targets. But then we have precious little in the way of machinery for debating the kinds of public services we want and the goals that they should be expected to deliver. Secrecy being the cement of the constitution, we can only assume that social cost benefit analysis does not take place. Market research is certainly a step forward and the ESA should be complimented on the steps it has taken in this regard. However, much more needs to be done which is not within the gift of any of the agencies. Again, leaving freedom of information aside (though why we should is a trifle baffling in a democratic society), one clear improvement would be the establishment of an Employment Advisory Committee along the lines of a beefed-up version of the Social Security Advisory Committee. This is not to advocate a parliamentary committee but one representing all shades of opinion with expert advice available to it, a research capacity and a *modus operandi* that was essentially public. It would need to have available to it all papers circulating within the Employment Department itself. Anything less is bound to be unsatisfactory.

Next Steps has been a limited success on the evidence presently available. It is interesting, however, that the emphasis has been on management rather than policy formulation. This is particularly important given the catalogue of policy failures which have characterised the intermediate past. We have not moved forward, for instance, in terms of fixing responsibility for failures on individuals in the way New Zealand has attempted since 1989. This is an enormous gap but one which, in all fairness, the Next Steps exercise made few claims about.

It is worth repeating that after Next Steps much information is available that previously was not. The author personally knows more about Employment Services than he did before 1989 but every slight lifting of the veil indicates the titillating concealment of whatever else the veil conceals. Next Steps has clearly undermined much of what limited credibility attached to parliamentary accountability without putting in its place a regime of administrative law. The fabric of the emperor's clothes was perhaps best revealed by the Home Affairs Select Committee (Home Affairs Committee, 1991) when it disclosed that it had been prevented from seeing the draft framework documents by the Home Office. The explanation given was that 'the internal relationships within a department are not exposed to parliamentary scrutiny'! (para. 8). Precisely, and there is no point in pretending that it has ever been otherwise in our lifetimes. Because the Committee was somewhat baffled about lines of responsibility under the new arrangements it was moved to ask for 'a short simple leaflet' available to MPs and the public, which explains where responsibility lies and to suggest the correct course of action to be taken (para. 26). The naiveté of the suggestion is almost charming.

My peroration is a quotation, which I believe summarises many of the dilemmas of delivering on public services:

> ... the problem for the users of public services may be that changes in structure or rules of behaviour by public servants may have unintended adverse consequences. The pursuit of profit might accidentally extinguish a right to equitable treatment. The pursuit of efficiency might so impoverish the workforce that service standards deteriorate. 'Freedom of choice' for one set of consumers may eliminate the rights of others to choose. The value dilemmas can cause managerial paralysis at a time of change. In some cases the paralysis might be beneficial. The real trick is for public sector managers to preserve public values while producing efficient and effective services. (Common et al, 1992, 137)

The Employment Service Agency has, in my judgement, performed extremely well in difficult circumstances, not least in the way it has sought out public views and opinions and sought to make itself answerable to its clients. My judgement, of course, is based on partial information. Only a constitutional reformation can alter that.

References

Common et al, 1992:
Richard Common, Norman Flynn and Elisabeth Mellon, *Managing Public Services: Competition and Decentralisation*, Butterworth Heinemann, 1992.

Department of Employment, 1990:
Employment Service Agency: Framework Document, March 1990.

Employment Committee, 1993:
The Work of the Employment Service, Report from the Employment Committee, HC 598, 1992-93, July 1993.

Home Affairs Committee, 1991:
Third Report from the Home Affairs Committee, *Next Steps Agencies*, HC 177, 1990-91, March 1991.

PCA Select Committee, 1992:
Second Report from the Select Committee on the Parliamentary Commissioner for Administration, HC 158, 1991-92, *The Implications of the Citizen's Charter for the Work of the PCA*, February 1992.

TCSC, 1991:
Seventh Report from the Treasury and Civil Service Committee, *The Next Steps Initiative*, HC 496, 1990-91, July 1991.

PART IV
Review and Conclusions

12

Next Steps to Where?

Philip Giddings

The Next Steps programme has changed the face of British central government. From Mrs Thatcher's announcement in February 1988 to the publication of the *Continuity and Change* White Paper in July 1994, 97 agencies were set up. Together with the 31 executive units of Customs and Excise and the 33 executive offices of the Inland Revenue, both of which operate on Next Steps lines, more than 340,000 (64 per cent) of civil servants were working in an agency of one kind or another by July 1994. (Cm 2627, 1994) In 1993 16 new agencies were launched, including the Prison Service (the third largest) and the Child Support Agency, set up under the Child Support Act 1991—the first unit to be set up from the outset as an agency. (OPSS, 1993,6)

By the end of 1993 the Government had identified the main areas of civil service activity which were potential candidates for agency status in the hope that most of those that were to become agencies could be launched by mid-1995. Agencies and announced candidates for agency status included the Court Service, MoD Police and the RAF Training Group and 35 other activities (21 in the Ministry of Defence), covering a further 67,000 civil servants (and 43,000 other staff, mostly military personnel). The total programme thus amounted to 78 per cent of the total civil service. Or, to look at it the other way round, only about a fifth of the civil service lay outside the agency programme, which the Government itself has described as a transformation, one which has 'fundamentally altered the way in which the Civil Service is managed'. (OPSS, 1993, 10 and 16; Cm 2627, 1994, 13)

In this study we have examined how Parliament has responded to this transformation of Britain's central administrative structure. The speed and scale of the programme, as we noted in the first chapter, prompts the question whether it really has been a fundamental change or is little more than organisational cosmetics. At the heart of that question is the delegation of managerial responsibility which is fundamental to agency status and the corresponding ambiguity which it has brought to ministerial responsibility and accountability. As we saw in Part I, it prompts a series of further questions: can delegation of so-called 'operational matters' to a chief executive be genuine if—as the Government has repeatedly insisted and reiterated twice in its July 1994 White Paper, describing it as a 'key constitutional principle' (Cm 2627, 1994, 2 and 16)—the minister's responsibility for *all* the work of the department, including agencies, remains unchanged? Is the distinction between 'operational matters' and 'policy objectives and resources' robust and viable? If there really has been significant delegation of responsibility from ministers to chief executives, then the transformation wrought by the Next Steps initiative has brought fundamental change. But if total ministerial accountability remains unchanged, then the initiative looks more like window-dressing, which critics of the Conservative Government might see as the presentational preparation for significant reductions in state functions through contractorisation and privatisation.

In this respect parliamentary accountability is important not only its own right but as an indicator of the extent of the change which has occurred. In her statement in February 1988 the Prime Minister said that MPs would be encouraged to raise operational matters with chief executives rather than directly with ministers, since ministers would themselves refer such matters on to chief executives. In this study we have seen that agency chief executives are answering MPs' questions (Chapter 7) and responding to departmental select committees (Chapters 4 and 5), the Public Accounts Committee (Chapter 6) and the Parliamentary Ombudsman (Chapter 8). That suggests that delegation of managerial responsibility has been accompanied by a substantial delegation of accountability as well.

In assessing how Parliament has responded to these developments, we have first to discuss the theory and practice of parliamentary accountability. It was clear from the beginning of the Next Steps initiative that its implications for Parliament would be a major concern. Although the proposals of the Ibbs Report were based on a critique of the inhibiting managerial consequences of the constitutional doctrine of ministerial responsibility, Prime Minister Margaret Thatcher firmly re-asserted that doctrine's fundamental status when she made her statement to the House of Commons accepting the Report's proposals in February 1988. That line has been doggedly maintained by successive ministers and senior officials since then and is given a prominent position in the July 1994 White Paper:

The key constitutional principle ... [is] that it is Ministers who are accountable to Parliament for all that their departments (including agencies) do'. (Cm 2627, 2 and 16)

Yet, as we have seen in the earlier chapters, the central feature of Next Steps—delegation of managerial authority from ministers to chief executives—seems to many to be in conflict or tension with ministerial responsibility, especially when it is expressed in this traditional form. It is helpful to an assessment of Parliament's response to Next Steps to analyse that tension more closely.

Civil Service Management and Ministerial Accountability

The central question is: can a 'fundamental alteration' in the way the civil service is managed take place without any change to ministerial accountability? That central question raises inter-related issues which lay bare the important implications of Next Steps for our understanding of public and parliamentary accountability.

The first issue is the relationship between *accountability* and *responsibility*: must the two go together or can they be separated? Can responsibility for decision-making be delegated while accountability for decisions taken is retained? There is a tension here between two lines of argument. On the one hand, it may be argued that if delegation of managerial authority is to be genuine, accountability must go with it, otherwise authority is not *fully* delegated. On the other hand, it may be argued that, providing the scope and limits of delegation are made clear, *final* authority can (and should) be retained by the delegator, otherwise the authority is transferred rather than delegated. Clearly, the crux of the matter lies in the ability accurately to delimit the scope of the authority to be delegated and the clarity and robustness of the limits so determined. The second issue concerns the relationship between ministers and civil servants, particularly chief executives. If ministers are responsible for all that their departments do, who is accountable when part of that responsibility is delegated? This is not a new question. It already arises when, for example, junior ministers are given specific remits within a particular department and when senior civil servants issue statutory instruments or administrative guidance (such as DFE circulars) on behalf of their secretary of state.

It is a commonplace to assert that final responsibility lies with the secretary of state. But when a decision by a junior minister or senior official is challenged, and the secretary of state declines to substitute for it a 'final' decision of his own, who is accountable: the junior minister or senior official who made the 'original' decision or the secretary of state who has not (explicitly) endorsed or overruled it? To endorse (*a fortiori* to overrule) an 'original' decision creates an 'appellate' role for the secretary of state which could defeat the purpose of the delegation of responsibility if it were to lead to all, or most, or even many, decisions being challenged in this way.

On the other hand, if the secretary of state repeatedly denies himself the opportunity to review, endorse or overrule the decisions of the 'original' decision-maker and so effectively plays no part at all in the making of such decisions, has he (the secretary of state) not ceased to be even the 'final' decision-maker? And if he plays no part in the making of the decision, how can he be held accountable for it?

If the secretary of state is not the final decision-maker, should Parliament 'hold to account' whoever is—i.e. the junior minister or, more controversially, senior official, to whom the responsibility for making the decisions has been delegated? The 1994 White Paper points out that 'there is a growing range of circumstances in which civil servants are called to give a direct account of their work'. (Cm 2627, 16) The experience of departmental select committees has shown that this works reasonably well when 'an account of their work' means nothing more than an exposition of what that work is. As *Continuity and Change* says, 'it is part of a civil servant's constitutional role to explain *policy* but it is ministers who must be accountable for it and defend it'. (Cm 2627, para. 2:29, emphasis added) But when does officials giving an 'account of their work' or 'explaining policy' become officials defending or justifying what has (or has not) been done? The answer depends upon how one interprets the notoriously elusive term 'policy'. The formal convention, which is designed to protect the political and partisan neutrality of the civil service, is that civil servants give evidence to parliamentary committees, not on their own account, but *on behalf of ministers*. Who, then, is 'accountable'? The answer is hardly clear.

The third issue is the relationship between parliamentary and other forms of public accountability. Again to quote *Continuity and Change*:

The Financial Management Initiative, Next Steps and the Citizen's Charter have all promoted greater transparency about what the Civil

Service does, what is to be achieved, and who is responsible for achieving it ... The effect has been to strengthen accountability to both Parliament and public, building on the existing framework of ministerial accountability and the particular responsibilities of Accounting Officers. Clarity is an essential part of Parliament's ability to hold the executive to account. (Cm 2627, 15)

Senior civil servants have acquired a more visible public profile over the last thirty years, largely as a result of the reforms which followed the Fulton Report, the evolution of the select committee system and the televising of committee hearings. The public role now taken by chief executives seems to be a natural extension of this, particularly in regard to the work of select committees. This was demonstrated in the decision to designate chief executives as agency accounting officers. (See Chapter 6) As senior civil servants generally, and chief executives in particular, appear before parliamentary committees and, perhaps more significantly, press conferences and other media events to give an account of their work, the role of ministers in providing a channel of accountability to the public is reduced—as the Ibbs report originally intended. This underlines the fact that there are other channels of public accountability for the work of agencies in addition to direct ministerial answerability to Parliament.

The fourth issue is Parliament's interest in the management of the civil service. In principle, given traditional understandings of parliamentary sovereignty, no aspect of government is immune from parliamentary investigation and involvement. In practice, the tension between Crown and parliamentary prerogatives which lies at the heart of the British constitution has normally been resolved in favour of the former in the field of governmental organisation.

It is not that parliamentarians have lacked interest in the workings of Whitehall or failed to realise the importance of efficiency and effectiveness in public administration. Rather, they have combined their instinctive preference for discussing broad policy issues with a recognition of the desirability of keeping large representative, legislative bodies out of matters of administrative detail. Generally speaking, therefore, governments—in effect prime ministers and their senior civil service advisers—have been allowed a virtually free hand in the way Whitehall has been organised and managed.

This relative freedom from parliamentary oversight has been most evident in governments' preference for, and MPs' acceptance of, non-legislative methods of reform or reorganisation in Whitehall. For example, the implementation of those parts of the Fulton Report accepted by Harold Wilson's government in 1968 was carried through by administrative means, not through legislation. Similarly with the Next Steps initiative: the possibility of proceeding by legislation was considered and rejected, though as the programme developed certain detailed aspects (e.g. trading funds rules) were found to need legislative action. The Next Steps initiative has been carried through without a full parliamentary debate and, indeed, without explicit parliamentary approval even though it was, in the government's own words, a fundamental alteration to the way the civil service is managed.

Part of the explanation for this lies in the relative absence of partisan controversy in this area. We have noted earlier (Chapter 4) that the TCSC was used a vehicle to cultivate bipartisan support of the Next Steps programme and that those Labour MPs who were, or became, particularly interested in this area were strong supporters of the agency concept (in spite of anxieties about privatisation), even if critical on matters of detail. In an adversarial culture, with an overloaded parliamentary timetable, matters upon which there is no inter-party controversy do not feature strongly in most MPs' priorities, especially not front-benchers' priorities.

In consequence parliamentary consideration of Next Steps has been at best fragmentary and episodic, as our study has clearly shown. In particular, there has been—at least until the 1993 TCSC enquiry—no general consideration of the implications of Next Steps and other associated government initiatives for the overall shape of the civil service and the role Parliament should play in deciding that. The implications of the Next Steps for a unified civil service was one of the recurring themes in the TCSC Sub-Committee's hearings up until the 1992 general election but that hardly amounts to a general parliamentary discussion of what is a very important issue for the way in which the country is governed. To its credit the TCSC has included this as one of the issues to be covered in its general enquiry into the civil service (TCSC, 1993), though whether this will lead to a general parliamentary discussion is not clear at the time of writing. It has to some extent been overtaken by publication of *Continuity and Change*, although parts of that document are explicitly of a consultative nature and the Government has said that it wishes to take account of the outcome of the TCSC's own enquiry. (Cm 2627, 1994)

The fifth and final issue is the effectiveness of parliamentary scrutiny. Even though parliamentary consideration of the Next Steps has been episodic, it is evident from this study that the development of the Next Steps programme and the work of some of the agencies have been subject to a good deal of parliamentary scrutiny. How this has taken place and how effective it has been has formed the main part of our research. Although subject to much criticism, parliamentary procedures provide many opportunities for enquiry about the activities of government departments, including agencies, and later in this chapter we shall review how effectively those procedures have been used and what more might be done now that agencies are the chosen format for the delivery of most of the public services provided by central government. But first, we must address a crucial underlying question: what is accountability for?

The Purpose of Accountability

In a system of representative government the accountability of those who govern to those who are governed is axiomatic: together with free elections such accountability provides the democratic basis for parliamentary government. Its purpose in the democratic schema is two-fold. First, it provides the means for democratic political control, for ensuring that the persons, policies and programmes sanctioned by the electorate are the persons who become ministers and the policies and programmes which they carry out—and *vice versa*. It is essential for the dynamic of democracy that the elected government, and those who act on its behalf, give to the electorate an account of what they have (and have not) done as well as of what they will (or will not) do. That enables the electorate to make, through its choice of those who are to govern, its choice of the policies and programmes which are to be carried through in its (the electorate's) name. Such is the theory. Accountability is vital to the mechanism of democratic control by which the electorate is able (in theory) to determine the principles and priorities of public policy. Democracy is about more than choosing who governs; it is also about choosing how those who are chosen to govern will govern. And that requires accountability. (Holden, 1988, 52 and 102)

The second purpose served by accountability is concerned not so much with democratic political control as with the public's interest in the efficiency and effectiveness of government. Whatever public services it is decided should be provided, those services should be delivered with the maximum of efficiency and effectiveness. Accountability is an essential means of determining both whether this is so and of encouraging it to be so. The notion of 'stewardship' is often called in aid here. The steward renders an account to enable his principal to assess how effectively he has discharged his responsibilities on his behalf. The requirement to render an account (and the implicit threat of sanctions if the account rendered is deemed unsatisfactory) is held to be a strong inducement to satisfactory performance by the steward. This general inducement may be supplemented by rewards and penalties attached to different levels of performance. Such incentives can only be effective if the required levels of performance can be clearly demonstrated to have been achieved—hence the need for the rendering of an account.

The principle behind this is easy to apply when the steward has to satisfy one master. It is considerably more difficult when a team of stewards (the government) have to satisfy a large and disparate collective master (the electorate) through a divided group of intermediaries (Parliament), whose requirements are manifold, changing and sometimes mutually contradictory! Nevertheless, accountability is clearly a necessary means to the realisation of the public's interest in the efficiency and effectiveness of the government for which it pays and by which the services it requires are provided.

The importance of laying bare these two underlying purposes of accountability is to draw attention to the possibility that they may conflict—and to the fact that some people wish to separate them from each other because they believe that they do conflict. Democratic political control must entail the possibility of changes in policies, including methods of administration, solely on grounds of public choice, even if this means higher costs or reduced efficiency. Keeping open the option of such changes may also entail costs and reduced efficiency and/or effectiveness. Representative democracy requires that parliamentary majorities, governments, ministers may change. Such changes may reduce rather than increase the efficiency and effectiveness of public administration. This is said to justify insulating as much as possible of 'administration' from the consequences of such 'political' changes, an argument which sees the 'de-politicising' of the administrative machinery of government as a contribution to the efficiency and effectiveness which the public interest requires.

A similar line of argument emerges from another example of the 'cost of democracy'—the consequences of public accountability mechanisms themselves. Parliamentary and public answerability needs to be serviced. In particular, it requires extensive and detailed record-keeping so that the whys and wherefores of what was or was not done can be explained if required. It may also require priority to be given to the immediate and the political to the neglect of the longer-term and the essential. These by-products of accountability are well-known, as is the response of minimising accountability (e.g. restricting it to principle rather than detail and limiting the availability of official information) in order to avoid them.

Thinking of this kind was evident in the annex to the Ibbs Report and robustly repudiated by the TCSC, as we have seen. (Chapters 2 and 3 above.) But it has a much longer, and arguably more distinguished, history. It can be clearly seen in the debates about the arrangements to be made for nationalised industries which took place in the Labour Party in the 1930s and more widely in Parliament in the 1940s and 1950s, debates about the tension between the twin needs of commercial efficiency and public accountability. The organisational device of the public corporation was developed as a way of reconciling those twin needs. The judgement of the 1970s and 1980s was that it was not a very successful device. The conclusion drawn was that one need (commercial efficiency) could best be achieved in the private sector where, so the argument ran, competition or regulation could more effectively realise the objectives of accountability. Such was (in part) the rationale of the privatisation programme.

Executive agencies, however, remain within the public sector, part of government departments and thus within the ambit of ministerial responsibility. They are, nevertheless, subject to the same tension between the requirements of democratic political control (the accountability of ministers) and the public interest in efficient and effective public services (the managerial responsibility of chief executives). The agency concept seeks to resolve this tension by circumscribing particular activities—administrative or managerial activities—from direct ministerial involvement and delegating authority for them to named officials (chief executives). However, the tension remains, and is to a degree intensified, by the continuing insistence that, whilst authority has been delegated to chief executives, ministers 'remain accountable'.

So we return to the central dilemma which the Next Steps initiative poses for Parliament—a Parliament which is interested both in democratic political control and in efficiency and effectiveness in delivery of public services: does managerial delegation entail reduced ministerial accountability and fundamental changes to the arrangements for parliamentary scrutiny? Or can those scrutiny arrangements, like the key constitutional principle of ministerial responsibility so frequently re-affirmed by the Government since 1988, remain unaffected?

In his discussion of ministerial responsibility in Chapter 2 Pyper has shown how the Ibbs report and the Next Steps initiative have oscillated between a form of constitutional radicalism, which would lead to a rethinking of the doctrine of ministerial responsibility, and a desire to placate constitutional traditionalists. Pyper's analysis of responsibility and accountability underlines the importance of sanctions in relation to the latter and points out that in practice these lie with the prime minister and the government's parliamentary party rather than with Parliament as such. With the creation of agencies, Pyper shows, the issue is how to clarify responsibility and accountability for management. The Ibbs report intended that the confusion and ambiguity it observed in this area should be resolved: in a well-managed department ministerial involvement should normally only be necessary by exception. (Efficiency Unit, 1988, 16) But does the reduction in the role of the minister leave a gap in accountability?

Winetrobe argues, following Day and Klein, that there is more to accountability than creating and enforcing linkages between agencies, ministers and Parliament. He suggests that Parliament is both trying to integrate the new agency system into its existing mechanisms and feeling its way towards evolving a radically different method of scrutiny of the Executive, though it is not yet clear what form this might take.

The Process of Scrutiny

Certainly the picture emerging from our studies of the process of scrutiny in Part II is one of adaptation of existing parliamentary processes to the new governmental forms. This is illustrated by the debate about parliamentary questions. As Evans shows in Chapter 7, this has focused largely on the issue of accessibility (of questions and answers) rather than the substance of accountability but from this there is emerging a form of direct accountability of agencies to Parliament which by-passes traditional notions of accountability through ministers. The settling of the dispute about the publication of chief executives' replies to MPs' questions by their publication in Hansard has maintained the appearance that these arrangements are little more than an extension of the arrangements for other questions to ministers. While this leaves the issue of the distinction between 'policy' and 'operational matters' as unresolved as it was in regard to the nationalised industries, the new arrangements do in fact bring the responsible officials (chief executives) much closer to Parliament. Thus, although the continuation of the parliamentary questions system may have appeared to conflict with the rationale of the Next Steps initiative because it is based on the traditional notion of comprehensive ministerial responsibility, it may—almost accidentally, as Evans puts it—be bringing about a form of direct accountability to Parliament of officials, by-passing ministers, an outcome which would be very much in tune with the philosophy of the Ibbs Report.

The incorporation of agencies within existing arrangements for accountability is clearest with regard to the jurisdiction of the Parliamentary Ombudsman. Here, as Chapter 8 shows, there has been no change to the operational arrangements for dealing with complaints of maladministration referred to the Ombudsman by Members of Parliament; indeed, agency cases figure very prominently in the Ombudsman's work and that of his associated select committee. Whilst this corresponds with assurances given by the then Prime Minister in her initial statement on the Ibbs Report, it has less to do with the philosophy of Ibbs than with the way in which the Parliamentary Ombudsman's governing statute is drafted: the inclusion of the key phrase 'any action taken by *or on behalf of* a government department' (emphasis added) in section 5 of the 1967 Parliamentary Commissioner Act secured the Ombudsman's jurisdiction (and therefore the select committee's remit) with regard to 'arms-length' public bodies, whatever the nature of their relationship with the government department; indeed it covers organisations in a contractual relationship with departments as well. While this may have been fortuitous, the continuing operation of the Ombudsman's jurisdiction has shown that agencies, through their chief executives, are accountable to Parliament, both in the form of the Ombudsman (an officer of Parliament) and of the Select Committee, just as all other parts of government departments are. And this is accountability for (mal)administration, which relates predominantly to day-to-day operations. Hence the chief executive in his dealings with the Ombudsman and the Select Committee in relation to his agency is acting in a capacity equivalent to a permanent secretary in relation to a department and may, as we have seen from the illustrative cases cited in Chapter 8, act in conjunction with the permanent secretary when agreeing a resolution of the case or answering to the Select Committee.

Natzler and Silk's review of the activities of the departmental select committees also shows that the creation of agencies has not altered their remit either in theory (the standing order) or in practice. The select committees have been thought by some to have been slow to exploit the opportunities created by the agency format to investigate the way departments are managed. After all, distancing agencies from ministerial control should act as an incentive for Parliament to ensure that the public interest in the delivery of the public services for which the agencies are responsible is not neglected when ministerial involvement is reduced.

The explanation for the relative lack of committee interest in agencies lies as much in the culture of the committees as in the organisational features of the agencies. Apart from the fact that for some departments' agencies are very peripheral, committees prefer to set their own agendas and tend anyway to concentrate more on policy than administration. They have to consider whether scrutinising agencies—meaning management and administration—should be given priority over other possible topics, particularly policy issues which are usually of more immediate political concern. Moreover—and there is a parallel here with the development of the select committee on nationalised industries (Coombes, 1966) —committees have to be aware that close parliamentary scrutiny could undermine the greater managerial freedom which agencies are intended to have under the Next Steps initiative. However, it is equally possible that the committees could develop a 'protective' role in regard to an agency's (relative) autonomy when encroached upon by the core department (or the Treasury), just as the SCNI and Energy Committee did in relation to the managerial autonomy of the boards of the nationalised industries. It has to be said that evidence of such a development has yet to emerge.

Nevertheless, the regime established for agencies does provide considerable opportunities for select committee investigation. The agencies are part of the Government's programme for enhancing the efficiency and effectiveness of the public service. The Committees are (with the PAC) the only way in which Parliament can make a well-informed input into an assessment of that programme, both as a totality (the particular role of the Treasury Committee, as demonstrated in Chapter 4) and for individual agencies. The publication of framework documents, performance indicators and annual reports and the increased visibility of chief executives all provide departmental select committees with material and a focus (some would say target) for scrutiny. Moreover, it is clear that chief executives themselves expect this—and some have been disappointed at the failure of select committees to follow through in this way. While that perception may indicate a lack of understanding of the culture and political chemistry of the committees, it does suggest that the committees would find little resistance from chief executives to a more sustained and systematic approach to the scrutiny of the agencies, an approach which would have more of an audit character. Indeed, chief executives might find this positively attractive as it could strengthen their hands in their dealings with their parent departments and the Treasury.

The record of select committee work, as Chapter 5 shows, is varied. Most committees have had some contact with the work of agencies and some have paid considerable attention to them. If the frequency of appearances of agency witnesses and the volume of memoranda are valid indicators, the agencies have certainly not been neglected. The examples of the Employment Committee, in relation to the Skills Training Agency, the Home Affairs Committee in relation to the Passport Office and the Forensic Science Service and the Social Security Committee in relation to the Benefits Agency and latterly the Child Support Agency, demonstrate the possibilities. It is to be expected that other Committees will in due course follow suit—perhaps particularly the Defence Committee as managerial delegation in the MoD is worked out to its full extent. But this is unlikely to amount to a sustained and systematic scrutiny of agency performance across Whitehall as a whole unless there is a fundamental change to the way in which departmental select committees order their priorities—a move towards a more cohesive, centralised programme of work, which is very unlikely to be acceptable to select committee members, as the Liaison and Procedure Committees have discovered.

If there is to be a more sustained and systematic scrutiny of agencies as a whole, it is likely to come from one of two quarters—the Treasury and Civil Service Committee or the PAC. Chapter 4 shows that initially the TCSC, through its civil service sub-committee, took a close interest in the development of the Next Steps programme and indeed played a vital part in its development. The dialogue between the TCSC and the Next Steps Project Manager and, to a lesser extent, the Cabinet Secretary and the Treasury, over the first four years of the programme not only recorded the evolution of the programme but secured its place as an enduring feature of the reorganisation of Whitehall. On issues such as accounting officer status, the procedures for appointing chief executives, and parliamentary accountability itself, the TCSC played a significant, and possibly decisive, role. However, given the broad and politically significant remit of the Committee, it was not surprising that the pattern of annual reviews of the progress of Next Steps could not be sustained in the face of many competing priorities. Whilst understandable, this was unfortunate from the point of view of systematic scrutiny, because it is the regular return to managerial issues like the definition, implementation and monitoring of targets and performance indicators and, even more significantly, the revision of framework documents, which is crucial to effective scrutiny. The TCSC in the 1987-92 Parliament showed what might be done in this regard—and how significant it could be when it was done. Scrutiny through continuing dialogue works by forming one significant element of the framework within which departments and agencies operate.

Continuing dialogue is a key element of the culture of the National Audit Office and the Public Accounts Committee. As with the Parliamentary Ombudsman, the statutory basis of the NAO (the 1983 National Audit Act) meant that the creation of agencies did not directly affect their relationship with the audit system. As Priscilla Baines shows in Chapter 6, the working out of the detailed audit arrangements has not been quite so straightforward. The PAC system has always provided a unique form of direct financial accountability of senior officials to Parliament, in contrast to the form of accountability through ministers which operates in regard to general administration and policy. The decision to designate chief executives as agency accounting officers indicated that this form of direct accountability was to be applied explicitly to agency chief executives and Peter Kemp rightly saw this as a decisive breakthrough in the working out of the nuts and bolts of managerial delegation. Whether this designation has clarified the respective roles of chief executive and permanent secretary is another matter, as both the Fraser Report and the PAC itself have indicated. Yet in practice, as Chapter 6 shows, the twin roles do not seem to create problems when a permanent secretary and chief executive are before the PAC any more than they do when they are before a departmental select committee or the Ombudsman committee. The PAC has made no attempt to divide the two or to exploit possible tensions between their respective responsibilities.

What is clear, however, is that the Next Steps initiative has meant a significant increase in the workload of the NAO and posed some ticklish problems in separating out an agency's accounts. Moreover, the NAO's explicit value for money remit places it in an ideal position to explore the issues of quality of service, performance measurement, efficiency and effectiveness which are at the heart of the agencies programme. The NAO and the PAC, while endorsing agency status as a practical means of improving public sector performance and commending the agencies' efforts in that direction, have been more sceptical about whether the improvements really are directly linked to agency status and whether the generally laudatory picture painted by agencies and ministers in, for example, their annual reports can be justified in detail. The vigorous exchanges between the PAC and the Treasury about the Vehicle Inspectorate which are chronicled in Chapter 6 illustrate this and show, as Baines points out, how close is the link between monitoring performance and policy issues, which are 'off-limits' for the PAC and NAO. How this will develop when the larger agencies such as the Employment Service or the Benefits Agency are dealt with will be a crucial test of the robustness of the National Audit Act system when managerial responsibilities are being redefined within Whitehall. Certainly, the NAO/PAC's value-for-money remit provides the basis for the sustained and systematic scrutiny which it is often argued is required for the agencies which deliver public services.

The case studies of agencies reported in Part III underline, in their different ways, the need for sustained scrutiny. The high political profile and proximity to central government of the Benefits Agency and the Employment Service underline the difficulty of differentiating between policy and operational issues and yet also the necessity of developing effective machinery for assessing managerial effectiveness and quality of service. As Norman Lewis points out, it is too easy to place the emphasis upon inputs and to neglect the wider issues raised by qualitative assessments of public services and the goals agencies should be expected to deliver. Although he acknowledges the improvements made by the Next Steps initiative, particularly the greater availability of information, Lewis—drawing upon overseas experience—advocates major constitutional reform and the creation of a comprehensive framework of administrative law as the only way of achieving the radical extension of accountability which is required. As he makes clear, this would not be confined within an exclusively parliamentary framework as in his view that cannot provide either the representativeness or the expertise which is needed for effective accountability.

The study of Department of Environment agencies by George Jones and his colleagues underlines the switch from ministerial accountability. The process of agencification, they conclude, has led to a decline in ministerial accountability to Parliament for the work of the civil service, largely because of the practice of referring PQs to chief executives. Nevertheless, they acknowledge that the greater openness about targets and objectives which has come with the agency programme provides an opportunity for greater accountability to Parliament for both ministers and senior civil servants since what is publicly announced is more easily scrutinised and monitored. Much of the parliamentary interest in agencies which they report reflected concern about the process of agencification, particularly its impact on the working conditions and career prospects of civil servants, so it might be expected that this would decline as the agencies become more established. However, the continuing development of the government's reform programme, with prior options, market testing, contractorisation and privatisation, suggests that parliamentary concern about the impact of these processes on both the providers and the beneficiaries of public services will continue.

That concern about impact will also be evident in the social security field. Patricia Greer's study of the DSS agencies illustrates both the opportunities and the problems for scrutiny which agency status brings. More and better information is available to Parliament about the workings of the Department and its agencies, though it is not yet clear whether Parliament will be willing and able to make the most of the opportunities for scrutiny all this information provides. But the high political profile of social security benefits and its policy content makes the differentiation between policy and operational issues problematic with the result that there is some ambiguity about who is accountable to Parliament for what.

Future Directions

Our researches have shown that the system of parliamentary scrutiny of executive agencies is continuing to evolve. The agency programme may mean fundamental change in Whitehall but so far it has only meant evolutionary change at Westminster. How might this evolution develop? There are two likely directions.

The first is a growth in the direct accountability of civil servants, which would reflect and reinforce the growing distance between the ministerial core of government departments, with its emphasis upon policy and politics, and the service delivery/administrative functions which would increasingly be conducted *on behalf of* government departments rather than directly by them. This has obvious parallels with what has occurred in local government and seems to be the direction in which the present government is moving in its recent pronouncements. It also has close affinities with the Swedish model which attracted the Fulton Committee in the 1960s. (Fulton, 1968, 61) The key issue here would be the point at which it would be formally recognised that the traditional concept of ministerial responsibility needed to be re-formulated, if not abandoned, and what would replace it.

This could occur as part of a much wider package of constitutional reform. Or it could emerge as a simple recognition that, over the years the constitutional fiction that ministers are directly and personally responsible for all that their departments do has been less and less useful as it has corresponded less and less with what actually happens. The growth of direct accountability to Parliament of civil servants, particularly those in senior managerial positions like chief executives, would render indirect accountability through ministers nugatory. This would not be unprecedented: the direct accountability of accounting officers has a long and distinguished pedigree. If that can co-exist with undoubted ministerial responsibility (individually and collectively) for public expenditure decisions—which have a high political content in every sense—then it ought to be possible for direct accountability of civil servants to co-exist with ministerial responsibility in other areas too. There would be the obvious objection that there would be difficulties in determining the dividing line between the two—but those difficulties are already manifest in current arrangements, as has been illustrated by the debate over accountability of agencies themselves.

The second direction in which accountability arrangements might evolve is through the select committee system. We have already seen that moves towards a more systematic and cohesive scrutiny system would require a change in committee culture and in the perceptions MPs have of their role. In present circumstances it is not easy to see how that would occur without a significant change in the composition of the House of Commons—i.e. a substantial period in which no one party had an overall majority. But short of that it is possible to see some evolution of the present system as agencies themselves become more prominent by virtue of the growth of the Next Steps programme. When that programme is complete, most civil servants will be working in agencies, and most of those who are not will have done so at some time in their career. Agencies will, in other words, become the norm and committee scrutiny of departments' 'administration, policy and expenditure' (to quote the current Standing Order, No 130) will perforce be scrutiny of agencies. How systematic and cohesive this will be will remain a matter of the political chemistry of the individual committees and the moral suasion of the Liaison and Procedure Committees but the element of familiarity, if not regularity, which will come from repeated contact with chief executives will itself generate some degree of 'system'. How much will necessarily depend upon the degree of continuity within the committees themselves.

Another important factor in the way the committees evolve will be how the NAO and PAC develop. There are two aspects to this. The first is the extent to which the NAO and PAC pursue the issues of quality of service and managerial effectiveness and whether the relationship between the NAO and the PAC on the one hand and departments, agencies and the

Treasury on the other continues to be broadly co-operative or becomes more adversarial. In the NAO and the PAC there is a seed which might grow into a substantial system of independent (of government) assessment of departmental performance. However, it is doubtful if under our present arrangements ministers of any party would see it as in their interests for that to occur: it would too easily be seen as guaranteeing a continuous supply of well-documented ammunition for critics of the government.

But even if that does not occur, it is possible to envisage, as a second aspect, a closer relationship developing very gradually between the PAC and departmental select committees which would enable Parliament to exploit more fully the wealth of material about the agencies (framework documents, performance indicators, annual reports, replies from ministers and chief executives to PQs, evidence to select committees) which is already available, and will grow as more NAO reports are published. However, there is no systematic analysis of all this information and no assessment of its quality. What is needed is a mechanism for evaluating it and drawing Parliament's attention to whatever is particularly significant—a role which the C&AG performs for the PAC with NAO material. It is to be hoped that this will enable parliamentary scrutiny to develop from the episodic and selective, even random, arrangements which apply at present to something more systematic and cohesive. It would require the committees themselves, including the PAC, to escape from the confines of their own departmentalism. And that would be an adaptation of existing scrutiny mechanisms which would be fully in line with the evolutionary style of the Westminster parliamentary tradition.

Both those developments assume a continuing focus on Parliament as the principal mode of accountability. But if we take the example of local government, there is also the possibility that external accountability mechanisms—perhaps an analogue of the Audit Commission—might come into play. Parliamentary scrutiny derives its legitimacy from its democratic base. It may, coincidentally, engage the expertise and professional competences of MPs, although in most circumstances MPs are performing the role of lay critics. There is a case, and some would say—e.g. Norman Lewis—it is an increasingly powerful case, for public services to be subject to independent expert, professional assessment as well. The emphasis here is as much upon the independent—meaning from outside the public service—as upon the expert and professional, for it is not meant to denigrate the expertise and professionalism in these areas within the public service itself. Rather, it is to stress that, however effective internal audit systems are, there is a need for an external audit as well, the independence of which acts (ideally) as a guarantee of public confidence in the outcome. In the case of executive agencies 'audit' here means not just financial and managerial audit, but the wider assessment of efficiency and effectiveness.

The traditional argument against such moves has been that the public services are so different from the 'outside world' (usually characterised as 'commercial', though there are many other forms of organisation, particularly in the social and educational fields) that only those within the service can be expected to be sufficiently attuned to its requirements (the political context and public service ethics are often cited at this point) to be able to assess its effectiveness.

It is indeed true that the public services are different. What is at issue, though, is *how* different they are and whether those differences prevent the application of 'outside' skills and techniques of assessment. Much of the motivation behind the Next Steps initiative has been to enable fuller use to be made of commercial and managerial skills within the public service, particularly in operational areas. It would therefore be singularly appropriate for such skills, more prevalent outside the public service than within it, to be applied to assessment of effectiveness. This could be done either through the establishment of an independent institution like the Audit Commission or the National Audit Office or by use of commercial accountants or management consultants or some mixture thereof. The material so produced would be available not only to MPs but to the public at large who would be able to draw appropriate conclusions about the management of these public services. It would then be for Government and Parliament to take whatever follow-up action seemed to be required.

Again, there is the question of the political circumstances in which ministers would see it as in their interests to establish such an independent system, particularly when they are, or see themselves as, ultimately responsible for the effectiveness of the government departments which they head. But if the distancing of ministers from the management of their departments which is detectable in the philosophy of the Next Steps initiative takes root and grows, then it is possible to envisage circumstances in which ministers would see external assessment as a useful instrument for themselves in their dealings with agencies. There are already signs of this kind of thinking in the (albeit controversial) use of outside management consultants.

There are doubtless other possible developments upon which one might speculate. But the key point is that how the system of parliamentary scrutiny might develop, or needs to develop, is not at present clear. An important factor in this is that the way in which the civil service will develop is not entirely clear either—though it may become more so as debate develops on the 1994 White Paper. What matters, therefore, is that Parliament itself should address these issues—both what the shape of the future civil service should be and how Parliament should relate to its work. These are undoubtedly issues which are being thought about within Whitehall, though whether the horizon of that thinking extends much beyond the next general election is open to doubt. But they are issues which are too important for our democratic system to be left entirely to government, in either its political or bureaucratic form.

Indeed, it is arguable that these are issues which are too important even to be left to Parliament, given its present over-loaded agenda. What is needed is a full-scale enquiry, perhaps by a Royal Commission, to examine the future shape of the civil service and the appropriate mechanisms for its accountability and control. Such an enquiry would need to go well beyond the parliamentary dimension and reflect the different interests and perspectives involved—those of senior politicians from (at least) the three main parties, senior civil servants, independent management consultants, and interest groups representing public service clients. The purpose of such an enquiry would be to ensure that the Whitehall-Westminster relationship for the next century is the product of considered and informed analysis, reflection and debate rather than being, as at present, the product of political and administrative happenstance. The 'Next Steps to where' need to be informed and considered steps, not unwitting stumbles dictated by day-to-day events.

References

Cm 2627, 1994:   *The Civil Service: Continuity and Change*, Cm 2627, HMSO, July 1994.

Coombes, 1966:   David Coombes, *The Member of Parliament and the Administration: the Case of the Select Committee on Nationalised Industries*, Allen and Unwin, 1966.

Efficiency Unit, 1988:   *Improving Management in Government: the Next Steps*, Report to the Prime Minister, (the Ibbs Report), HMSO, February 1988.

Fulton, 1968:   *The Civil Service: Report of the (Fulton) Committee, 1966–68*, Cmnd 3638, HMSO, June 1968.

Holden, 1988:   Barry Holden: *Understanding Liberal Democracy*, Philip Allan, 1988.

OPSS, 1993:   *Next Steps: Agencies in Government: Review 1993*, Cm 2430, HMSO, December 1993.

TCSC, 1993:   Sixth Report from the Treasury and Civil Service Committee, Session 1992–93, *The Role of the Civil Service: Interim Report*, HC 390, July 1993.

Bibliography

This bibliography is divided into three sections. Section 1 is a select list of works on the general topic of Parliamentary Accountability. Section 2 is a list of works on the Next Steps and management of the civil service. Section 3 lists those British Official Publications which deal generally with Next Steps. Publications dealing with individual agencies, such as reports from departmental select committees, the Public Accounts Committee, the National Audit Office and the Parliamentary Commissioner for Administration and its associated select committee are listed at the end of the relevant chapters.

Section 1 **Parliamentary Accountability**

Coombes, David, *The Member of Parliament and the Administration: the Case of the Select Committee on Nationalized Industries*, London, Allen and Unwin, 1966.

Day, Patricia and Klein, Rudolf, *Accountabilities*, Tavistock Publications, 1987.

Drewry, Gavin (ed), *The New Select Committees: A Study of the 1979 Reforms*, second edition, Oxford, Clarendon Press, 1989.

Erskine May, *Treatise on the Law, Privileges and Proceedings of Parliament*, twenty-first edition, London, Butterworth, 1989.

Finer, S.E., 'The Individual Responsibility of Ministers', *Public Administration*, Vol 34 No 4, London, Royal Institute of Public Administration, 1956.

Franklin, Mark and Norton, Philip (eds), *Parliamentary Questions*, Oxford, Clarendon Press, 1993.

Garner, M.R., 'Auditing the efficiency of the nationalised industries: enter the Monopolies and Mergers Commission', *Public Administration,* Vol 60 No 4, London, Royal Institute of Public Administration, 1982.

Giddings, Philip, *Agencies and Parliamentary Questions*, University of Reading, 1994.

Gregory, Roy, 'The Select Committee on the Parliamentary Commissioner for Administration', *Public Law*, London, Sweet and Maxwell, Spring 1982.

Gregory, Roy and Hutchesson, Peter, *The Parliamentary Ombudsman: a Study in the Control of Administrative Action*, London, Allen and Unwin, 1975.

Harden, Ian and Lewis, Norman, *The Noble Lie: the British Constitution and the Rule of Law*, London, Hutchinson, 1986.

Holden, Barry, *Understanding Liberal Democracy*, Oxford, Philip Allan, 1988.

Johnson, Nevil, *Parliament and Administration: the Estimates Committee, 1945-65*, London, Allen and Unwin, 1966.

Lewis, Norman, 'Regulating Non-Government Bodies: Privatization, Accountability and the Public-Private Divide' in Jowell, J, and Oliver, D, (eds), *The Changing Constitution,* Oxford, Clarendon Press, 1989.

Lewis, Norman, 'The Case for a Standing Administrative Conference', *Political Quarterly*, Vol 60, Oxford, Blackwell, 1989.

Lewis, Norman and Birkinshaw, Patrick, *When Citizens Complain: Reforming Justice and Administration,* Buckingham, Open University Press, 1993.

Marshall, G, *Constitutional Conventions: the Rules and Forms of Political Accountability*, Oxford, Clarendon Press, 1986.

Prosser, Tony, 'Democratisation, Accountability and Institutional Design: Reflections on Public Law', in McAuslan, P and McEldowney, J, (eds), *Law, Legitimacy and the Constitution*, London, Sweet and Maxwell, 1985.

Prosser, Tony, *Nationalised Industries and Public Control: Legal, Constitutional and Political Issues,* Oxford, Blackwell, 1986.

Pyper, Robert, 'The Doctrine of Individual Ministerial Responsibility in British Government: Theory and Practice in a New Regime of Parliamentary Accountability', Ph D thesis, University of Leicester, 1987.

Pyper, Robert, 'Ministerial Departures from British Governments, 1964–90: A Survey', *Contemporary Record*, Vol 5 No 2, London, Frank Cass, 1991.

Rawlings, R, 'Parliamentary Redress of Grievances', in Harlow, C, (ed), *Public Law and Politics*, London, Sweet and Maxwell, 1986.

Robinson, Ann, *Parliament and Public Spending: the Expenditure Committee and the House of Commons, 1970–76*, London, Heinemann, 1978.

Ryle, Michael and Richards, Peter G, *The Commons Under Scrutiny*, third revised edition, London, Routledge, 1988.

Section 2 **Next Steps and Civil Service Management**

Carter, Neil and Greer, Patricia, 'Evaluating Agencies: Next Steps and Performance Indicators', *Public Administration*, Vol 71 No 3, Oxford, Blackwell, 1993.

Chapman, Richard A., 'The Next Steps: A Review', *Public Policy and Administration*, Vol 3, 1988.

Common, Richard, Flynn, Norman and Mellon, Elisabeth, *Managing Public Services: Competition and Decentralisation*, Butterworth Heinemann, 1992.

Davies, Anne and Willman, John, *What Next? Agencies, Departments and the Civil Service*, London, Institute of Public Policy Research, 1991.

Drewry, Gavin and Butcher, Tony, *The Civil Service Today*, second edition, Oxford, Blackwell, 1991.

Drewry, Gavin, 'Forward from FMI: the Next Steps', *Public Law*, London, Sweet and Maxwell, 1988.

Drewry, Gavin, 'Next Steps: the pace falters', *Public Law*, London, Sweet and Maxwell, 1990.

Dunleavy, Patrick, 'Bluehall, SW1?', *Strathclyde Analysis Paper Number 11*, University of Strathclyde, 1992.

Flynn, A., Gray, A., and Jenkins, W., 'Taking the Next Steps: the changing management of government', *Parliamentary Affairs*, Oxford, Blackwell, Vol 43 No 2, 1990.

Fry, G., Flynn, A., Gray, A., Jenkins, W., and Rutherford, B., 'Symposium on improving management in government'. *Public Administration*, Oxford, Blackwell, Vol 66 No 4, 1988.

Greer, Patricia, *Transforming Central Government: the Next Steps Initiative*, Buckingham, Open University Press, 1994.

Greer, Patricia, 'The Next Steps Initiative: the Transformation of Britain's Civil Service', *Political Quarterly*, Vol 63 No 2, Oxford, Blackwell, 1992.

Greer, Patricia, 'The Next Steps Initiative: an Examination of Agency Framework Documents', *Public Administration*, Vol 70 No 1, Oxford, Blackwell, 1992.

Hennessy, Peter, *Whitehall,* London, Secker and Warburg, 1989.

Hunt of Tanworth, 'The Cabinet and "Next Steps"' in F. Vibert (ed), *Britain's Constitutional Future*, London, Institute of Economic Affairs, 1991.

Jordan, Grant, *Next Steps Agencies: From Management by Command to Management by Contract*, University of Aberdeen, 1992.

Kemp, Peter, 'Next Steps for the British Civil Service', *Governance*, Oxford, Blackwell, Vol 3 No 2, 1990.

McDonald, Oonagh, *Swedish Models: the Swedish Model of Central Government*, London, Institute for Public Policy Research, 1992.

Pliatzky, Leo, 'Quangos and Agencies', *Public Administration*, Vol 70 No 4, 55–63, Oxford, Blackwell, 1992.

Price Waterhouse, *Executive Agencies: Facts and Trends*, No 3, London, Price Waterhouse, 1991.

Price Waterhouse, *Executive Agencies: Facts and Trends*, No 4, London, Price Waterhouse, 1992.

Section 3 Official Publications

'Official Publications' are published by, or available from, Her Majesty's Stationery Office, London.

A: Government

Cabinet Office:

Improving Management in Government: the Next Steps, Report to the Prime Minister, (the Ibbs Report), February 1988.

Making the Most of the Next Steps: the Management of Ministers' Departments and their Executive Agencies, (the Fraser Report), May 1991.

Next Steps Project Team, *Next Steps Briefing Note*, July 1992.

Waldegrave, William, *Speech to the Institute of Directors*, Office of Public Service and Science Press Release 18/92, 1992.

Command Papers:

Cmnd 2767, *The Parliamentary Commissioner for Administration*, October 1965.

Cmnd 3638, *The Civil Service: Report of the (Fulton) Committee, 1966–68*, June 1968.

Cmnd 8293, *Efficiency in the Civil Service*, 1981.

Cmnd 8616, *Efficiency and Effectiveness in the Civil Service: Government Observations on the Third Report from the Treasury and Civil Service Committee,* 1982.

Cmnd 9058, *Financial Management in Government Departments,* 1983.

Cmnd 9297, *Progress in Financial Management in Government Departments,* 1984.

Cmnd 9841, *Civil Servants and Ministers: Duties and Responsibilities: Government Response to the Seventh Report from the Treasury and Civil Service Committee,* 1986.

Cm 78, *Accountability of Ministers and Civil Servants: Government Response to the First Report from the Treasury and Civil Service Committee 1986–87, and the First Report from the Liaison Committee 1986–87,* 1987.

Cm 524, *Civil Service Management Reform: the Next Steps: Government Reply to the Eighth Report from the Treasury and Civil Service Committee, 1987–88,* November 1988.

Cm 841, *Developments in the Next Steps Programme: the Government Reply to the Fifth Report from the Treasury and Civil Service Committee, 1988–89,* October 1989.

Cm 914, *The Financing and Accountability of Next Steps Agencies,* December 1989.

Cm 1261, *Improving Management in Government: the Next Steps Agencies Review,* October 1990.

Cm 1263, *Progress in the Next Steps Initiative: the Government's Reply to the Eighth Report from the Treasury and Civil Service Committee, Session 1989–90,* October 1990.

Cm 1599, *The Citizen's Charter,* July 1991.

Cm 1730, *Competing for Quality,* November 1991.

Cm 1760, *Improving Management in Government—the Next Steps Agencies Review 1991*, November 1991.

Cm 1761, *The Next Steps Initiative: the Government's Reply to the Seventh Report from the Treasury and Civil Service Committee, Session 1990-91*, November 1991.

Cm 2101, *The Citizen's Charter First Report: 1992*, November 1992.

Cm 2111, *The Next Steps Agencies: Review 1992*, November 1992.

Cm 2290, *Open Government*, July 1993.

Cm 2430, *Next Steps: Agencies in Government: Review 1993*, December 1993.

Cm 2627, *The Civil Service: Continuity and Change*, July 1994.

HM Treasury:

Executive Agencies: A Guide to Setting Targets and Measuring Performance, HMSO, 1992.

Civil Service Statistics, published annually by HMSO.

B: Parliamentary Publications:

House of Commons Expenditure Committee:

Eleventh Report, 1976-77, *The Civil Service*, HC 535.

House of Commons Committee of Public Accounts:

Thirteenth Report, 1986-87, *The Financial Management Initiative*, HC 61.

Thirty-eighth Report, 1988-89, *The Next Steps Initiative*, HC 420.

Second Report, 1989-90, *Accounting Officers' Memorandum*, HC 527.

Tenth Report, 1989–90, *National Audit Office Estimates 1990–91 and Corporate Plan 1990–91 to 1994–95*, HC 42.

Twenty-ninth Report, 1990–91, *National Audit Office Corporate Plan 1991–92 to 1995–96 and Estimates for 1991–92*, HC 413.

Tenth Report, 1991–92, *National Audit Office Estimates, 1992–93*, HC 207.

House of Commons Liaison Committee: First Report, 1986–87, *Accountability of Ministers and Civil Servants,* HC 100, 1986.

House of Commons Select Committee on Nationalised Industries:

First Report, 1967–68, *Ministerial Control of the Nationalised Industries*, HC 371.

House of Commons Select Committee on Procedure:

Second Report, 1989–90, *The Working of the Select Committee System*, HC 19, October 1990.

Third Report, 1990–91, *Parliamentary Questions*, HC 178, May 1991.

House of Commons Select Committee on the Parliamentary Commissioner for Administration:

Second Report, 1991–92, *The Implications of the Citizen's Charter for the Work of the Parliamentary Commissioner for Administration*, HC 158, February 1992.

House of Commons Treasury and Civil Service Committee:

Third Report, 1981–82, *Efficiency and Effectiveness in the Civil Service*, HC 236, 1982.

Seventh Report, 1985–86, *Civil Servants and Ministers: Duties and Responsibilities*, HC 92, 1986.

First Report, 1986–87, *Ministers and Civil Servants*, HC 62, 1986.

Eighth Report, 1987–88, *Civil Service Management Reform: the Next Steps*, HC 494, July 1988.

Fifth Report, 1988–89, *Developments in the Next Steps Programme*, HC 348, July 1989.

Eighth Report, 1989–90, *Progress in the Next Steps Initiative*, HC 481, July 1990.

Seventh Report, 1990–91, *The Next Steps Initiative*, HC 496, July 1991.

Sixth Report, 1992–93, *The Role of the Civil Service: Interim Report*, HC 390, July 1993.

National Audit Office:

The Next Steps Initiative, HC 420, 1988–89, June 1989.

Index

Figures in italics refer to tables.